CH00833471

"A fine book that was a joy to read, describing in a simple and honest way Panos's journey through life. I especially liked the many pearls of wisdom he brought with him from his childhood home, which have been and remain very useful today."

ERIK SELIN
Property developer and CEO, *Fastighets* AB *Balder*

"I had the pleasure to spend my life as a travelling professional showman and worked with magic and entertainment for many years around the globe! Panos had the same journey — he worked with passion, focus and mystery in his lifetime and finally got to learn his tricks. Like any great magician he mixes hard work, business and understands his audience. I won't be revealing my secrets but I enjoyed reading all of his!"

JOE LABERO
Magician and illusionist

"A true modern Odyssey. Panos takes the restless Greek entrepreneurial spirit to the shores of the Mediterranean and all corners of the earth. With stubbornness, perseverance and hard work, he honoured Greece and especially his parents who were always the precious light of his life."

GEORGE LOGOTHETIS
Author, biographer of Mikis Theodorakis and Ulf Palme

"Nothing can be more inspiring than a true success story! It is touching to read about the little Greek boy who dreamed about a better life. It was fortuitous that the boy ended up in Sweden, and that he started to produce swimwear, which we loved and bought.
"The rest is history, a successful international company and an entrepreneur recognized and praised by the corporate world and the King of Sweden."

LENA APLER
Chair, Collector AB *and Collector Bank*

"His grace, belief in values, and incomparable courage shine in his first literary work, so sincere and absent of hagiography, an almost confession from a psychologist's couch, drawing us breathless travellers into his days, and into his shoes that took him from the slums of Greece to conquer an entire world."

CHRYSA SAMOU MITRENGAS
Journalist, ERT3 TV, *Greece*

"A unique story of a life-driven man."

RITA TAINOLA
Finnish journalist and writer

Published by
LID Publishing
An imprint of LID Business Media Ltd.
The Record Hall, Studio 304,
16–16a Baldwins Gardens,
London EC1N 7RJ, UK

info@lidpublishing.com
www.lidpublishing.com

A member of:

BPR
businesspublishersroundtable.com

Printed by Gutenberg Press, Malta
ISBN: 978-1-911687-12-2
ISBN: 978-1-911687-13-9 (ebook)

Cover design: Caroline Li
Page design and typography: Jack Yan
Fabric patterns: Panos Papadopoulos

PANOS
MY LIFE, MY ODYSSEY

PANOS PAPADOPOULOS
WITH JACK YAN

MADRID | MEXICO CITY | LONDON
NEW YORK | BUENOS AIRES
BOGOTA | SHANGHAI | NEW DELHI

Contents

Prologue

I HAD HUMBLE BEGINNINGS. As a small boy in Paralia Aspropirgou, on the outskirts of Athens, I experienced hunger. I saw the dirty, poor environment around me and wondered if this world was for me. I had decided, at the age of five or six, that I had to do something to escape this misery. I knew that it was more than a mere dream, listening to the music of Tolis Voskopoulos, one of the legends of modern Greek music, and hoping for the best. My parents showed me that any progress had to come from hard work. Real effort. Walk, not talk.

In 20 years' time I would be in my new home of Sweden, proud of having earned my academic degrees, and starting a business from zero.

I may have had an inkling that it would become a multi-million-dollar enterprise, but I knew the key to growing it was still hard work. When you don't have money, there is no substitute for making it. It's not about 'manifesting,' or some vague hope, but tapping into that drive inside you. And then, being brave enough to tell the world about it, not the other way round. This is where so many seem to have got it wrong: those who brag without having done the work, with some vain hope that reality will suddenly happen around them.

But, it paid off. In another two decades I would be on a plane heading to Mexico with the King and Queen of Sweden, embarking on a state visit with them. A day later I would sit at a lavish dinner table with the President of Mexico and them, surrounded by fabulously wealthy business leaders.

There was no privilege afforded to me at the start of my life, other than parents who loved me and nurtured me, regardless of how busy they were. Both had their schooling interrupted by tough circumstances, and my mother was illiterate. Yet, they set an example of such dignity and self-respect that it informed my every move in life, for the better.

When I left Greece as a teenager, to seek greener pastures in far-away Sweden, I had faced difficulties that some might deem impossible to surmount. When you are born outside privilege, though, you have this innate push to see things through. You may be hungry because you don't have enough money to buy a meal. 'Down to your last dollar' isn't just an expression to me, but a lived experience. You really have nothing to lose, so why not keep pushing on? You're alive, after all.

As wonderful as my parents were, in the days when not everyone had telephones — this is within living memory for a lot of us — I couldn't rely on their counsel because that would have meant an expensive call, armed with coins in your hand in a cold phone booth. Who can call when you've barely enough to eat with? Sometimes I felt I lacked emotional support, too, not just financial means. You don't feel like the world's your oyster, but your obstacle. Yet, this happens every day to so many people in our world, for many different reasons. They find themselves alone in a desert, naked and afraid, with dark skies, strong winds and scorpions all around.

It's the journey, the odyssey, that one faces that builds up one's character.

I'm not saying that it will always yield obvious rewards. I've had to endure tough times, and treaded a fine line with the help of people who bent the rules for the sake of doing the right thing. (In some cases, I've continued to protect their privacy and have changed their names in this book.) Those were valued rewards, indeed, although not necessarily in a monetary or celebrity sense.

But, this is also a life where I've met royalty, including prime ministers and political party leaders, been invited to the Nobel Prize ceremony, worked with international stars, chaired a football team, had disputes with Donald Trump, and worked with some of the best talents in their respective fields. I wound up leading my industry, and the press dubbed me 'the King of Swimwear.' It was not a crown that I found easy to part with, but you also have to know when to start a new chapter.

Now, I have the opportunity to share this story with you. This book should serve as a reminder that you have inner strength, and that good values trump the pursuit of fleeting, shallow gains. My 38 years running my apparel brand, Panos Emporio, gave me great joy (for the most part), and I really could have kept it going, because I never pursued anything fleetingly. I always looked to the long term. I worked 18-hour days, so it felt like I had put 76 years into the business. When I found success, I knew I wanted to keep it going, not just for myself, but also for all those around me. That was my reward.

I know some of you will read this book for lessons in business, learned from my success over nearly 40 years. Just as I've done in my work,

I've attempted here to cater to the customer — to understand what you want. Those lessons, the primary ones in each chapter, appear in **bold type**, recalling the points at which I learned them myself.

For others, the reward may come in the form of a great relationship or a wonderful family, which are immensely important in life. Certainly, for my parents, that mattered. Their satisfaction and joy came in being able to look back and know they did the right thing and were honourable. I know they had a clear conscience. They had their own journeys to make.

This is ultimately a story about values. There is some truth to the old adage, "Show me a boy of seven and I will show you the man." When I look back, much of my character had been formed by that age. Everything else sprang from that, and I've never had to change the early values my parents instilled in me. The advice they gave, the events that followed and the experiences I've had are all built on those solid foundations. Those formative years, my first quarter-century on earth, continued to shape me, setting the stage for my business. There were years of frustration and dead ends, which compelled me to leave my home and go through even more trials and tribulations. But they were well worth it. They remind me that the lessons I'm now able to share — lessons about marketing, business, wealth and fame — are all founded on simple, down-home values and respect for other people. That is the simple truth. What follows is not just a personal odyssey — and as a Greek man, I use that term advisedly — but an altogether humanistic journey.

1
Nothing but pride

LET ME TAKE YOU BACK to the very beginning ... to the southern region of Peloponnesos, Greece, in the spring of 1958.

EVERYONE has a story about their name, and while the world knows me as Panos Papadopoulos, it was not the name I was baptized with. I came to have it through circumstances that no mother should have had to endure. Had it not been for this incident, you might not have known me by this name at all.

My parents never completed their schooling due to World War II. My father, Ioannis, who went by Giannis, was born in Kertezi, in the Kalavryta municipality in Peloponnesos, and had one brother and one sister. He had about three years' schooling before the misery of the war. And it was quite a miserable wartime childhood for him and everyone he knew. Kalavryta was the site of the Nazis' worst atrocity in Greece, in December 1943. It is now known as the Massacre of Kalavryta. The Wehrmacht set out to exterminate the entire male population, ruthlessly executing more than 500 civilians and burning the town to the ground.

My father was a handsome gentleman, always well dressed. That was unusual for that time for someone who came from a small village and moved to an industrial ghetto. I remember his brown eyes, with the glance of an achiever, but not one who would be prone to arrogance. He had a voice that was quiet but powerful, not too soft or too polite. His hair was always well groomed and combed without exaggeration.

He was a man of few words, and in meetings he did not argue with others without reason. He avoided political banter, even if it was typical in the Greek mindset to argue over such things. If someone was considered 'too stupid,' he would let it pass.

He could be quick to anger, often erupting like a volcano, although in times of celebration he became another person altogether. He'd start to smile, dance and entertain others. He was a very good dancer, like a real-life Zorba. His posture was excellent. When someone wanted to join in, he would open his arms in welcome, and let them lead the dance.

He was a thinker, someone who could solve difficult issues. His mind was well organized and everything he did was done properly. He stored everything neatly. He had skills in many areas: building, carpentry, painting, repairing and gardening. He would regularly mend our shoes. He was very careful about details, and despite little formal education, he behaved as though he had academic acumen. "Just use your brain and what you have," he used to say. He was a hard-working person, and never seemed to stop — I never saw him relax.

It is emotionally tough for me to look back, because after he passed away in 2008, I seemed to lose a good deal of my energy, happiness and strength. Some of my roots were suddenly gone.

He always treated my mother with respect. On Sundays, he made his coffee, and one for Mum. He would call to her, "*Ela* Maria!" But it wasn't just, "Come, Maria!" Not at all. His *tone* made all the difference. I learned from him that the tone in our voices was important. He never explained this in so many words, but like any animal, we see and feel how our parents act, and we learn. During dinner, he would always fill her glass with wine. They always had one glass of red wine that they bought from the village. Dad refused to drink wine in bottles, as he believed that it should be free of chemicals and preservatives. "It must be real, and that's balsam for our bodies," he said, "but the wine bottles are killing us."

My mother, Maria, was born in a small village, Lagovouni, an hour from Kertezi. She came from a family that had had only daughters, and there was no opportunity for them all to go to school. She stood just under 1.6 m, and was slim, with dark eyes and hair. She was beautiful, and despite being illiterate, and having to sign with her thumbprint on official documents, she was very clever. She felt no handicap from not knowing how to read or write. When we were at school and they needed her to sign something, she would proudly say, "Give me the ink and I'll use my fingerprint to sign." At the local markets, I could see how quickly she calculated the sums and could find out when they were trying to fool her. She would ask us, her children, to read the amounts on the banknotes so she knew which ones to use, though she eventually came to know the denominations by their colours.

Mum was a great cook and mended our clothes. She was physically strong, and capable of working alongside men, doing physical labour.

She was very active in the church, and tried to help them raise money.

Every night she would light a candle and pray to God. Every Sunday morning, at the break of dawn, she would head to church for a couple of hours. My father would only attend on specific occasions, and did not like the priests, saying they were only after money. He had a point. I'd seen how the priests would ask for money to perform a funeral service. If you gave less, the ceremony would be shorter! He believed the priests were 'the devil' and would say that if God is in our home, why did we need to attend church? My mother would insist, *"Asto na to pari to potami."* (It doesn't matter.)

By 9 AM on Sundays she would return home to prepare the food for the day, before heading to work again.

She always had a smile, and a hopeful sense that better days would come.

All the family members who got a salary would give it to my mother. She would plan for the family and budgeted where it would be spent. She always had a little bit extra money somewhere, to surprise my father. When something important and unexpected came up, Mum had a bit of a buffer that could help solve the problem. Budgeting seemed to come very naturally to her.

Mum was also a good dancer, and Dad always invited her to join in. She loved that glass of red wine with dinner and enjoyed Dad's coffee.

When a neighbour was in need, or someone passed away, she was always there to help. In Greek tradition, when a person died, the body would remain at home for 24 hours before the funeral. It had to be washed and dressed. Mum always pitched in with this task and was emotionally strong. She could help calm people during tough times. Her favourite words were, "Do not blame them; they did not want to harm you."

When I watch on Animal Planet how a chicken might protect its off-spring from an eagle, I remember my mother. When I was six or seven, I was in our garden, trying to get some figs from a tree, when suddenly she jumped up, high above me, with scrubbing brushes to protect me from a viper that was about to attack.

In the summer we slept with the windows open because of the heat. One night, my father worked the night shift, so only Mum was there to look after us. A burglar jumped into our room but Mum ran in, ready to fight with him. Do not test a parent's anger when they are protecting their own; the power is incredible. Even at 79, when Dad was ill in bed, Mum attacked another intruder and started to hit him with the first thing she could grab, screaming angrily. The police later caught the would-be burglar, and Mum wound up on the television news.

While they were rich with love, they weren't well off financially. My mother worked as a labourer in the fields in Peloponnesos. There was no way she could stay at home. She had to help provide for me, my elder sister, Panagiota ('Giota'), who was two years my senior, and my brother, Spiros, who was four years older.

My parents would share their responsibilities without argument. It was all very natural. By the time I went to Sweden, I was both shocked and humoured how couples planned to the letter how they would divide up the smallest tasks. "You wash the dishes today, and I'll do them tomorrow." "But tomorrow we're having a bigger dinner, so you must do two rounds next time!" "But then who takes out the trash on Tuesday?" Yes, I respect equality, but micromanaging routine household chores like this didn't seem very human or respectful to me. It's like an artificial filter that we simply don't need.

ALL THREE OF US CHILDREN were born in Kertezi. And while we all grew up in those humble surroundings, my siblings didn't have quite the dramatic start to their lives that I did.

One day, my mother took me — her two-week-old infant — out into the fields, and tragedy struck. One of the horses that was helping the workers collect and transport the harvest from the field got startled by a snake. Jumping and kicking in fear, the horse managed to kick me.

My mother described me as looking blue, bruised and unconscious, and I was expected to die. An Orthodox priest who heard her screams from across the field ran toward her to see what had happened. Believing the kick would prove fatal, he quickly asked, "What is the boy's name? Is he baptized?"

"No, he isn't," replied my mother.

In Orthodox tradition, one has to be baptized to get a burial and go to heaven, and everyone gathered there believed I was done for … in this life and the next. With no time to waste, the priest performed the rites of baptism and gave me my name right then and there: Panagiotis Papadopoulos. The name means 'all holy,' deriving from the Greek epithet *panagia*, for Mary, mother of Jesus.

The experience didn't kill me, fortunately, and I went on to have a long, happy childhood, humble as it was.

To support the family, my parents applied for work just outside Athens when I was three or four months old. They secured jobs in a metal foundry, Viomichania Chalyvon AE.

Paralia Aspropirgou, where we settled, was 16 km from Athens and situated by the sea. The shore was only 300 m from our door, and the water wasn't too deep. Workers would fish there after their day to get their food. At the time, there were numerous factories concentrated in a small area. It was mostly poor people from other parts of Greece who came to get jobs there. My parents rented a single room for all five of us, which was relatively large by their standards at the time. It had a little toilet and an outside 'kitchen,' which was really just an open area beyond a door where they could cook. If you've ever seen cooking areas in refugee camps, you can picture it.

Renting, my family used to say, was like sleeping on the beach: you never know when a wave might come and take you away. It was an insecure feeling, so after two years they managed to save enough to buy some land there, and later we built a one-room dwelling. All this was illegal in those days; it was impossible to get official permission to build, so it was done without any urban planning, inspection or approval. We would work on building the room during the late afternoon and at night, so the local police would not notice and try to stop us. The family and our neighbours helped, and soon our little house was ready ... but for the ceiling. We needed one more day to do that.

In the morning, Mum and Dad had to work, and we kids stayed together to guard the new home.

Sure enough, a police car approached and asked where our parents were. I was shaking; a sense of doom enveloped my heart. They asked a few more questions, drove away, and a bulldozer arrived a few hours later to demolish our room-cum-house. They forced us away, and within a few minutes it was in ruins — just a heap of small pieces of brick and wood.

The neighbours tried to bring us into their homes, but we stayed on the demolition site and cried. I wondered, why these people were like that. What was wrong with having somewhere to stay? Who was making these decisions? Were they even human?

The bad news reached my father and mother during their working day. Dad came running back, to try to save as much as he could, but it was futile. His face when he saw the wreckage still haunts me: it was so very painful to see your strong, proud father so sad and weeping.

That evening, we started to sort out the undamaged bricks so they could be used again. This was all done in utter silence, but I could sense my parents' desperation. They said not a single word as they worked all night to sort out the mess. That night, we kids curled together like a snake on a small mattress and exchanged no words.

A few days later, my parents organized more neighbours to help, and after one Saturday and a Monday morning, the room was ready and we could put up a ceiling. That would help secure us from more police harassment, as the authorities would need more documents now that this was now a dwelling with a roof, and not just four walls. The mattress and our possessions were in moved in, and we felt no one could push us out.

The police returned a few days later with a bulldozer, ready for round two. They showed my mother some documents that claimed they had the right to destroy our house. Mum said, "I can't read," Mum said, "Go away!" There followed screams that sounded like the angry cries of a captured animal. Many words came from her mouth and they remain in my soul. She might have been small in stature, but her voice scared the police and the bulldozer operator. The only words I remember are, "You are not human! We have nowhere to go! Let us be, and don't destroy our dreams. We have nothing left."

My brother and sister were crying. As for me, I was stunned. I could not cry, and I couldn't say anything. My little heart and brain wondered why the heck I was even born. Why had no one asked me if I wanted to be here on this earth?

A few years later, we would have three rooms and a small garden, which provided enough vegetables to eat. And, a few chickens joined us.

MY PARENTS generally worked different shifts in order to look after us. Dad often worked nights, from 10 PM to 6 AM, while Mum worked 6 AM to 2 PM.

My parents' workplace was 1 km away from home. My older brother and sister were in school by then, so Mum and Dad would come back to feed me, and then return to their work. I was not happy being alone, and that still affects me. To this day, when I travel, I always make sure a friend is waiting for me at the airport when I arrive.

There were no other relatives here, so my parents only had each other to care for their three small children amongst a community of strangers who'd also moved there for work in the surrounding factories. They worked six days a week, Monday to Saturday. These were tough times, but experienced as a small child, you don't remember much of the struggle in later years. Food was the most important thing for survival, and then a home.

However, being poor also meant that we developed a keen sense of survival, and we had to find ways to be tenacious. **We would conquer each struggle one by one, and I learned at an early age to never give up.**

Above: With my family in Kertezi.
Above right: After we moved to Paralia Aspropirgou outside Athens. I'm the smallest in both photos.

By the time I started school, we had very little money to buy clothes or books. However, three to four times a year, we were able to go to the cinema together as a family. The films ignited my imagination, and I dreamed that one day I could be a hero. I believed that anything was possible. That could start with tiny things: my packed lunch for school might have just been bread and water, but I'd add sugar to make them more palatable. We each found ways to make what little we had more enjoyable.

One of my childhood idols was a singer and actor named Tolis Voskopoulos. His first songs and movies were like a balm for my vulnerable soul. He'd portray a poor outsider trying to become a singer. His character's struggle for survival was met by less-than-kind people who wanted to exploit him, or just insult him. I recognized his character's struggle to make a career and the obstacles he faced along the way. He didn't worship money like some did; he was a passionate person whose values attracted me. I knew most of his songs' lyrics intimately, with so many feelings and so much respect. Every time I watched an interview with him, I could see how his words connected to his soul: simple, authentic replies, with a soft voice. There wasn't that typical arrogance or a feigned air of superiority about him.

His way of acting and his life would be reflected in my later life. He was principled, and he wanted to be something of his own making without steamrolling others. In many ways, his values have been mine for my entire business life.

I remember the cold nights when I went to bed with an empty stomach. Just his name on my lips helped keep me strong and happy.

I have been uncompromising when it comes to showing pride, dignity and respect. In business, I have my unwavering principles. For instance, I have never bribed anyone to gain an advantage. There were many times when I was challenged to 'give a little' in order to get ahead in my career, but it was always a definite *no*. When the press offered editorial coverage as a sweetener for me to buy advertising with them, I felt so damned cheap. I told them I'd rather open Pappa Panos's Pizza, and eke out a living on that, than buy publicity. It just felt so humiliating to buy into something you did not deserve. All the passion I put in, and all the days and nights spent creating something, would be meaningless — erased in one swoop — if I bought some press.

Dad was a proud man of few words. He was maybe 1.7 m tall, but his pride made him seem far taller. And he never looked down on people. He propped me up by the neck when we walked, and if I slouched forward, he'd lovingly squeeze my neck and straighten me upright. He used to tell us, "Do not look down, but don't look up, either! Just tilt forward — it's where you're going!" Those were strong and simple words that I used to face every adversity. It is true that the weak are exploited in the animal world, but we humans are also animals, so why would we be any different? There are many in this world who wouldn't want to hold the hand of a weak individual, or sit next to one.

Tolis, my idol, portrayed the desire to get out of poverty and make a better life. On the big screen, he fought against the injustice and insults. Sometimes, it seemed light would come into his character's life, only for it to be snatched away by other events, destroying what little hope existed. And then, he would pull himself together and start again.

His movies were my guiding light, because he never gave up. I dreamed of his movies every night. His music could replace my food: here was something that really gave me nourishment and hope. I knew that one day I, too, could be somebody. Someone who did not need to eat dry bread soaked in water for it to go down. Someone who could take care of his parents in return for everything they gave us. A warm and comfortable home, and better food on the table. Someone who could give his own children a little more, so they could love more fully and not feel inferior to anyone else. I do not remember longing for any luxury that few had, and I do not today, either.

I realized that life wasn't always fair, and that some are just fortunate to have been born into an affluent household, though I never envied them.

Unlike some of my classmates, I really had nothing: no books, and certainly no encyclopaedia. The teacher would give a lot of homework, and I used to have to find excuses to visit my friends' homes so I could read their books. I experienced a feeling of chaos every day in trying to do my homework. Given my parents' lack of education and how little money we had — not to mention how little time they had, with how hard they worked — I couldn't ask them for either their input or for those books. I knew the money wasn't there. I couldn't ask them to buy an encyclopaedia, and I knew that saving up for one would take time. **My family's values were that we would never buy anything on credit if we did not have enough money, and that we always prioritized the right needs. My father used to say, "I have enough to think about when I go to sleep, and I do not want to have lenders chase me in my dreams."** These words are simple enough, but so many have destroyed their lives because they could not prioritize their needs with discipline and a plan.

When my parents could see that I was trying to ask for help elsewhere, they felt uncomfortable. But, I also remember that when I helped my father build our wall, he looked at me during a break and said, "Today, our neighbour should have been here to help me, but changed his mind at the last minute. **Remember one thing in life: never wait for someone else to solve your problems. Your life is in your own hands. Do not expect solutions from someone else.**" Whenever he absolutely had to see a doctor, he went ahead and did so, but he was disappointed, as this ran against his commitment to finding solutions ourselves. We know ourselves better than others, he felt, so listen to your soul and your body.

My family's words and values cemented themselves in my professional and private lives. I started with no money, but I never got a bank loan for my business, and grew it from zero into a multi-million-dollar enterprise without a single borrowed cent. This was something few understood and many thought strange. But everything had to do with *a plan.* That was how Panos Emporio AB could go on to become a rock-solid limited liability company, for 35 years! Every year I received a certificate and could see that among half a million limited companies in Sweden, only 450 received this platinum status — and my company was among that select group.

MY MEMORIES of my primary school years were not terribly happy. The homework on weekdays was only part of it. On Saturday we had to attend church, where one could not sit — we had to stand for the service. Our teacher would check to see if we were in church or not. I hated that, because I could not just stand for hours. That was torture for my brain as well as my body. Even today I hate to stand for a long time, even in the fun setting of a bar or nightclub. I want movement, or I want a seat.

During the breaks on school days, we could buy something light to eat, but that necessitated having a little money. When there are three kids, and all of them needed a little, there just wasn't enough to go around in our family. As soon as the bell sounded, the children would run out of the classroom. Not me. I just walked out and other thoughts came to mind. I looked at all my schoolmates running for no reason. Some were rude to others; others played with a small ball. I did not want to waste my energy; I had more things to do later on.

One day, while everyone was running around the playground, I had the idea to start a theatre.

I began thinking about how the stage would look, and what sort of performance it would be. What would it be about, and what role would I play? Should I be alone on stage? How much could I charge? And, why would they come? What were they really paying for?

I asked my father to help me build a podium and a simple stage on the roof of our house. He didn't object, but was very clear that I had to be careful up there. We didn't want the roof caving in on the family's heads! I couldn't have any other activities there, including playing with a ball.

I had figured out that I would have to be alone on stage, as I couldn't afford to pay anyone else. And, I didn't want my schoolmates to know what I was doing or how simple it was.

I started to think what they talked about on their breaks, their opinions and reactions, and their interests inside the classroom. I decided to play a hero, someone who helped others. But, I'd then need a couple of friends to play simple supporting roles. I carefully chose two of the most popular children in the class, boys who came from the upper classes. I thought that if they were involved, others would come and see them.

I prepared everything, and wrote the script. I came up with a few words — a sales pitch — to interest my would-be cast mates, so they'd hear out my explanation of why they should take part. I would keep the audience size to ten, as my father said that was all the roof could handle. Everyone would have to prepay. There would be a complimentary drink, which I'd make from the oranges in our garden. It would be watered down, to stretch it, so I'd add fresh basil to make it more palatable.

Finally, during a break at school, I made my appeal to these two classmates, and they accepted their roles. I asked them to tell me which other students might want to buy tickets. They were so excited, and made a list of who could be in the audience. I said no more that day, but everyone began asking what was going on, which generated great interest.

I replied that they'd have to buy a ticket, so they should bring money for that. The following morning, all ten had been sold — all to boys, since the sexes did not play together.

Finally, the big day arrived. I had to choose a day when neither my parents nor my siblings were home, as I wanted to be alone there. I started preparing all the details and asked my two cast members to come before the others were to arrive. I did not want them to change their minds or start asking questions.

It was a perfect day, a holiday, and it was very quiet around us. Even the neighbours had gone to the countryside for their time away from work. That was perfect for my theatre because the neighbours' roofs were just one metre away from one another, so they were more or less connected. That suited my 'action film' scenario, since a hero can't stand on stage and just talk about how good he is. He needs action — rooftop to rooftop, if necessary. I already knew that action helped me to be creative, and find the right words to tell others.

Everyone came on time. This was unusual, because some of them often arrived at school late. That made me feel like a real actor, so I felt that was halfway to success.

I started serving the orange drinks, which impressed everyone. At least they showed no sign that they disliked theirs. I put on some music, looked into their eyes and studied their faces to get into the mood to start. Then, suddenly, I was speechless. I had forgotten my lines. I looked at my notes but they were only words. The energy and the power had gone, and I knew they would not capture my audience.

Time passed and I had to act. Fortunately, the inspiration returned and I found the right words to start. My imagination flowed and I started to act as a real hero: a man who will do good things for others, one who is fearless, who could not be touched. No evil would confound him. Like a powerful angel, even the devil would quake in his presence. Within a few minutes the applause could be heard from many roofs away!

Action is my natural drug: it's difficult to explain how much my heart and soul love it and crave it. I started running around on our roof, but it was more exciting to use our neighbours' roofs, too. The audience began following me over, to stay with the action. We hopped from roof to roof, and one of them fell between two houses! He broke an arm, which healed just fine, but with that unfortunate accident, my first business ended on a disastrous note. Back at school, everyone knew what had gone down and talked about my mad production. I felt deep shame over how badly it had ended, and I knew I could not try it again. No one would come, and my parents certainly wouldn't allow it.

However, once an entrepreneur, always an entrepreneur. I might not have wanted to be a theatre producer again, but I knew I was creative. You simply cannot extinguish that part of your soul when it's so innately there. I knew that inspiration would hit again, and the next time I would have to see it through to a successful conclusion. I also knew that it wouldn't involve dangerous stunts that would see a paying customer hurt.

THERE WAS A SMALL NEIGHBOURHOOD SHOP 300 metres from our house where you could buy newspapers, sweets, clothes and toys. It was there that I saw a crocodile-skin belt in Bordeaux red that I really obsessed over. It was expensive, and I knew it would take me months of saving to afford it.

Every day I passed that shop and went in to say hello, but it was not a place where one felt welcome. The owner, Giannis, was not an outgoing, sociable person, so it wasn't easy for him to say hello and be welcoming — particularly to a little kid who wasn't really buying anything — day after day.

On one occasion, I hung around longer than normal, and Giannis began talking to me. He asked why I stopped there every day, not just in the mornings, but also in the afternoon. I told him that I loved the belt, and had even thought of stealing it, but that I would never actually do so. I'd been sorry that the thought had even come to me, and felt disgusted for a long time that I had even contemplated it. I had already been to the priest in confessional over it.

I could never steal anything; I couldn't even pick up things I spotted on the road. My parents' pride and their life values were rooted very deeply in my heart.

Giannis replied, "Yes, I saw that in your eyes, and I could also see that you will not steal. Your eyes are going to be your Achilles' heel. You will give yourself away. This will attract a lot of pain in your life, but also great success."

I asked him why he hadn't been able to sell some of the things he'd had in the store for years, gathering dust. He said that no one wanted them.

I jumped at the opportunity. "Give me a chance to sell those things for you," I said. "Let me be here before you open the shop, because I want to make some changes."

He laughed and nodded his head. Before he could even utter a word, I said to him, "Tomorrow morning is Saturday. Before I go to church, I'll be here at 6:30 AM. Can you open for me?"

All night I thought through why people were interested in certain items, why he couldn't sell those particular products, and what changes I could make. I couldn't sleep a wink. Thoughts ran in and out of my mind, but the belt made me feel so happy.

The next morning I was there at 6:30 sharp, but Giannis did not turn up until 7, with no explanation. He opened the door and turned the light on. Then he left me alone and locked the door behind me. He said he would be back at 8, so time was of the essence.

I stood still for a few minutes and looked around the store. Time was too limited for major changes, but I needed Giannis to sell these items.

I touched some of the toys on the top shelf. They were dusty and felt disgusting. My reaction was to clean them, and place them on the shop floor in front of the door where people came in. They were toys for children, yet they had been out of their sight. I decided to clean and remove as many items as possible, to make the shop look different and new.

At 8:00, Giannis returned and shouted, "What have you done? Don't put these on the floor; people can't get in!"

I was very sure of my idea and too young to know otherwise. I told him, "Let it be for two days, and if I'm wrong, I'll put everything back. But if you sell some of these, I'll need the belt as a gift."

I headed to church, but my mind stayed on his shop and all the toys I had placed in front of the door. My first reaction was that he would sell it all, but a few minutes later, my rational brain kicked in and I was filled with doubt. Maybe I was wrong. But at the same time, something told me, "Your first instinct is the right one. Do not change it now."

After the church service, I headed to the shop. A few metres from the entrance, I contemplated whether to go in or not. I was just outside the door when a father with two children came out with some of the once-dusty toys that I had cleaned. They were shining. I remembered my father's advice: stand tall. I straightened myself up and waltzed into the shop with a big smile. Giannis looked at me, but he had to tend to the customers looking at items I'd put on the floor. After serving them, he said, "You were right. People said the new toys were nice, or 'My son has his birthday tomorrow.' I've already sold three pieces that had been here for years! Come after school or before school, and help me make some changes. I'll pay you. I'm tired and I hate my job. I'm waiting for the day I can retire."

And right then and there, he gave me the belt. You cannot imagine how proud I was. Not so much about the sales Giannis had made but about the belt that I had longed for. Now it was mine. I had earned it. My confidence was at an all-time high, and I knew I could stand up and explain my ideas. I had dared to make changes, and it paid off

I felt like a big man at nine years old. Now I could go to school wearing that belt, and it did not matter that I stood in the last row every morning. (We used to line up in rows of three, with the tallest students in front.) Everyone will see me! Panos is here with this unique belt.

Sure enough, every one of my classmates was crazy about it — my first adventure in fashion. Most people will never discover their talent, and I think 80% are working at the wrong things, without passion, and not innovating in any way.

I FELT A REAL SENSE OF INJUSTICE over our family's financial status when I was a child. Leaving poverty was a firm dream, for poverty equalled endless torment.

In our class were a few children whose parents were higher up in society, and they had plenty of books at home. Makis, a friendly child, lived a few hundred metres from us and his father had some decent work with the government. Their house, in my eyes, was like a castle. One time he invited me to play with him after school and to visit his house. For me, that was a major event. I was anxious to see his books, toys and bicycle.

We became friends, but as I didn't come from the same class, his family made me feel it. They talked to me in a way that made me feel unwelcome. However, Makis allowed me into his room one time, to go through his encyclopaedia set as I did my homework. It was overwhelming looking at these six huge books, filled with so much information and so many photos.

This was the norm when I was six to nine years of age. We never really had enough, and luxuries were hard to come by.

Makis had a low-profile personality but he was clever. He wanted to be my friend, and there was a symbiosis. I might have been poor but I had style — I had that belt — and knowing me brought him joy.

I realized then that it does not matter who you are and what you have. If you can find someone to have that sort of close, mutually satisfying relationship with, you can feel better and more complete as a person.

You can only discover your talent when you feel free. I understand now that I could nurture my talent when I was young, and I already had an interest in creative pursuits.

There was definitely creativity in the family. My father often worked at night so he could carry out construction on our small house — which he'd built with his own two hands, along with a couple of friends — during the day. He had to paint the walls and roof every two years because of general wear and tear. He was particularly focused when he was doing this. When I was eight or nine, I decided I would take my father's brush and paint a tree on an outside wall. Then, I painted birds of different colours. He asked, "Do you want to make the whole wall like this?" I said that I did, and he let me deface the whole wall with my art. Thinking back on it now, I'm sure it looked positively awful. Even the neighbours would ask, "What on earth happened here?" But my father didn't mind. He encouraged me, and gave me this kind of freedom. That's something we should all nurture, in ourselves and our children.

ALL THE VALUES WE HAVE as adults come from our early years. I've always disliked people who cannot behave or control themselves, because they're drunk or on drugs. It's not so much that I am passing moral judgement on others, but I hate that alcohol and drug abuse takes people away from whom they really are. They don't realize just how much goodness they bring, or can bring, to others' lives when they're clear-eyed and standing tall.

It wasn't uncommon in the 1950s and 1960s for the men to go out drinking, and come home drunk. I remember neighbours, friends of my father, doing so, and all that flowed from it: the arguing, the domestic disturbances. But my father never came home drunk. He always said to me: "Don't lose your control." That always stuck with me, and I understood innately just how wasteful and purposeless it was to see men drink to lose who they were. As an adult, I can smoke a single cigarette or have one drink without becoming hooked. I never got to a point where I couldn't control something like that. I've never been drunk, nor have I ever engaged in unruly behaviour.

It was also common to see them gamble. Greeks of that era would play cards for money, and this could lead to disastrous consequences, with many losing what meagre earnings or savings they had. My father might play for a tiny amount, but he always knew when to stop. Come six or seven o'clock, he would be home. "Never play cards, never gamble," he would say, and to this day I still refuse to. Once again, I couldn't see the purpose behind it, especially if it led to the sort of disharmony I witnessed in other families around us.

My father smoked, but he had respect for others and was careful about where he lit up. He never once smoked inside our house. I can't think of any Greeks back then who would smoke outside. That impressed me a lot, and it taught me about consideration for others. It also sent the message that I should have control of my body, including my pain and my desires.

This has a downside, too. If you tolerate too much pain, you may well pass the limits of what is healthy. I've done that with my body and with my soul. I've gone to the dentist and insisted I didn't need anaesthesia. One time, in the 1980s, when I didn't have a good dentist, a nurse fainted during a procedure where there was a lot of blood. I always wanted to remain in control of a situation, but that can create other issues.

I IMAGINE it was Dad's own sense of self-worth and pride that he wanted to convey to the three of us. "Even if you are poor," he'd tell us, "you are rich enough to be clean." That was another one of his sayings, and he stuck by it.

My parents managed to find a balance, and everything developed slowly. I remember that the dry bread I had to soak in water and sometimes put powdered sugar on became bread with oil, and later with margarine. The sugar gave way to jam. I remember that the winters were cold and the bed even colder. As soon as I climbed into bed at night, I pulled the blanket over my head and started breathing quickly to warm the air under the covers. That was after we had gone out to wash ourselves with icy water before going to bed. That was pure torture.

My parents seemed happy enough with how life was progressing. They made sure that we were washed properly every Sunday, and that we wore clean clothes and shoes. Dad sometimes pulled up the blanket when he came home from work in the morning, to check on whether we had properly washed our feet. At that time, everything was muddy. There was no paving, and our shoes and feet turned black. If you had not washed your feet for a couple of days, they might have turned permanently black. Children are bound to get their clothes and shoes dirty from play, and I was no exception, but it wouldn't be tolerated for long in our house.

In addition to the feet inspection, Dad would check our shoes each morning. If I failed the inspection, he would say, "They are not clean. Go and clean them." To this day I still keep my shoes spotless; it's a habit that never left me. As an adult, women regularly complimented me about my clean shoes.

My father was a proud man, and with that pride came other lessons. "You are always to be kind," he told us. Kindness came with pride, automatically. We were never allowed to be rude to anyone. Others might shun Gypsies, but we never did. When they asked for money, we had to decline, as we were barely better off ourselves, but we were always polite to them. "Be proud of what you are and what you have," both my parents would say. "If you have kindness, then you are a good person." I saw how helpful they were to everyone, and how they spoke with respect for others, no matter whom they were. I am convinced that you must have the right attitude toward everyone. One cannot be respectful to some and disrespectful to others.

We also learned to be tolerant of others. And if you borrowed something, you returned it on time. Mind you, one thing my parents never had to tell me was to be on time, because I always was. In fact, I'd usually be early for everything. Those little things all added up.

In those days, it was so easy for those of us children who had very little to take the wrong path in life. Many resorted to petty crimes, which usually led to greater criminal activity. I am so thankful that my parents instilled in me their values. We might not have been affluent, but we had a lot of love in the household, and were raised to place greater value on who we were as people than what physical possessions we owned. My outlook has not changed one bit.

My father worked hard to feed the family, and bring about little, incremental improvements, so we could have a better life. My mother worked full-time, and took care of the family budget and our finances. She might not have gone to school, but she could count on her fingers. Dad never insulted her by bringing up her lack of schooling. In fact, I never heard them argue about anything in front of us, even though they surely had their differences at times. It's a lesson modern society could learn, as today I see couples who find it acceptable to argue in front of others, even strangers. This remains very unsettling for me. Here my father didn't have a saying, but I witnessed how a loving couple behaved, and knew to do the same.

I find I'm very sensitive about anything artificial, and this probably informs my attitude toward drugs. As a boy, our neighbour's grapevine grew across to our side. They tended to put chemicals on it, to keep insects away and promote a greater harvest. We relied on our little garden, but my father never did that. "I don't want this poison in me," he said.

He could see that people were poisoning their own food, even though we lived in an industrial ghetto filled with thousands of poor workers from all over Greece, where money and food were limited. Nevertheless, he would say, "Better we don't have 10 kg of these grapes. I'd rather have fewer, but have them be purer."

Growing up, it was perfectly natural to kill chickens and lambs, since they provided something to eat. But, it was important in our family that this was done with respect. That's something I've witnessed in many cultures around the world, especially indigenous ones. When my father killed a chicken, he never did it in front of us. Because of this, I can't fathom how we've become a world that doesn't treat animals with respect, where farmers use intensive procedures to force cows to make more milk or feed hormones to chickens that barely have room to move. Fundamental respect for nature seems to be so lacking these days.

One time I did see my mother cut the neck of one of the chickens outside. She normally did it when we weren't home, so we wouldn't see how they killed the animal. She realized I was standing there and told me to go away, dropping the knife. At this moment, the chicken freed itself from her other hand and jumped around, its blood gushing everywhere. She tried to push me back into the house. She understood that it wasn't good for me to witness this, and saw how those few seconds affected me. I know full well the trauma other children around the world have experienced when they see terrible things, like killing and war.

Now, I can't pass judgement on whether vegetarianism or veganism is right or wrong, but I understand those who object to eating animals, since society has crossed a line in some of our farming practices. Look at how our crops are grown, for instance. As a child, I knew that after we harvested the tomatoes, we would have to wait. First, we'd have to fertilize the soil properly with animal by-product, and then we planted, because that was what a natural process demanded. Today, many farmers put chemicals in the soil to get those tomatoes in more quickly, and this means we consume those chemicals. Most of our food is poison. We once treated nature with respect, and in the West that's gravely missing. We could do well to learn from the past, including from those cultures that have thrived for millennia, and who have kept their agricultural and farming practices pure. They'll still be around long after the West has exhausted its livestock and land, and is racked with health problems.

In recent years, I've realized how important all this was and how great an impact it had on my personality. In our family, we learned to be proud, polite, clean, and to show respect for everyone and everything. Not only sentient beings, but also toward our plants. We got to see how respectfully my parents treated the animals and plants that would later become our food. They always did that little bit extra to nurture them and make them healthier. It was also about respecting ourselves, since how we treated the animals and plants would affect us.

I remember a little goat that I took and slept with in my bed until it was three or four months old. I remember the relationship I had with my kitten, Chico. And my little chickens, which would leave the property each day, walking down a few hundred metres to greet me as I came back from school. There was one in particular that remains in my thoughts.

The chickens produced eggs for us, and I accepted that some would be slaughtered for their meat. However, among the newborn chicks was one with a crooked beak. I named it Stravomiti, Greek for 'crooked nose.' Every time we fed the chickens, this one never had a chance to eat as much as the others. And so, I always took it aside and fed it separately. Despite this attention, it always remained small.

It is impossible to describe just how happy it was every time it saw me. I would shout, "Stravomiti!" and it would run to me.

One day I returned from school and noticed that it was not waiting for me along the road as usual. It would always accompany the hens and chicks in that greeting ritual. I had the strangest feeling. I was just a small child, but my body was telling me something. It was as though a strange blanket enveloped me, filling me with dread. I screamed, but no one came forward. My Mum then heard me, and ran toward me. "What is it?" she asked.

I looked her in the eyes and felt that she was concealing something, that something was wrong. I told her that Stravomiti was missing. "We can check together," she said. "It may be a little further away." I felt like she was buying time. I stared into her eyes and started crying.

She responded, "The cat has taken it!"

"You're lying!" I screamed. "What have you done with my Stravomiti?!" I screamed more and more loudly. She tried to hug me but I refused her. I ran to our rubbish bin but it was not there. I ran to our neighbours' bin, and there I saw a bag with its bones.

I became so weak. The little boy who could lift heavy things, dared to walk in dark streets and jumped from roof to roof — suddenly, I was as light as one of Stravomiti's feathers. I had known that that the bigger chicks would outlive it, and it would one day be gone, but that small living thing had been mine to protect and care for.

My biggest disappointment was my mother's explanation. Mum, who was the most righteous in the eyes of God!

She laid me gently in my bed and tried to hold me in her arms. My strength surged back, growing into a strong aggression. I spied a man on the steps who was fixing our neighbour's electrical cables. I saw his eyes staring at me, and I could see he was the reason they slaughtered my Stravomiti. It was his payment for the work, and he had eaten it! I pushed my mother from me, quickly jumped up, ran towards him and pushed him so hard that he fell down the steps, hitting his head on a table and drawing blood.

I can still remember the blood gushing from his wound and his screaming. Mum had no time to stop me. My siblings arrived when they heard the commotion, as had the neighbour, who wanted to help. My sister Giota took me away while the others tended to the electrician.

I was inconsolable. I shouted that I wanted to kill the bastard who ate my Stravomiti!

Why I was particularly upset, despite knowing that my parents often slaughtered chickens for dinner, was because I knew Stravomiti was fragile. It didn't have the same opportunity as the others to survive. I simply could not accept its disadvantage. Maybe we had something in common: neither of us had the right opportunities at the start of our lives. It was weak and I was poor. It could not defend itself, and I saw his killing as a grave injustice.

I seem to have always had a gift of being able to read the situation before it's explained to me. From that point I developed a greater ability to understand things, reading those signals and knowing what my body was telling me. I still remember hearing my mother ask the neighbour, "How could he see from the electrician's eyes that he had eaten his chicken?"

I was severely depressed for a few weeks. Everyone tried to comfort me, enticed me with everything I could wish for, but it was pointless.

Mum explained that we needed to fix the electricity at home so we could light the lamps, and the electrician wanted fresh chicken to eat while he was doing the job. That made me even angrier.

Afterwards, my Mum told others this story with a sense of pride. She was proud of her little boy, who wanted to protect a weak creature. She saw how the electrician had looked at me, and I know that, deep down, she thought his punishment fit the crime.

It's no wonder that at a very early age I took action against the harming of life, and against environmental pollution. I had been inspired by my parents' actions. I was doing what Greenpeace would do, and this came to a fore in my teenage years. Children see and hear more than we think, and that affects them deeply.

EVERY SUMMER, parents had the challenge of figuring out what to do with their children. They had to work, but school was out for the holidays. We needed to get some fresh air and grow stronger. Those Greeks who could afford it sent their kids to camp for a few weeks. There, they would learn good habits: to wake up, clean their room, eat regularly, explore the forest, be together with others and, most importantly, get some fresh air into their lungs.

Sometimes the government gave coupons to poorer people so their kids could experience this, too. I was given that opportunity, but it didn't agree with me. I was counting the days and hours before I could go back home. I hated sleeping with so many others in the same room, and having someone else decide what you would do every minute of the day. This was very stressful for me. I missed my little animals and my freedom.

The other option my parents had was to send me to some relatives in the countryside. Mum had many sisters, and one was living in Diakofto, a very nice summer destination in the west of the country. I was around seven or eight when they put me in a bus, with a packed bag, headed to Diakofto for the first time. The bus had a smell — the exhaust fumes — that made me feel sick. It was a six- to seven-hour trip, but it felt like years. I would feel sick to my stomach in waves, and didn't know what to do.

The bus drove around the wild mountains and I could not see any life, just barren, rocky landscapes. When the bus passed the Corinth Canal everything got worse: it seemed that we drove around in a circle, rounding mountain after mountain. Finally, I could not control myself and vomited all over my clothes, producing another terrible smell.

The driver stopped and asked me to get out. My small eyes looked for a place to disappear to, as it was embarrassing and I smelled so badly. I wanted to go back home.

The bus had stopped on a very high mountain, and I was just a few centimetres from the edge. I looked down and had a sudden sense that I would lose my balance and fall. I had never been on such a high vantage point, and looking down, all I could imagine was hell. After that, I've always been scared of heights and can't be close to the edge of anything high.

They took me back into the bus and the driver told me, "Don't be afraid, we only have three hours to go!"

Three hours? After that, I lost it. I started to cry, but what would my parents say if they saw me like this? They were proud of me because I was a big boy — in their eyes I was someone who'd showed an early sense of responsibility in everything. I was a youngster who could sit next to older people and get involved in their dialogue. Suddenly, this big boy was acting like a baby, crying, scared of the loneliness of the road. And I hated being on the edge of this terrible, ugly mountain. I could not understand why people loved mountains, where they must fight to stay up there and not fall down to hell.

Finally, the bus reached Diakofto. A round, bald man was waiting for me: it was my mother's sister's husband. One cousin was also waiting. They hugged me, but I could not get any words out. Silence took over my soul and controlled my body. My first reaction was that this place looked nice and didn't smell as bad as home. During the long walk to their house, I saw that the natural surroundings were very green. The place was thick with trees and bushes. There were donkeys that transported people. I saw a long train and could not count how many wagons it had. When we arrived at their house, more cousins were waiting. They had a big family of nine children.

All my cousins were older than me and were involved in work, on the fields or in the workshops. One of the older brothers had private workshops making windows and doors.

One of my cousins, who was around 18, used to catch octopus, and one early morning, at 4:30, I joined him. He chose a rocky place where the water would get deep very quickly, just a couple of metres from shore. I stood on a rock in the water, as I couldn't swim. I was impressed with my cousin's skill: he just jumped in with a knife in one hand, and I enjoyed watching how he freely moved up and down in the water. A few minutes later, he had already caught a big octopus. He came out of the water and wrestled with it on the rock. He eventually subdued it, and then jumped back into the water.

I wondered what would happen next, when I spied a small octopus next to me in the water. Without a thought, I dipped my hand in to catch it. The octopus caught my hand and pulled me into the sea. I tried to come up again but that was not possible. The little octopus seemed stronger than me, and was used to being in the water. In those precious seconds, thousands of thoughts came flooding into my brain. Why? Where are my parents? I'm dying.

My cousin came up on land and did not see me on the rock, but he could make out the black shape of the octopus under the water. He realized what had happened and dove back in to look for me. It would have only been seconds, but it felt like hours to me. He pulled me out of the deep water, and lay me down and shook me. Water came from my mouth and ears. My eyes rolled back and I began to lose consciousness as I saw him cut away the octopus that was still clinging to my hand.

This wasn't the only mishap out in Diakofto. One day, my cousins and their parents had to go into the fields before dawn, and they didn't want me tagging along. They said they would be home in a few hours and let me sleep. I woke up soon after they left, and was waiting on the balcony, looking at the garden. Some goats, a lot of chickens and a couple of pigs were just outside, so I didn't feel so alone.

On the table was some dry bread and, as they always had in the villages, some tomatoes and olives. I'd had so much of these during the last few days and was tired of them. I went to the table and touched the bread, and it was too dry to eat. I went out and tried to hug a pig, and could not understand why it reacted so aggressively. The chickens were not like mine — these were more wild — and they didn't want a hug from me either.

I went back to bed but started to feel alone, and a lot of tears came. It was better to be up because as soon as I sat down, I started crying again. Time went very slowly and I started to feel more anxious. My hunger was becoming stronger and my stomach hurt. I touched the bread again but I didn't want to have it so dry. I put some water on it, but it was still impossible to eat.

I love milk, but there was none. They had either forgotten to milk the goats or it was too early. I went outside again and started playing with a ball they had in the garden, but I was too hungry to keep playing. I saw the goat's big hanging teat, which I imagined had plenty of milk. I ran to get a bowl, to try to milk the goat. I tried for several minutes but could not get a single drop. I had seen my cousins to do it every day, and it had looked so easy for them.

My hunger was getting unbearable. I stretched out under the goat, put the teat on my mouth and tried to drink her milk. The goat did not like it a bit and started running. In her nervousness, she defecated at the same time. All I managed to get out of her were some faeces in my mouth.

ON SUNDAYS, my mother worked an extra job, cleaning the factory office and the small home of the manager, Mr Savvas, which was adjacent to it. I used to follow her there and scrub the floor, even when I was five or six.

I loved doing it. I would be there till 1 or 2 PM, and that was the best day of the week for me.

Mr Savvas was a short, generously proportioned bald man, though he had once been blond. I couldn't make out any eyebrows above his huge eyes. He resembled the stereotype of a big, strong, rough-looking man in an American movie. He walked a little strangely, and sweated a lot. He never dressed like a boss — he wore a huge white T-shirt every day. He was a clever man, with a polytechnic education. He had diabetes and other health conditions, and was often in a bad mood.

Savvas drove a beige Volvo Amazon, which I also cleaned each weekend. Having a Volvo in those days was like having a Rolls-Royce to us, but he never really bothered with its cleanliness or appearance. He usually just sat at his desk with dozens of pieces of papers around him, and made calculations.

I did not understand how he could find what he wanted on that cluttered desk, but my mother was careful not to move anything from its place. She'd pick up paper after paper, dust and polish the desk, and then place each paper back in precisely the same spot. She was careful when she breathed, so that she did not blow something away from its place. Savvas appreciated this.

A couple of times a month, he would go around the factory for an impromptu inspection, to see how efficient the workers were. That, along with shuffling through papers on his desk, seemed to be the sum of his duties at Viomichania Chalyvon AE.

He tried to show a hard, almost heartless exterior, perhaps not unlike some men of his generation who couldn't display affection by saying things like "I like you," or "I love you." I never heard my parents say that to each other, either, but I never thought much of it, since the way they acted showed that they loved and respected each other.

I still remember the shock I had the first time I went to London, with everyone calling each other, "Love." I asked the family I was staying with what the English used when they went to greet their real, true love. They looked at each other for a moment, smiled and told me with a shrug, "Love."

Savvas often worked weekends and Mum cooked his special omelette. He ate eggs all the time.

One Sunday — I must have been ten — he called for us but my mother was not there. I ran over to see what he wanted. "I must have an omelette," he said, "at once!"

"Mum will be there in a few minutes," I told him, "but I can try to make your omelette."

He glared at me, but then gave a small smile. I ran to the kitchen and jumped into action. I whipped the eggs and warmed the tomatoes. I had an idea: I would do something to surprise him. I noticed that every time I picked up his plate after he'd finished eating, there was tomato peel. I remember that because he always licked the plate, leaving it shining, save for those red tomato peels. I had listened to his comments about how much salt and pepper he wanted, so I knew how to season it properly.

Others used to whine about his strange demands, and were always forced to apologize when he complained that the omelette was not to his liking. So, I knew he was demanding.

I knew what to do.

The omelette was ready, along with the tomatoes. I grabbed the plate and ran to his office. I knocked on the door but he did not answer. I quickly opened the door. Savvas sat there exhausted, having lost his strength, despite his hefty body. His large belly hung over the desk. In one hand he held the black telephone receiver, as though he were trying to call someone. In the other hand was his insulin injection. I spied it, and I panicked. I went close to him and I shook with fear. He suddenly moved a little and said, "Well, did you come to give me the omelette?" His eyes looked strange and I could not stop trembling for several hours. It was not the first time I had seen him collapsed at his desk. I have had a lifelong fear of seeing someone die, and not being able to do anything.

Savvas began eating and his energy gradually returned. When he had finished, he stared at me with his angry gaze and yelled, "Who made this omelette?"

I replied that I had, because my mother was not there.

He raised his powerful hand and beckoned me to come close to him. I didn't know what would happen, and I was still trembling.

He put his heavy hand on my shoulder and said, "It was the best omelette I have ever eaten. However did you come up with the idea of *peeling the tomatoes?*"

Even as he praised me, his gaze and tone remained angry, but I had learned to see through that façade. I only saw his inner thoughts, his innermost soul. I felt that he was a kind person, but a bit primitive in his demeanour. Everyone was afraid of him, but there was something deep down that told me he had a big heart.

Working was always a great pleasure. It helped me grown and develop, because I had the right attitude. No matter what I did, I wanted to do it better than everyone else. I would even compete with my own mother. The little matter of the tomato peel — my attention to doing it right, and the praise and satisfaction it brought — would come to characterize how I approached everything in life. I recognized the importance of listening and interpreting the need, instead of imposing one's will on others.

I would like to say that my knowledge of sociological marketing was developed even then, at an unconscious level. Listen to the need and strive to satisfy it. How can you fail at that? Being observant — seeing the details, and responding appropriately — were what I took with me from that moment. Showing respect to the person who pays your salary is a basic quality that is unfortunately lacking in today's society.

After this, I developed a very special relationship with 'the angry boss.'

He paid private doctors to examine me. I got a litre of milk every other day, and he carefully checked to see if I was growing. He also bought my first encyclopaedia, which helped me tremendously with my homework. In many ways, he became an additional parent for my siblings and me.

SAVVAS BELIEVED IN ME. This gave me a boost. Here was someone who could see the glow in my eyes, and had a big heart, even though he was angry all the time. Why would a boy of ten leave such an imprint on this big man, he who was so much better off, always angry and impossible to talk to? He was the terror of most of the workers in the factory. He was alone, with no immediate family. He probably had relatives somewhere who were waiting for his last day to come.

I still remember one day when he addressed me in a different tone than the one he took with his siblings' children, who happened to be there. I stepped into his office with my big, wondering eyes. I could sense the other children thinking, "Just who do you think you are?" I felt their jealousy, and it didn't take long before they wanted to put me in my place.

On the way out, through the long corridor that my mother had just scrubbed clean, they intentionally spilled coffee and scattered food. They ran back and forth and laughed, stomping through the mess, as if to mark their status. And because I was still small in size, it was easy for them to look down on me physically.

I could not understand why this seemed to be so much fun for them, soiling the place and jumping around like wild animals, looking for trouble.

I had a thought to lay into them, but my Mum appeared, saw what was happening and pulled me aside. "They are just kids," she whispered. "It does not matter. We will redo it later, when they've gone."

I heard that sentence again and again, as long as she lived. It does not matter. She was always so caring, forgiving people before they even asked for forgiveness. She made it clear that the hateful incident in the corridor didn't matter. I was angry, but I did not know what to say. I was silent the rest of the evening, my child's brain bombarded by various images. It felt like it was too much for me to handle. After a while, the kids left the building and sat in the boss's car, which I also polished every weekend.

On the way home, my mother tried to talk about other things to make me forget the incident. She understood that it had been a traumatic humiliation for her son. I remember that night as though it was yesterday. It has stayed with me for more than 50 years.

One day, I wanted to design a desk in the factory's carpentry shop and asked if I could do it after work. I wasn't allowed in the workshop due to my young age. Savvas questioned whether I was capable of what I was suggesting. "Are you just going to buy one in the store, and I pay for it?" I insisted that I had an idea and promised that I would not handle any tools, but get help from an older worker. He relented. I set to work, with the idea brewing inside me so strongly that I can still summon up the feeling. In fact, the desk is still there, and is just as nice half a century later!

I got to try all sorts of jobs at the factory. While I was in primary school, I could work in the afternoon for a few hours, and again on the weekends. By the time I was in high school, I would put in time on the technical production line. I was working on contract, and could deliver in four hours or less work that was timed for eight … and got paid for eight hours. The fact that I got to work so early in life gave me a great deal of satisfaction. I could find solutions to problems, meet adults and work with them. I learned to handle different situations, work through tough challenges, and see the positive results I'd achieved with my own two hands. Above all, I saw my dream of leaving poverty — something I'd yearned for since I was very small — coming true. That job shaped me, both my strengths and weaknesses.

I was officially employed in Greece from the age of 14 and worked there until the day I moved to Sweden at 19.

WHEN I REFLECT on how my Saturdays and Sundays looked, as well as my holidays, it explains a lot about me as an adult. I cite that formative backstory whenever my own children ask why I work so much every day,

Sundays included. I've learned to trust in myself, because you should never expect anyone else to solve your problems.

I believe that every successful person will tell you that they have one thing in common when they look back: they started being the person they came to be at a young age. If you follow your first instinct, do not change it. Don't let others put doubts in your head, just because they do not dare do what you do. Don't let your rational brain make you doubt yourself, either. Stay on your true path. You have your goals, regardless of what anyone else says.

**Listen to your inner self,
and let the best values guide you.**

2
From actor to activist

ONE THING MY FATHER DID DISCOURAGE, due to the tensions in Greece at the time, was involvement in politics. He said he wasn't into politics, but I remember seeing political books under his bed. He was at heart a socialist who believed in social democracy, but it was dangerous to believe in anything democratic in Greece at the time. This was ironic, as Greece had given the world the concept of democracy, and the word itself.

During the 1950s and '60s, and then during the *metapolitefsi* period, when a military junta took control from 1967 to 1974, Greece was a politically turbulent place. When Georgios Papandreou's Centre Union party won the election in 1963 and he became prime minister, certain political forces inflamed tensions, leading to his resignation. There were cultural conflicts in the country as well, as long hair, rock 'n' roll and the whole counterculture movement became fashionable. In 1967, four colonels led a military coup and declared martial law. King Constantine II, who lacked military support and failed with a counter-coup, was forced into exile. Civil liberties were suppressed, and even long hair was banned. Opposing political parties were outlawed and the military junta instituted censorship. By 1973, the junta had abolished the monarchy, and this was ratified as law soon after.

Under this dictatorship, my father warned, "You are too young to read about politics. You need to be reading about other things." He pushed me in another direction, but events were soon to take place that would bring me head to head with these political forces.

ONE DAY IN 1973, a well-dressed insurance agent from Proodos SA of Athens visited Viomichania Chalyvon AE when the boss was out. I opened the door for him. I was 15, but I always acted as though I was older in meetings or on the phone, which was why Savvas allowed me to get involved in things. However, he was worried that the authorities might find out that he'd given an underage kid such responsibilities.

The agent started to explain to me how he wanted to meet with our workers during their breaks to sell life or accident insurance. I asked him to come back the week after, or to call my boss. I explained it was unlikely that he would be allowed on the factory floor.

He was on the way out when I stopped him and said, "Give me your card. Maybe I know someone who can do that here for you. Explain a bit more to me, and we can see."

We sat down and went through what he did. After a few minutes, I said, "I want to work for you in my free time. I know more factories, so I'm sure I can sell a lot."

We decided to visit their head office together and explore the possibilities. It was located on Andrea Syngrou Avenue, a major artery in central Athens.

I was prepared for the meeting and ready to show his boss, Cleanthes, what I could do for them. It would be a perfect second job for me, because I could do it any day, at any hour, and make a lot of money. I had called other insurance companies and proposed the same, to see how easy it was to get a job like this, and to compare prices and packages. **It's a basic principle in business: do your research on the competition, and understand the environment.**

I could see how this type of business could expand quickly, but approaching regular people, from the lower and middle classes, to propose insuring them posed a major hurdle. They were suspicious, because there were bad stories everywhere about insurance companies that never paid up, or closed shop, losing all the workers' money.

When I came into their office I was impressed. There were huge, clean windows and amazing views. All the staff wore suits and carried themselves professionally. I went with Cleanthes and several of his colleagues into a large meeting room.

Cleanthes was an interesting man, with a sympathetic voice. Many bosses were rather rude in those days, but I used to say that he was 'human educated,' someone who would not show off his position through shouting or intimidation. Once we were in the office environment, he carefully studied me, for a little too long. I started feeling uncomfortable. My first thought went to my clothes, which were very basic in a room full of suits.

"If you are thinking about my clothes," I said, "I must say that I've done some exploration of how potential customers in a factory setting react to insurance salespeople. Now, I don't know how to say this …"

"Tell me what you have to say," Cleanthes said, in his calm voice. "Don't worry … it's important for us to know."

I continued, "They call out, '*Koustoumakias* coming!'" A *koustoumakias* is a person who wears a suit, but the term has negative connotations. In English it might be equated to a *tosser* — an altogether obnoxious, self-absorbed person.

After I said the word, there was silence in the room. They looked at each other, and, of course, they were all wearing suits.

"Now, I'm not going to wear a suit," I added. "I'll wear presentable clothes when I meet my clients. My plan is to work with people around me, and appeal to them on their level, and see the results."

Most of the staff got up and silently left the room. It was not clear whether it was me, and what I had told them, or if they legitimately had to go for some other reason. Cleanthes was still there, along with one very young, beautiful secretary, who smiled and kept her composure when I said "*koustoumakias*."

An hour passed, and I was still there, going through their policy and their goals for sales representatives. I pointed out how important it was not to promise things that the company couldn't deliver on, just because it was a way of getting new clients. That was why insurance companies had a bad reputation. **I understood the consumer, whereas they didn't. Academics call this adopting a market orientation.** It's something so simple, that's been proven to help drive sales, yet many business people still don't do it.

I wanted that job, because this company had something that set it apart, and it would be my trump card to persuade a new client. I'll come to this shortly. Most people did not believe these insurance companies would be around for the long term because they had to pay out a lot. All the factory workers had said the same.

I also knew that the insurance companies were always after new salespeople, so after a lengthy discussion, I wanted to close the deal. I had no time to come back to central Athens.

I asked if we could go through the contract and make it ready, because I had already been in contact with a few of their rivals. "Let's talk about commission," I said.

The beautiful secretary left the room to get some contracts. She returned a few seconds later and gave me one to read. It was many pages long, and that made me uncomfortable. I hated reading page after page of dry contractual language, and still do today. "Let's talk in percentage terms," I said. "How much, and for how long a time will you pay me a commission?"

They had different percentages depending on sales volumes. I negotiated that if I could get a certain number of new clients beyond what had been planned, I should get the highest percentage from the first day.

They seemed to like the idea, but Cleanthes said, "No, because we believe in a long-term relationship."

"Yes," I replied, "but I won't be here for a long time. In a very short time I can get more customers than you can imagine. That's great for you, too, so let's sign now."

The secretary started filling in the contract and asked for my ID. I gave it to her; she stared at it for a moment, and her eyes got wide. She looked at Cleanthes, exclaiming, "He's only a kid of 15!"

"I'll be 16 in a few weeks," I said.

Cleanthes seemed a bit confused, and said with the same calm voice, "It's not allowed under the law. You must be 18! But I like you, so come back in two years."

I said, "No way." I told him that the other companies I'd talked to had asked about my age, and were willing to pay me using my brother's name on the official documentation. "You pay the salary to him, but it's me who does the work," I responded. "Where's the problem?"

I left their office with a signed contract in my hand, and a lot of brochures so I could start the day after. I worked there for more than two years, had the top sales figures every month and made a lot of money.

The company was in insurance, but it had an extra word in its name: *antasfalistiki*. It was a reinsurer. That meant it insured other insurance companies. This was the additional feature I mentioned earlier. This, for me, was a huge advantage in persuading customers to sign up. It would alleviate their fears that the operation would shut down in the dark of night.

A company called American Insurance was prepared to offer me a better arrangement, but being with an *antasfalistiki* would help me seal the deal. I knew from my research that no one wanted to feel insecure, and this would help settle the matter quickly. It was an early example of how sociological thinking and marketing became so helpful to my success.

IN MY BUSINESS, I worked with many international celebrities. When I look back, show business kept pulling me in.

I started to write songs when I was ten. It wasn't only Voskopoulos who inspired me, but also a singer and guitarist named Kostas Hatzis. His songs had philosophical messages about humans and how we act.

I wrote some songs that I imagined would be perfect for Voskopoulos, and my dream was to meet him. Despite not having an actual instrument, I would pretend to play music with my hands — air guitar. There was no possibility that I could buy an actual instrument. My father could see that I had a dream, and when I was 13 he surprised me with an unbelievable present. He'd bought me a guitar, and a beautiful one at that. It immediately took the kitten Chico's place: I slept with it, hugging it tightly in my arms.

Days passed and the guitar stayed with me. I wanted to learn to play something, but how? I got frustrated because in films it appeared that you just moved your fingers up and down the neck, and wonderful sounds emerged.

I had to do something, but nobody offered guitar lessons in our suburb. The centre of Athens was an hour away by bus, but at that age — years before my insurance venture — I had never been there.

Soon, however, I learned that our class would go on a field trip to visit the Acropolis. That day, my eyes looked around, absorbing every detail of every house, every store, every sign. I was impressed with the city's size and how many people there were.

When we walked from the bus station to the Acropolis, we passed music schools, and I asked my teacher if I could go into one for a minute and enquire. I returned with my head down.

"What happened?" she asked.

I told her that it was too expensive.

I knew that if my father were there, he would remind me again to stand up, straighten my shoulders and look forward! I did, but as we walked around the Acropolis, all I thought about was that music school and how I could manage to go there.

It wasn't just that day. I thought all the time about music and what I could do to learn how to play. I felt very unlucky and sad as I dwelled on it. At my school, we had a music lesson once a week, with a teacher who had a very angry face. It was strange to be a music teacher and look like that, I thought. His tactic was to surprise students by saying they would be examined. Normally, if you had been subjected to an examination, you could feel safe for a few weeks, until your turn came again.

He had given me a surprise exam a week earlier, and I hadn't been prepared, although I managed to pass. When he came to the classroom this time, he looked around and carefully studied our faces. I was nervous, because I still hadn't had time to look at the lessons, and he sensed that.

He asked me to come up next to him. "You did not expect that I'd examine you again," he said. "Remember, all of you, that at any time I can see if you've done your homework or not."

I could not look him in the eyes, as they seemed capable of drilling into your soul and taking your energy. They were full of such sadness and anger.

"I will ask you ten questions," he said, "and you have to give at least five right answers to pass. Each question is worth two points, and you'll need at least ten points."

He started asking his questions, one after another. I don't know what happened, but I answered them all quickly, and correctly. He stared at me with an even angrier face, and then broke into applause!

For the first time, I got 20 points. Prior to that, I would pass my subjects with 12–14, tops. He could not believe what had happened, and after the lesson he asked me to stay. I was more nervous now; did he want to take back my points?

After everyone had left, he came close to me and said, "You have talent. What do you want to be? I can see that you could be a good actor. You can go after gymnasium to a school in Athens to study acting for three years."

I looked at him and asked, "Why do I have to wait so long? I see a lot of kids playing in movies."

"You can do that," he said, "but you must visit the talent school and take some exams. If you pass these, they will take you, even if you aren't 18 yet. They will demand that you finish your basic education, so, you'd have to go to two schools at the same time."

That was not possible because I lived far away, and I would not be able to maintain my work.

I asked him to call the talent school and tell them I wanted to visit, even if it would be impossible for me to take the course at that time. Just to visit a place of my dreams might be enough to help me calm down and wait for the right opportunity.

Days later, I made my way back to Athens and met a teacher at the school. Walking through the hallways I passed some famous faces from movies. I was stunned. It was a nice feeling; I somehow felt at home. I thought that if they could keep me there, I would stay.

The teacher started asking many things, and said, "I can give you some material to read, and then call you back after a month so we can decide when the next examination will be. We have a jury of five actors and actresses, so be ready. Some students who are already here will also be watching you. You will be alone, on stage, doing your performance."

I took the pages and held them tightly in my hand, so nothing could happen to them. In the weeks ahead, I spent virtually every moment of the day studying and trying to memorize everything. I play-acted by myself, went through the motions and spoke loudly so I could hear my voice.

The day of the examination came, in front of 50 students who had already passed this stage. Some actors I did not recognize were also there to examine me.

They led me onto the stage and turned off the house lights. I had visited the toilet beforehand, but now, just five minutes later, I felt that I had to go again. I asked if I could, and they gave me permission. My body was shaking, and I felt that I had to pee, but it wouldn't happen.

I returned and the lights went down again. There was dead silence … but not only from them. I couldn't start, or find any words. I started crying and said, "Sorry, I forgot my lines, and the truth is that I can't play anything if it's not real." Even today I can never do that. How could I stand in front of people and just recite meaningless sentences that I had read to myself?

The lights came back on and the students started leaving the hall. The teacher gave me a sympathetic look and said, "This is what it's like to be an actor, and you're not ready yet. So go home, and maybe you can come back one day."

It had all come crashing down in a moment. I was crushed.

Every night, I stared at my guitar with sad eyes and felt that my dream could never become a reality. I hated reading lines, memorizing others' words and then repeating them. Even today, if you tell me one small sentence of five words, and ask me to repeat it in front of a camera, I'll fail. But let me stand up and speak my own words, and I can surprise you. Yet, as an actor, you can't do that. You have to perform with others and you have your script.

A year later, I decided I would go around to the theatres and ask for work. It didn't matter what the job was. I'd work as a cleaner, ticket-seller, whatever. I wanted to be at these places, even if I was never going to become an actor. To research where I would go, I picked up a magazine that had stories about singers and actors. Once a month, the publication allowed readers to visit their offices in person and meet an actor or singer. I took the opportunity and did it a few times, meeting some of my idols there.

When I was waiting in their office one day I saw an ad for an upcoming charity performance that was looking for actors. I took down the address and went there directly. I arrived at an apartment with a sign on the door that said, "Actor, book author, producer." I rang the bell and a man opened the door. Next to him was an older lady who wore a pungent perfume, the thought of which still makes me ill.

She asked me to wait in the living room, where a number of others were already waiting. After a while, it was my turn to meet the producer, a man of around 60. I immediately felt at ease because of the way he said his first words. He looked a little tired after so many meetings, but he asked me to sit and asked if I had experience.

"This is my dream," I said. "Let me try to show my skills." He stayed on my eyes and face for a while. I felt comfortable because there was a good reason for him to study me in that way. He asked if I could come back in a week to audition.

I did, and got a small role as a policeman. A few months later, I fulfilled my biggest dream at that point: to stand on a stage in Athens' most famous theatre, where Greece's most famous actors had played. Glory, in the heart of the city!

Of course, my parents and siblings were there. I could see how proud the whole family was, even if my father used to say that being an actor was not a job that would feed your family. "You need a real job. Finish your education, and get a diploma," he would say. But he accepted my choice, and in a nice way, with his silence, he let me try to do things my own way, in pursuit of my one dream.

To be on stage in that legendary theatre at 16 was an indescribable feeling. That evening, after the show, some audience members visited the actors and asked them to sign their programmes. I was shocked when some of them asked for my autograph. Me? Someone who could not manage to say a single word on stage a few months before? Me, who without any lessons had managed to perform in Athens' best-known theatre? In that moment — then and there — I became much older. I felt like a man. I was a man with a vision and clear goals.

AFTER THAT NIGHT, which was impossible to sleep through, I decided that I would become an actor. But, at the same time, I needed to study something and have a real job. A job, my father said, should be able to get you food and a roof over your head.

Weeks later, I won a small role in another 'free' theatre troupe, which travelled around Athens and played in a few places.

One day, the lady I'd met at my first casting call asked me to visit her because she had "something big" for me. She looked like someone out of an old movie: a big woman of a certain age, wearing too much make-up, and too artificially polite, using French words to impress others. And that perfume! She asked me to come over the following day, at around 6 PM.

Come 5:30 PM, I was already in the lobby. It was in a huge hotel, the Omonia, in Athens' Omonoia Square. At 5:59 PM, I asked reception to call Madame. She gave the OK for me to go up to her room. I knocked on the door, and she said something in French. I could see that the door had been left open a bit. I went in and Madame came from the bathroom wearing a bathrobe. Her hair and face were too dry for someone who had been in a shower or a bath.

She went to the sofa and asked me to sit. She offered me coffee or a drink, but I said, "No thanks."

I don't know why, but until I was 20 years old I always said "No thanks" to whatever people offered me. It could be strangers, or in friends' or neighbours' homes — I always declined. Even during my first two years in Sweden, until I changed my behaviour, whenever people asked if I wanted a tea or coffee, I would offer the same reply. Maybe it was because my parents used to say, "Do not show your hunger, even if you are starving."

Eventually, a Swedish family explained that it was not polite to say, "No thanks." People would be disappointed if I didn't accept their hospitality, they told me.

Madame started to ask about my life and gave me compliments on my first performance. She said she would help me become a famous actor. She was sure about my talent.

Time passed, and I started to feel uncomfortable because she never talked about the supposed big gig. After her second or third drink she stood up and asked me to come closer to her. I could smell her bad scent — I hated heavy perfumes, and hers was the worst. It reminded me of my kitten Chico's diarrhoea after I fed him milk. She grabbed my bottom, and hugged me hard against her bosom.

I was confused; my heart was pounding and I felt I was about to vomit from the smell. I was not a man, only a 16-year-old. I had never been with a woman. I pulled myself back but she held me tightly. She began to laugh loudly, and became more aggressive. She moved about, her breasts heaving up and down, and uttered more French words.

I broke free of her and walked to the door. "If you want to go, the door is open," she said, "but who is going to give you a role? I played with you just like in a film."

It was getting late and I had to run to get the bus home. On the way, confusing thoughts ran through my head. I wasn't sure what had happened, but I've never forgotten the smell of Chico's diarrhoea on her, or the way she touched me. What should I have done? She reminded me of a hungry hyena who could have torn my body apart in seconds.

After this experience, I met another producer. I arrived at the studio at the appointed time, but had an uneasy feeling. It was dark and empty, and I got scared when he opened the door to his office in the back. He acted differently from the day I'd first met him. He looked at me, and immediately tried to touch me. I had never met a gay man before, and knew nothing of homosexuality. I couldn't understand his advances, and my quick reaction was to say that my mother was waiting outside, and asked if we could step out to the well-lit lobby to talk.

Predators seemed to be everywhere in the acting business, and on both occasions I felt that I'd walked into a wild animal's den, and could be eaten alive at any moment.

After these experiences, my father's words came back to me more strongly. Get a diploma and be somebody, or you will die hungry. I stopped thinking about acting, and focused on school and the other jobs I had.

"CLOSE THE WINDOW!" Mum shouted. These words came quite often. Our house and the others around Paralia Aspropirgou were surrounded by all sorts of factories and refineries. There were steel, cement, and gas and oil works, along with other unclean industries.

Dark dust would drift regularly from the cement factory, and if our windows were open, everything would get terribly dirty. Some mornings there would be an odorous stench in the air.

I could hear my parents talk to the neighbours about it, and saw their worries for their children's health. But all the discussions ended with the same sentence: "Be quiet, because if they hear us, we'll be out of a job." This was the case year after year.

I eventually decided that we'd had enough. It was after the return of democracy in 1974, but at that point we had another headache: a crisis with Turkey and war in Cyprus. I could not breathe sometimes, but knowing that we were at war, you didn't have the wherewithal to think about justice and the environment.

By 1976 I could barely breathe, and my eyes constantly stung. The odour, like bad eggs, was very intense in the early morning. This came from the seaward side. I decided to find out where on earth this smell was coming from, and spent many nights searching. One day, the smell came in the early afternoon, so I ran toward the sea to start looking for something there. The stench was so strong that my nose led me directly to its source: a drainpipe leading to the sea. I ran to get a sample of water in a bottle.

At the foundry, I had a good connection with a polite young chemist. I gave him my bottle and asked him to examine its contents. He ran an analysis and explained that it was contaminated with thiourea dioxide, or formamidine sulphuric acid. The noxious substance was associated with the production of paper, specifically the bleaching process.

I contacted the Health Ministry and the government's environmental departments, pressing for quick results. I wrote a petition and gathered names and signatures. I made contact with newspapers. And, I wrote directly to the paper factory.

A big surprise came in the post: the factory invited me there to show how good their environmental procedures were. I went, but was unconvinced. And the problem was wider anyway, so I began contacting the area's cement factories and asked them to stop polluting.

People started to speak negatively about my actions. "What are you doing?" I was asked. "Do you want to cost us our jobs?" The very people who complained every day about the pollution suddenly decided that it wasn't a problem.

Even my angry boss called me into his office. "Are you a communist? What do you want?"

I replied, "I respect everyone who runs a factory, but I also have respect for my own and others' health. There is a balance if we want to have an acceptable life on this planet ..."

He did not let me finish. He started shaking, and waved his large arms around in anger. And then, most of the workers who had signed my petition asked me to remove their names. I remember that afternoon: it was sunny and hot but my heart felt cloudy. How could people change their minds about their health and wellbeing so suddenly?

A few days later, a daily newspaper called, wanting to interview me by the sea so they could understand what was going on. A young reporter came, enthusiastic about the story. We were lucky that day that the smell was stronger than usual. He took photos and promised me that this would be a big issue for the Ministry.

Two days later, the newspaper closed down, and the article died with it.

I was frustrated. I felt alone among the people whom I admired for their passion and their hard work to feed their families. I could read the exhaustion on their faces. How could we humans have it so bad in our lives? I fought my thoughts constantly.

ONE VERY WINDY AND RAINY MORNING, I passed the bus stop close to the foundry, where workers from different factories waited to go to work. I spotted one of the oldest workers, Kostas, a very kind man. He had suffered a lot through his life. During breaks, he used to sit next to me and speak very slowly and quietly. That is not unusual for us Greeks, but he seemed too subdued. Sometimes I felt he didn't have enough energy to talk, but I was wrong. He liked to talk with me about life. He used to say that he could see in people's eyes whether they were good or not. He had a very philosophical way of explaining things, and in a nice manner in general.

Now this tired old man sat on the ground in the rain at 7 AM. I ran to him and asked what had happened. He could not talk properly and I saw that he needed medical help. I panicked, and tried to stop people in their passing cars, but no one pulled over. The hurriedness and stress of the traffic only worsened my panic. I jumped out in front of a big lorry, startling the driver, who managed to stop just short of hitting me. I never thought for a moment what might have happened if he hadn't hit the brakes in time.

The driver leapt out and started shouting at me, but then saw Kostas and realized we needed help. He took Kostas into his truck and drove him to the nearest hospital.

A few days later, Kostas returned to the factory. He told me he had been waiting since 5:30 AM for the bus the day I found him, but because the bus drivers could not see him slumped on the ground, they failed to stop. Others were so packed that they could not take another passenger.

The situation angered me, especially as I noticed that there was no weather protection for any of the workers who used this stop. I knocked on Savvas's door and came in quickly. He did not like it this time. He looked at me and demanded, "What?!"

I asked if I could go with a colleague from the workshop to build some sort of bus shelter for our workers. He replied that this was not allowed, since the bus stop was in a public area.

Soon after, the boss took ill and had to go to hospital. While he was away, I went to the workshop and said I had the OK to make a simple shelter for the workers. The foreman knew I had a good relationship with the boss and didn't question me.

A few days later, the shelter was erected at the bus stop. I felt proud, but also nervous, because Savvas would surely learn of my big lie when he returned to work. It would be the first time I had disappointed him.

I arrived at the factory and saw his car in his parking spot. I did not know what to do ... whether to go in, or go home. I chose to go straight to his office.

I knocked on the door and could hear a very weak reply, *"Empros."* (Come in.)

I stepped slowly inside and looked at him. I did not know what to say, and kept quiet.

"You are here early, as usual," he said. I nodded my head.

"Boss," I said to him, "I missed you. When you're not here, it is like everything stops. We need you, so please stay healthy."

He didn't respond. He just sat staring at me.

I continued, "I also want to say that old Kostas was close to dying, and some of our other workers had big problems with the buses every morning. It's winter now, and I have built a simple shelter for the bus stop until the Ministry of Transportation can decide what to do. I've already written to them and have their reply, saying that they're looking into this matter."

Savvas seemed so tired that he could not manage to lift his eyes to look at me. He just gave a weak flutter of fingers toward the door, which was my signal to leave the room.

A few months later, the Ministry decided that they would put shelters up in and around Athens. The newspapers published the story, and I still have the Ministry's official reply.

Kostas asked me how I had managed it. It was such a big thing for a boy of 17 to achieve that. "Are you not happy?" he asked.

"Yes," I said, "but ..."

For the first time, Kostas summoned up his full voice and put me on the spot. "Are you not very happy with this big achievement? I can read in your eyes that you do not belong to Greece. Greece has hurt your heart too many times, and people do not understand you. It's like a bad relationship: you can keep fighting, but it will never get better. Go away. You will find your place somewhere." He said that because he had relatives in other countries, and I used to ask him how I could manage to go somewhere else at some point, to try my luck.

ONE DAY I asked Kostas to tell me about women. He was a good-looking man, even at his age. I could not understand why some people could still be attractive at that point. I later came to understand that they have charisma. It's how you feel, and how you project that, and the more real you are, the more attractive you will be.

"Women are the most beautiful souls we can have in our lives," Kostas began. "Without them, life is too boring. But they are like fire. You must take care, otherwise they will burn you. At least do not get your heart burnt too many times. In my generation, we had to find a woman to secure a family, but I do not think this will be the same for your generation. I had only two women in my life, but I can see you will have a lot!"

I asked him why he said that.

"Don't take this in a negative way. You are a man who wants to make a long trip with many adventures. You will never stay and wait. You will keep running, regardless of whatever is happening to you. Even when it's time for Charos [the God of Death] to come and get you, he will be dismayed at your speed, and he will let you keep running and make a long journey."

He said it would be a long and wonderful journey, and that I'd see things that most people would never know about.

"You will meet many good people, but bad ones also. Women will enrich your trip but they also await much sadness. But this is real life. You have the eyes a mother-in-law wants to see in her daughter's man, so you will have her always on your side. To have her mother on your side gives you and your wife the freedom you may need to develop your relationship. If I had a daughter, I would be happy to have you in our family. But, there are many outside waiting for you. Just remember to never lose the respect you have showed me all this time we've known each other. Never lose it!"

BY THE TIME I WAS 17, I was acting as though I was 30–40. I had enough confidence, but I had seen so much misery and pain, which made my daily life difficult. At that age, I was making quite good money: I had my salary from the factory, where I worked three hours and got paid for eight. I would soon have my gymnasium diploma, having done electronics studies. And, there was my commission from the insurance company, which was quite good.

So, why should I have a care in the world? I had left the working class and lifted myself into the middle class. **I could see how easy life would be if we were less egoistic and had just a little bit of *respect* for each other.**

Yet Greece, which had shone so brightly in the past, was becoming miserable. The poor were getting very poor, and the rich so arrogant that the only thing they cared about was making more money. In fact, everyone — poor or rich — was out to make a drachma. The pursuit of money was the end goal, and there was little respect or confidence left for the country's leaders. Without this respect, what was the point of following any rules? Politicians themselves were just working toward their re-election, not for the people. Such a society boiled down to everyone for themselves, and themselves only. It was like the Soviet Union, where no one trusted anyone else, and they did not know what the plan was for the next day. It was just for the now. Tomorrow ... who knows?

I thought back to all that when I started to do business in Russia, in the early '90s. In our negotiations, when I tried to explain to them longer-term goals — for as soon as the following year — I could see in their eyes that they found the concept very strange. They didn't want to even try to understand anything I had to say along those lines. "A plan for next year? Are you crazy?!" So, after a few meetings, I changed my approach, and only talked about the here and now. That helped me a lot in doing business with them. Just a short meeting, and the deal was done! I love to move quickly, and hate a lot of talk where you do too much of nothing. **You should always aim to understand the cultural context of the people you're talking to, as well as their age, so you have an idea of what experiences they had during their lives, and how that-shaped their world-view.**

Anyway, by the time I had reached my late teens I felt that the pervasive injustice in Greece had become intolerable. One day, there was a ghastly accident at the factory. One of our colleagues, a 22-year-old man, lay dead in front of us because someone had neglected to screw things together properly, on a machine that was too old to begin with. The machine had broken, and then exploded, cutting his body in two.

He was a nice guy, who had a big motorcycle, and he loved speed. He was handsome, and many of the workers who had daughters tried to interest him in becoming their suitor. His father also worked there, but wasn't present when the accident happened.

I was in the office and called the ambulance, and then ran over to see what had happened with my own eyes. I can't begin to describe the grisly results, but in the days and nights ahead I became increasingly angry.

A big, dark cloud loomed over the factory and on everyone's faces. People who saw what had happened told others what they'd seen. Production slowed dramatically as everyone processed their shock. And, everyone expected that justice would come.

Normally, in the event of a fatal accident in a factory, the police would come and someone would be immediately arrested, be it the managing director or some other responsible person. Not this time — the authorities never showed up.

The funeral took place a few days later. I was there, along with most of the workers. Only a skeleton crew stayed behind to keep the machinery running. The silence was deafening, with the expectation of what would happen to the owners or a responsible foreman.

But weeks passed, and nothing happened.

Then, the father was promoted from a lowly position to a better one at the factory. And, his wife got a job there.

I was surprised, and I wasn't the only one. The workers talked quietly among themselves about how no legal authority had taken up the case. Nothing added up. Why had no one been arrested? And now, his parents had better jobs there!

Mr Savvas was in a good mood one day. We had some big clients visiting from Italy. After a series of successful meetings, he stayed at the office to sleep, as it got too late to drive home. I made the tomato omelette for him, and as he ate, and looked satisfied, I asked, "Boss, who is going to be arrested? I'm worried about whether you or the other owners will be in trouble now."

He looked at me as though he were a cow: huge, polite eyes and his head hanging to the floor. "We solved things with his parents and we can't bring him back."

Savvas was normally a nice soul, a man with humanity, but at that moment I saw him as a monster! I exited without saying more. Each time I saw the parents, I felt disgusted. I refused to look into their eyes.

Weeks later, there was a smaller accident. This time, it wasn't so serious, but for me that was it! It happened to my friend Giannis, an older man who had tried to teach me about life, telling me to laugh even when it was painful. He was very calm, his words coming from the ancient Greek philosophers. He meant a lot to me. He used to spend time sitting next to me and say, "Come my son, do not worry so much."

When Giannis was injured, I was so furious that I could have killed someone. After the ambulance arrived, I ran to the boss's office. He was not in the factory. I was manic, running around like a crazed, wounded animal. I went to the second-in-charge, although I knew he was very seldom in the office and never talked to the workers. I barged in through his door, with my voice quivering.

He asked me what had happened, and I exclaimed, "We must stop production and check that the factory is still safe for us all!"

His face was blank. There was no reaction at all. All he managed to get out was, "Go home, you're upset. I'll talk to Mr Savvas about this."

Savvas was the man who protected me. He was my guardian angel. No one could do anything to me with the boss on my side. I was his favourite, and the only one he looked after.

I contacted the Health Ministry and wrote letters about workers' accidents in our area. I sent letters to the press and some articles were published. I demanded of the Ministry that they open an emergency hospital in our district, which had the heaviest industry in the country concentrated in a small area. Nonetheless, there was only a small, non-emergency clinic, some 10 km away. The nearest emergency hospital was 25 km away, and it could take an ambulance an hour to get there. In those days, ambulances were few and far between. We would normally drive people in a private car, because if we waited for an ambulance, chances were that no one would survive.

I checked for any kind of information I could get and tried to see if someone could force the local government to be accountable in a court of law. But, I did not realize one thing: people fought every day to put food on their table, and they were willing to fight for nothing else. To have a job was a privilege, and people had to focus on that to survive. My expectations were middle-class luxuries.

After much research, I found that the law 'allowed' five deaths a year in a *varia viomichania*, a heavy-industry facility. The law allowed hard conditions for the workers — accidents, pollution, and other health risks in these factories. As a trade-off, those who survived to middle age could receive their pension five years earlier than others, in more civilized settings.

Savvas began to get upset with me. He stared at me like he had that first day, when I found him at his desk looking as though he was dead. He had no physical energy, but he was angry and his eyes told me, "That's enough."

I stopped in front of him and faced him. I wanted to give him a chance to say something. I felt at that minute that I was becoming a man. I straightened my back, with my Papa's words coming to mind.

"Get out of my office," he said.

"Mr Savvas," I told him, "you know what has happened these past few weeks, and you know very well how much I care about your business, and how much you've done for my family and me. But to see our workers killed for nothing is too much."

He simply waved his hand to tell me I should go.

Time passed and people began to forget. Too quickly, it seemed to me. Workers and others looked at me in a somewhat disappointed way, as if to say, "What are you doing? This stuff happens. Don't make waves." These were the same people who, weeks before, had encouraged me to keep going.

My family also got noticed. My father lost his job without explanation. My mother's work in the factory worsened, and she had to do heavier tasks.

People can fear change, even change for the better. But I recognized I had to do what I did — I was the only one who would, and could. I was disappointed, and grew disillusioned, and decided I had to change my dreams. But I did not know what to dream of now, or how. I didn't recognize yet that every change has its season, and I might have been ahead of my time. Society is often slow to move, because people cannot see the larger picture, or just how their self-interests are being damaged. They need to be shown, and to recognize that life could be better for them. Unfortunately, it dawned on me that I wasn't in a position to get this through to them.

I WOULD FINISH MY STUDIES as an electrical engineer at the private Kontoravdis Technical School in 1977. This school had a great reputation, and graduates could easily find a nice job. To study electronics ensured a safe, secure future. The owner of the school, Mr Kontoravdis, was nice and very involved, and loved to see his students succeed in their careers. He was very helpful to all of us.

In Greece, when you studied at a private school, you needed to do a further examination from the state to get a 'real diploma' after receiving your private one. My plan was to study at a polytechnic university to get this state diploma. For my final three months at the technical school, I studied day and night. After the regular school day, I went to another school to prepare me for the examination. There, I met a student who came from a wealthy family, and we became friends. He was very relaxed and asked me why I pushed myself so hard. I explained that I had no time to lose, and I did not have the finances to do one more year if I couldn't pass the exam. That was very common for some students. If they didn't pass, they went to a private school for another year to prepare for taking the exam again, the year after. In my mind, that was crap.

One evening, after completing my studies at the evening school, my friend asked me to stop by a bar. He had one drink, and then another, in a very short space of time. I had lemonade and regularly glanced at my watch, because I didn't want to miss the last bus. A couple of girls he knew came and joined us, and I could see that he was trying to impress them.

"Relax," he told me. "If you're clever, you will pass, and I know how you can do it!" The girls started to laugh. He came closer and whispered in my ear, "I know the boss there. I can give you his phone number. You visit him, and you won't need to answer any exam question if you can't. You just have to write your name on the examination paper and that's all."

He explained that this special treatment cost only 200,000 drachmas, but it was worth it. "That's why I have fun and you are so stressed every day. Just give him the money and you will get your diploma." He said some other things that he shouldn't have, but the drinks and the girls affected his judgement. There is a Greek saying that you hear the truth from crazy people and from children.

This confused me, and I did not know whether to be angry or happy. I could not change my family values, and I wanted my parents to be proud that I achieved something through my own hard work. Dad would say, "If it is not worth something, then do not demand it! Leave it to someone else." I would feel like a fake if I bought the diploma; I would never know if I was actually capable of earning it myself. No good business person — indeed, no *good person* — would ever take the cheater's route. If they did, there would always be something gnawing inside them, casting doubt on whether their work was up to scratch.

It took a few days for me to gather my thoughts and understand what had happened, and what I needed to do. I went to Mr Kontoravdis and told him what I had heard, and he just said, "I know this is true and we can't do anything. This would risk closing down our school, and it is better that we existed, for you and for others."

He looked at me and could see a fire in my eyes, and knew that nothing could extinguish it. He asked me to stay after school to talk.

I did, and his advice was that we should get the signatures of parents, students and other interested parties to send to the Ministry of Education, and explain how unfair it was that those who attended private schools were treated differently. Furthermore, he said that the corrupt examiner should be removed from his job. We agreed that he must be stopped!

I followed Mr Kontoravdis's advice and arranged to send letters and a petition to the Ministry of Education, although I suspected that nothing would happen. Some newspapers started writing a few pieces, but that was all. As I've said, I am someone who hates talk with no action: I needed to see results, so I knew I had to do something.

I called the examiner and made an appointment to see him, not letting on that I was out to expose his corruption. He was very polite and helpful, and that made me feel uncomfortable. He asked me who had put us in touch, and I said the name of my friend — he had given me permission to identify him. When the examiner heard his name, his reaction was very positive. It meant they knew each other well and he could trust me.

He took only a few minutes and explained to me what I had to do during the examination, and he would arrange everything so I could get top marks and receive my diploma. He asked if I knew 'the amount.' It would have to be prepaid, of course. "Yes," I said, "do not worry."

I left his office with two different feelings. The first was that he seemed to be a nice, friendly person. The second, concurrent feeling was, "*Fuck him*, and all those around him. These bandits are being nice so they can pull you into their schemes." Now, I wanted to teach him a lesson. How can I get him arrested? Who could help me?

A name came to mind: Varvara Tsimpouli.

As I said before, I loved to write songs. I wanted to contact my idol, Voskopoulos. I tried to get his phone number or address through a magazine, but that proved impossible. One day, I read about a new song of his, and the lyric writer was a woman who had once lived in France: Varvara Tsimpouli. She must have another mentality than the old Greek way of doing things if she'd lived and studied in France.

I had been reading a newspaper and saw her credited as a writer and entertainment journalist. Her paper, *Vradyni*, a large, government-friendly daily, was located in the heart of Athens, en route to where I was going to school. I began formulating a plan for how I could deal with the examiner.

Before I met Varvara, I read the lyrics to her songs. They were nice, and sincere, and I concluded that she must be a nice person. Voskopoulos's songs are about love, and are so sweet and sensitive that I was certain Varvara must be the same.

I called the paper and acted as though I was an important person. No one could guess my age on the phone. When I heard her voice, I felt relieved — she did indeed seem like a nice person. She asked why I wanted to meet her and I said, "You write such nice pieces about my idol Voskopoulos, and I have something for you as both a person and as a journalist. But for now, it must stay between us."

Choosing this newspaper was a strategic move, because I wanted to win. The ruling party was Nea Dimokratia (New Democracy), which had been created after the military junta had been toppled in 1974. There actually wasn't much democracy in Greece at this point, new or old — the government was still dictatorial, as it was difficult to effect great change between 1974 and 1977.

Some had already branded me a communist, but I was never a communist or anything else. I refused to be connected with any political party, because none expressed all my beliefs. It seemed that anything one said or did in Greece back then would be attacked by the other side — that was the nature of politics. And the pushback wasn't based on any principle; it was simply a knee-jerk form of combative opposition. So, to work with a news outlet that was close to the establishment would at least keep the issue apolitical, since both sides needed the paper for their own authority.

Our meeting was not inside Varvara's office, but in the nearest café. Should the meeting have happened inside *Vradyni*, my name would have been taken down, as there were police guarding the entrance.

I said to myself that I would analyse her first words and then decide whether I could trust her or not. When you listen to someone, listen for their first words: if they seem to ring true, this can give you a good idea of where they stand.

She shook hands with me and said, "You are so young. I thought you were much older. Thanks for calling me; I want to hear what you have to say."

I replied, "First of all, I must say that your songs help make my hard work days very happy. They give me passion and energy. I'm proud to meet you."

She said, "I also want to give you Voskopoulos's phone number." She opened her address book and started copying it down on a piece of paper, without my having asked for it. Giannis had always taught me how to get something you wanted without the other person asking why, as you could get things you might not otherwise get. I took Voskopoulos's home phone number and put it in my pocket.

I looked around to make sure no one could hear us. I asked her, "What floor is your office on?"

"On the fifth."

"What I'm going to say now is too heavy to carry up so many floors, so please let it stay here only, until I know you can carry it up there." She gave me a kind smile and waited to hear more.

"Do you promise that whatever we might agree upon, only I decide who else will get to know this?" I asked.

"Yes," she answered. "It's your secret and I respect that."

I explained what had been going on for years with the examination bribery. She was stunned, and I could see that she was taking it all in. Yet, something was wrong.

She said, "I'm an entertainment journalist. It's going to be hard for me to go to my editor and sell the story to him."

I panicked. "This is not a story I want you to write about," I told her. "I want your help to catch and arrest him!"

"What do you mean?"

"He wants 200,000 drachmas. It's big money and I don't have it, and I don't know how to contact a prosecutor. I need your help organizing this and securing the money from your boss. You won't lose the money, and can you imagine how much goodwill your newspaper will gain?"

After thinking about it a few minutes, she said she would talk to her boss about the money. "We have great connections with the police, so they would mark every single banknote. This has to be done properly."

Varvara was excited after our meeting and I could see on her face how much she loved being a part of meting out justice.

She told me to wait at the café while she went back to her office. When she returned, she said she had talked to her editor, but they would not decide on anything immediately. She asked if we could meet again, as the day was getting late. I responded that I needed to pay the bribe within a few days, or the opportunity would be lost.

She said her boss wanted to know who the examiner was. I had not given specifics; I did not even tell her which school I went to and what education I had. I wanted to keep it safe until the day I carried out my plan. I had learned from my older friends, and my boss, never to say too much until you have an agreement in your hand. My father took this one step further: even if you have the agreement, you do not need to tell others about it without good reason.

We decided we would meet again in her office the following day. I went as arranged, and the police checked my ID before sending me to the fifth floor. Her face was different this time, more grey, and her glow and her beautiful, soft smile were gone.

"Come in," she said, and closed the door. Her voice was so low I could hardly hear her.

"Sorry, I'm really disappointed, but my editor said no. He said it wasn't our job as journalists. The police could work, so you should go to the police."

I became very weak and some tears came. A feeling of loneliness took over my skinny body. I began to shake, but I took her hand and said, "Do not write more songs about love, please." I shook my head, got up and left.

I had been so happy over the previous two nights, thinking we could stop this crime, and now I was alone again, walking the streets. I could not go home, and needed to think. Maybe I could go for a walk in Plaka, the old historical neighbourhood in Athens, and tell the gods there how I felt. Maybe they would reply.

I went to Plaka, walked around for a while, looking for the Acropolis, and felt a deep anger. How can we Greeks accept this life? A life where none of our values mattered, none of our Greekness existed? We were just walking shells that only looked human, seeing corruption but unwilling to fight it! Had money taken the place of our ancient gods, and the God of the Orthodox faith? This wasn't humanity. Our people had been stripped bare and here we were, seemingly content to let it carry on!

I had five days left before the examination would take place. I needed to do something, or just forget it.

The next morning, during a school break, another student from a lower class told me that he had heard about this examiner, and was saddened this was happening with no way to stop him. That emboldened me. I went to Mr Kontoravdis and asked him how the prosecutor worked and where I could find him. He gave me some advice without getting directly involved.

I left the school and headed to the main police station in Athens. I asked for the supervisor, who then took me to his room. Some curious policemen wanted to join in and listen, but I asked that he be the only one there.

I explained that I needed to contact a prosecutor because I had a very interesting case, giving some of the basics, but not the identity of the examiner. He said that I would need to tell him first, and he would organize it.

I said, "No, I want to tell them myself, and I want to know how they can secure the evidence, and I want to make sure they really will act."

He left the room and some other policemen came in, looking at me strangely. One asked if I was a communist, and another insisted I tell him about the case. "It's our job, we will fix it," he said. "Don't worry."

The atmosphere was increasingly unpleasant. The supervisor returned and said in an angry voice, "If you do not tell us the name, you must tell us which area he is in, because if it's outside Athens, it becomes the responsibility of another prosecutor."

I did not reply. I started to get up and said, "I'll be back."

One of the officers blocked the door. The supervisor asked me again to tell them everything, and demanded to see my ID. They became very rude and started slapping me.

They pressed me so hard that other policemen came in, wondering what the fuss was. They started asking who had sent me, who was behind this, and what was I up to. I'm not sure how long I was there, but it felt like years. They insisted on me telling them the examiner's name and where he was.

Next, they threatened me with a prison sentence of a few years, alleging I was trying to bribe an examiner, and made other threats.

They saw that I was not going to fold, and eventually let me go. But they succeeded in taking all the pride I'd had in my determination to pursue justice. I felt like a loser who couldn't win this round.

I came home late that night and my father was waiting. The local police had been by and had taken him in for questioning, demanding to know my political views. They had threatened him, too, and were rough on him.

Now I found myself on a police register. I was nothing but trouble to them, and they would follow me every step I took. Not only me, but apparently my family as well.

The coming days were the worst in my life. My feeling of loneliness became so strong that I decided to fight on and accept what was coming to me, or pack it in and leave Greece altogether. I was torn between the two choices. I needed to be strong to help my country and my people, but the reality set in that I would have to do it from somewhere else. It just wouldn't be possible in Greece. I had come to feel that the country was not my home. I'd never felt like so many of the other Greeks, the complacent ones, but believed I was a real Greek, connected to the strength of our ancestors, the civilization that gave the world democracy. I'm not so different from them, but I have a huge passion about life. I respect everything on this planet, and I love and demand a lot of love.

I had always been different, in so many ways, and I didn't feel welcome in my own country. I might speak Greek perfectly, and my parents are pure Greek, but I wasn't treated as Greek. Your identity, who you really are, what you must do in life, transcends nationality or ethnicity, and I came to realize this. I knew now that I was Panos.

3
Departures

I WAS VERY NERVOUS during the examination, not because I might fail, but I was worried I'd run into the examiner and didn't know if he had been tipped off. He had to have been well connected and protected by others. But my decision had been made: Greece was not my place. The country only made me upset and unhappy. Why should I ignore my values, just because the others who suffered when something went wrong merely accepted the situation?

Earlier that morning, a few hundred of us had gathered to take the exam. They divided us into different halls, each with around 100 students, observers ensuring that we did not talk to one another or take cheat sheets from our pockets. We were not even allowed to visit the toilet.

I tried to focus on the examination. I did not even notice who else from our class came. I felt that I could answer everything correctly, and was in fact one of the first to leave the hall.

I went to a café nearby and waited to see the other students, to get their thoughts. As I sat there, I began to feel quite confused, and something inside me stirred. Memories washed over me — from the police station, *Vradyni*, the factory, and my parents, with a look of worry on their faces. Was I a troublemaker? There was air pollution and I had wanted to fight the factories. The exam process was rigged to benefit those with money, and I'd set out to expose the corruption. What a shit-stirrer I was. What did I know about life, regulations, and the future? Maybe things should be the way they were. But why should people die on the job, and then it's all OK once you pay off their relatives?

There were too many whys in my little brain. Stay in Greece and do what? Get into a political party, so that one day I could be prime minister and make the changes? Was I the right person, or just an egotist who wanted to be something?

My father was an admirer of Giorgios Papandreou and his Centre Union party, and simpatico with his liberal–social democratic ideas.

I was, too. But when I saw politicians talk, I felt I couldn't be like them. I hated to talk and to dream, rather than getting out there and actually *doing it*. The thought of entering politics did not leave me with a good feeling. I used to say that if I were a political leader, I would like to be a benevolent dictator. I need things to be done, but I knew that just, compassionate dictators did not exist, not even in fairy tales. The notion of staying in Greece and going to university made me sad, too.

The Greek people suffered a great deal during the Second World War and the Greek Civil War that followed. Greeks were divided between left and right, with tremendous animosity between them. This was even so between siblings who held different political views.

I left the café where I'd been sitting and was walking on Panepistimiou Street, where the University of Athens was situated, when I spotted a small sign in a travel agency's window: "Interrail card, only $100!" I went inside and asked what that meant. An older woman gave me the information, showing that I could travel all of Europe by train for just $100. They could even help me sort out a passport.

I decided straight away that I would do it. I filled out my passport application, and a few days later, it was ready. I bought the ticket. Up to that point, I'd said nothing to my family. But with my passport and rail pass in hand, the heavy weight in my soul lightened, and I now felt I could fly. Nothing could keep me on the ground!

When the family gathered for dinner, I told them that as soon as I could gather up some dollars, I would travel around Europe. There was silence. My father said nothing — for the first time in my life his face sent no signals as to whether he approved or not. Mum gave me a smile after some time, asking what she could prepare for me.

That was a moment I wish many parents around the world would get right: do not fret, or ask your children why, or tell them how difficult it would be, and that they shouldn't go. Instead, make them feel loved and supported.

Dad went to the neighbour's small shop and bought a big bag for me, but still said nothing. I went to Athens and tried to change my money to dollars with tourists. At the bank, I could only change $120; if I attempted to take any more abroad I would be put into prison.

I had an older school friend who worked at a hotel in central Athens, which mainly hosted foreign tourists. He helped me change more money, and after that, I had $600 in total.

I tried to find out how I could hide the extra dollars without the authorities finding them. I talked to my father, and he opened the heels of a pair of old shoes I would take, putting $100 into each. A clever ruse, but it did render that pair useless for wearing afterwards.

We emptied a tube of toothpaste and put another $100 in there. I always carried a folder with my notebook, with photos of Voskopoulos glued to the cover. I carefully peeled them back and put $100 each on the front and back, covering the money with the photos.

I believed no one could find this money, and I was ready for the journey … one without any destination or plan. It was my first trip, save for the ones where my parents bundled me off to our relatives in the countryside. I only knew which countries the train would pass through, and that the end of the line was Finland, the country of Santa Claus. The only countries that I knew a little about were Sweden and Germany.

I KNEW SOMETHING of Sweden from the early '70s, mostly through newspapers and TV news. Not everyone in southern Europe of that era had a home, or a TV inside it, and even newspapers were a luxury. I was probably around ten when my father mentioned something about Sweden. He was disappointed about our own political situation. He did not like politicians and priests because they talked and lied a lot, and took advantage of poor and weak people. He had discussed Sweden being a much more free and open place.

I do not know how he knew about Sweden, but the fact he did impressed me then, and even more now. With his three years' education, he still occasionally read newspapers, though he refused to watch TV news. When I was older and asked why, he said, "It's corrupted news. There's nothing to see. They affect your soul, and suddenly your soul will be dirty, and will likely remain dirty. So, stay away from it if you can."

My father was fascinated with northern Europe. He knew about the region's infrastructure, and how the countries there had fewer traffic jams because of their bridges. He knew of their forests and lakes. He was sad because Greece gave civilization and democracy to the Western world, but it gave everything, so there was nothing left for us!

I remembered Dad's words and they created my own positive picture of what Sweden must be like.

I KNEW ABOUT GERMANY because when I was 16, I met a girl the same age from there. One summer, Mum took me on a two-hour bus trip to Kinetta beach, where a lot of people, mostly workers, went daily to immerse in the sea. The seawater, they said, would help calm our bodies and make us stronger for the coming winter. Seawater had salt and iodine and was believed to be therapeutic for humans.

It was a Saturday and there were a lot of people everywhere. I enjoyed that time because I loved to be in the sun. I could not swim, nor could my Mum. So, we ventured ever so slightly together into the edge of the sea. I could stand there with her in metre-deep water without feeling ashamed. Next to us was a beautiful girl with her father and mother. Her father was quite portly, a sign in those days that he had a lot of money. Her mother was very elegantly dressed and they behaved as though they came from the upper classes. We learned that they were staying at the hotel next to the beach.

The girl looked and laughed at me. I did not know whether it was because I couldn't swim or something else. She came up to me and said something I did not understand — they weren't the few English words I knew, such as, "Hello, how are you?" She came closer and wanted to talk more, and would not accept my silence. She finally said some words in English that I understood, saying that she was from Germany. I looked over for her father's reaction. In Greece at that time, if you spoke with a Greek girl and her parents noticed, there could be trouble.

She invited me to say hello to her parents. My Mum observed and said nothing. Her parents gave me a huge smile, especially her mother. We started walking around and talking, although it wasn't really a conversation since we only had some simple English words in common. I felt the girl was interested in me. I could see it in her happy eyes and how she looked at me.

Later, her family asked me to have lunch with them at the restaurant next to the taverna. I declined, because I remember what my parents told me: never show your hunger. They also asked if I was with my mother, and went over to her and said hello. My mother, as always, replied very politely in Greek.

They went to the restaurant, but afterwards the girl came to find me. She showed me around the hotel and — in a completely genuine, innocent way — invited me up to see her room. I was impressed. I had never seen a room like that, with all its luxury. In fact, it was not just one room, but two, with a big balcony and a sea view.

She got her tennis racquets and a ball out so we could play on the beach. Time passed quickly, and soon my mother shouted that the bus would be heading back in 15 minutes. I did not want to leave, but I had no choice. My mother looked into my eyes and saw my disappointment. The girl asked my mother if I could stay with them, and then her mother asked, in German, if I could.

Mum understood everything even though she knew no foreign languages. Sometimes I asked her how she could understand, and she would say, "I look at them, and I understand." It was a talent I developed myself. I've been in China, where I saw that people were arguing over important business matters, and before they could tell me what they were saying, I would shock them by indicating whether I agreed with their conclusions or not. I've been to China 50 times, but cannot speak one word of Mandarin. I've never tried to memorize the vocabulary, but I get a feeling, and an innate understanding of what's being communicated, and that's thanks to my mother.

I decided to stay, and Mum emptied her wallet and gave me everything. She asked me to take the bus the next day by myself, because she would be working that Sunday as usual. "Yes," I told her. "Don't worry."

With all this, and Mum's reaction, I was growing up faster by the minute. I was already quite mature for my age. Too mature, maybe.

In the evening, they asked if I wanted to join them for dinner. For the first time in my life, I said, "Yes, please." We could not talk to each other properly because they spoke mostly German, but the mother tried to explain what they did in Germany. Her husband worked for Mercedes-Benz — that was why he had a nice, large car — and they loved Greece. They came every year for their holidays. The girl suggested that I come visit them in Germany.

They invited me to stay the night in their suite, but I declined, instead heading to the beach. I wasn't alone there; there were a few others spending the night in the open air, but it was all very safe and orderly. I only had two towels and the night was chilly. The girl kept me company until midnight, when she headed back to the suite.

During the night she came down to see me again. She held my hand and could feel how cold it was. She asked me again to come up to the suite but I shook my head.

She went to her room and brought down a pillow and blanket for me. She stayed for a while, until her mother came down and took her back upstairs.

The next morning, I ate breakfast with them, and they gave me their address and home phone number so I could keep in touch. I took the bus home, returning with a nice feeling. I felt like a man, a real one. I had never really spent any time with a girl, let alone held one's hand. Imagine how I felt when this wonderful girl took my hand and tenderly held it in front of her parents!

We wrote and sent photos to each other afterwards. She was the only contact I had in Germany — or anywhere outside of Greece — and to me that was amazing. Maybe I could stay in Germany. I daydreamed about it endlessly, and envisaged my future there ... or in some far-off place.

I HELD my passport and Interrail card in my hand, ready to start a journey to destinations unknown. I wondered how close Finland was to the sky if Santa Claus came from there.

I dreamed of finding a peaceful place and seeing what was possible. My bags were packed with sandwiches, all made with love by my Mum. She was worried about the food abroad and whether I would have enough to eat. That was the only concern she had. She knew her son's survival in-stinct well: I would have the skills to overcome any issue or difficulty. She was very comfortable with that, just not the question of food.

I think that in all poor countries, we had a focus on food. That was the first thing we had to fight for. To feed someone was a privilege, and to see your kids grow and gain a little weight was a huge satisfaction for parents. But this is not strange. Look around our planet: all animals do the same.

THE BIG DAY CAME, FINALLY.

The day before, the whole family was home, anxious and looking at me all the time. Some neighbours also came by to say goodbye. The night was long, even though I had to wake up in the early morning. My mother could not sleep at all; she kept coming to my room and putting the blan-ket on me. When I get nervous I get very warm, and do not want to use the blanket. Yet, she came every few minutes, and would say, "Sleep now, tomorrow you will have a long trip." I believe most parents, or at least mothers, would do the same.

I woke up at 6 AM and began getting ready. At 7:00, a neighbour drove me in his taxi to the Athens train station. I was very quiet the whole way. He tried to talk to me but soon gave up.

I got into the long train. I had ridden the rails a few times to the coun-tryside, but had never been on one like this. It was very crowded, with people sitting everywhere. I found a compartment for four and settled in.

We would pass Thessaloniki, an ancient Greek port city on the Aegean Sea, before proceeding to the Yugoslavian border. It took a long time to get from Athens to Thessaloniki — a distance of more than 500 km —

as the train stopped at every city along the way. In Thessaloniki, most left the train and new passengers boarded. At that point, my compartment was empty but for me. An American student, a girl named Cate, came in and sat next to me, and then a Greek man, Giorgios, who was on his way to Germany. I did not like his eyes or his face. He had a sinister look, and it was scary having him there in the same compartment.

The border was not far from Thessaloniki and I started to get nervous. I wondered what kind of immigration and security controls they had, and if I'd have any trouble getting through. What would happen if they found my hidden dollars? How many years would I spend in prison?

Cate started chatting with me, but I had difficulty understanding her. I could read English, but other than a few words with the girl on the beach and her parents, I'd never spoken it in conversation before. We'd studied English at school, but it was in an old-fashioned way: read a text and translate it. There was a lot of grammar and translation, but we never spoke it. I wonder if our teachers could even speak English.

Giorgios could not speak English either, but he could speak German. He asked why I seemed so nervous, and if he could help me. "Maybe you need to get your money out of Greece?" he asked. "Give it to me and I can do it."

I shook my head to say no. "I don't have any. I'm OK." Cate put her head on my shoulder without asking, and fell asleep for a few moments. I felt safer being close to her. Giorgios left the compartment for a while and I tried to gently wake her. I wanted her to hold my hand, because I began shaking with the announcement that we were approaching the border and we needed to have our documents ready.

Cate reacted quickly. Maybe she wasn't really sleeping, and only wanted to be close to me. She whispered something into my ear, which I did not understand. She gave me a smile and kissed me on my cheek. She seemed to understand that something was not as it should be. "Calm down," she said. "I'm with you. Can I do something for you?'

"Just hold my hand, please, and stay with me," I said. "I don't want to be alone when the police come." Maybe she could help. Maybe the police would be distracted by this beautiful American girl and forget me. Aristotle Onassis, the shipping magnate, used to say that in hard negotiations, he always had a beautiful woman next to him. The whole atmosphere would become softer, and people would behave better in front of an attractive woman.

The Greek police came through and asked for passports. They stamped them and asked some questions of various passengers. They then turned to me and asked me to follow them. "Bring your bags with you." I could not let go of Cate's hand. She understood, and tried to follow me, but one police officer said sharply, *"Oxi esi! Monos tou!"* (Not you! By himself!)

They took me off the train and into a room. They asked me where I was going and what I intended to do there. I answered that I had just finished my studies and was going to northern Europe to see if I could attend university there.

One of the officers asked, "Are Greek universities not good enough for you, or aren't you good enough to get in?" The older officer was quieter. His face showed that he'd had a miserable life. Who knows what lives rest behind each person's face … how many problems or personal disasters lay behind them?

The older officer left, and I was alone with the vocal one. He asked me to open my bags. He was looking for something, and carefully examined all my items. He even opened my mother's food package.

The announcement that the train was about to leave came over the public address system, asking all passengers to embark. I tried to close my bags, but the officer said, "No. You're hiding something. Tell me what it is, so I can let you go. If it's drugs, then you're going to prison, but I don't think it's that. I can tell you never touch drugs. So just tell me!"

"I have nothing," I told him. "Nothing illegal!"

He became louder. "You're staying until we know what you're trying to take out of the country!" Tears began to run down my face. I kept saying, "I have nothing! Nothing illegal!"

"Oκ," he said, "but then, what do you have?"

I repeated, "I do not have anything illegal!"

I looked around for other officers who might help diffuse the situation, but it was just the two of us. I looked him in the eye and said, "I want to ask you something, sir."

I continued, "If your son was trying to travel to another country to have a better future, and he needed to bring something more — legal or illegal — in order to have some food for the first few weeks, what would you tell him?"

He did not hesitate. He put his hand on my shoulder, looked me in the eye and said, "Good luck, my son. Now, run back to your seat. The train is ready to leave." He took my big bag and followed me to the train.

I climbed aboard and went into the compartment with my bag. Giorgios had already returned, and Cate was there. Giorgios asked, "What happened? Why did you not give me the chance to help you? I travel every month on this train and I know what to do."

Cate put her hand on my knee and hugged me for a long time. There were no words. I did not want to cry but I could not stop my tears.

Giorgios left the train in Germany, leaving Cate and me alone in the compartment. The train would head to Denmark, where Cate would board a plane to go back to the US. We could not communicate verbally, but these hours together would prove to be deep and meaningful for us.

Cate led me to the toilet and asked me to come inside. My thoughts and worries were still swirling after my frightening encounter with the police, and there had been so many 'must not' messages from my past. I stood awkwardly outside. After the conductor passed, she dragged me in, and we made love. For many long minutes I was completely disconnected from reality. All my phobias, and the stress from my confrontation with the border police, and the uncertainty about my destination, were still there, but she was so soft and gentle, and acted in a way that had me follow her wishes. I felt safe next to her. After we returned to the carriage, she comforted me further.

It was my first intimate experience with a girl, and we were so connected that I felt we had known each other for years. My anxiety was gone, and I suddenly felt truly human, able to take love without feeling guilty or ashamed. It made me stronger, and despite having gone on to do so much in my life, my time with Cate is of course something I still remember clearly. For all of us, first experiences follow us and help mark our destination. So, I was lucky this was such a positive, loving, and tender experience. Good experiences make us happier long-term, while bad ones do the opposite.

We did not spend a moment apart from each other for the rest of the journey.

WE ARRIVED IN COPENHAGEN and my angel Cate left me. I wished the trip would continue, as I'd already had such memorable experiences. After a while though, I felt extremely tired and my stomach was a disaster. I did not like the food on the train and it was too expensive. I barely slept — only a few minutes here and there — from Germany to Denmark. Cate had been the first girl who had touched my feelings in this way, and awoken me inside, and I spent every minute thinking of her.

It was exciting to see what was outside: small wooden houses, all in white, with snow everywhere. I had never seen such vistas, not even on television or in magazines. This was amazing. But the pain in my stomach persisted. Something was amiss.

From Copenhagen onward I had a deep feeling of loneliness. The train had to be transferred on to a ferry, and we had to leave the carriages and board the boat. On board was a restaurant, and in front of it a huge queue of hungry passengers. The menu had photos, so it was easy to order. The choices were sausages with French fries, and hamburgers with mashed potatoes. Both were the same price, and I asked the man behind the counter to give me French fries with a hamburger. He answered, "No." I tried again, hoping he would understand that the two choices were the same price. It shouldn't matter. They were both potatoes! I couldn't get one kind of potato instead of the other with my burger? He did not give me a second chance, instead taking the order of the next person in the queue. I went without any food.

That was my first experience of the Nordic countries.

I did not understand their thinking. As we left the boat and got back on the train, I wondered where I was going, and how different people of different mentalities met and interacted. Why did he not want to substitute fries for mash?

I was very hungry and my stomach continued to hurt. My thoughts went back to the menu on the boat. I tried to understand the Greek policeman who allowed me to travel. There had been a crime, if you considered the letter of the law, and he knew it, but he used his humanity to see that it was not a terrible offense. There was no damage. But the man in the restaurant showed no humanity. That made me scared. Just where was I going?

My stomach pain became unbearable and I felt that I was going to lose my balance and topple over. I had no idea what would happen — it was the first time I'd experienced anything like that. I tried to gaze out of the window and enjoy the view, but that didn't help. The train would make a stop soon, but I didn't know where.

We ground to a halt and I disembarked with my bags. We had arrived in Gothenburg, a major seaport city on Sweden's west coast. I learned that it was Easter — celebrated on an entirely different day than the Greek Orthodox Easter I'd known all my life — and I could not see anyone out and about. The station was empty, and everything looked closed. My stomach churned again and I had to find a toilet, now. None were in sight. I ran like crazy, with my bags, asking for a toilet, but no one would help.

I got into a taxi and asked to be driven to the nearest, cheapest hotel, as quickly as possible. A few minutes later, we stopped at a hotel in the Vasastan district, in central Gothenburg. I ran to the reception without paying the driver, and left all my bags in the taxi. I asked for the toilet, went in, and was there for a considerable time. I discovered that I had soiled myself slightly. I threw out my underwear and put a lot of paper inside my trousers, and tied my pullover around my waist.

I returned to the taxi, where the driver was quite upset because he had to wait. I settled the bill, and checked into my room.

The next day, I woke up and could see people wearing white clothes. My eyes were foggy, and I couldn't make them out very clearly. I was scared that I had died and had arrived in either paradise or hell.

I could not understand that I was in a hospital. I couldn't remember how I'd got there. A few minutes later, a man of Greek origin came to interpret. He explained that the hotel staff found me on the bathroom floor and an ambulance brought me here. It seemed that I had become severely dehydrated on the trip, having had virtually nothing to eat or drink for several days. My diarrhoea only made things worse, draining my body of whatever vital liquid I had left. They said I was so debilitated from the journey that I'd drifted in and out of consciousness.

I was discharged after a day, and went back to the hotel, feeling much better after being given liquids. I walked all day and looked around. I was impressed at how clean and orderly Gothenburg was, with no traffic jams and no car horns honking. I tried to find some chewing tobacco, but it wasn't available.

The next morning I went to the university to get some information on what I needed to do to be able to study there. It was also a shock for me, but a positive one. It was so easy to find someone to give you information, without being asked to come back in a few days! They also had a person specifically responsible for foreign students. She was not there that day, but I was told that the principal could speak with me. The principal herself! She was an elegant woman of around 40, with a very soft voice and approach, named Irja Persson Utterhall. I couldn't believe that the principal of Gothenburg University was willing to talk to me directly. That would have been impossible in my country. She asked me to pull out all the papers I had, we chatted for a short while, and we made a follow-up appointment for 9:00 the next morning.

I WAS THERE at 8:45 AM. Mrs Utterhall's door was open, and I could see that she was sitting at her desk. I did not say anything; I continued to wait quietly outside. She saw me a few minutes later and came out with a polite smile. "You are early. Come in."

"I can wait," I replied.

"No," she said. "Come in. We can start."

She shared with me a funny play on words: 'the academic quarter' referred to the fact that most Swedish university students tended to show up 15 minutes (a quarter of an hour) late. "But you were here 15 minutes early," she said with a smile. "How nice." Hearing that made me feel good.

Her office had a lot of papers and books everywhere, but her desk was well organized. I liked that, because I once thought Savvas's chaotic desk at the factory was the sign of someone successful. He must have been important, I'd figured, to have so much paper everywhere that you couldn't fit a pen on the desk.

I gave her my diploma, along with a sheet onto which I had translated it in English. She took it and placed it on her desk without looking at it. "I want to hear about you," she said. "Tell me why you are interested in studying here in Sweden, if you have relatives, and what your plans and goals are. To me that is most important, so we can see if we can help you."

She was so polite. I'd never imagined that a university principal could be like that. She spent her valuable time with a foreign student trying to understand his vision. I said that my dream was to be an actor, but I'd studied electronics. I had considered pursuing electrical engineering, because I thought it was the future.

Her eyes lit up. "There is a nice school in Gothenburg if you want to be an actor," she told me. "If you want to study engineering, we have Chalmers University of Technology. Both are right around here." She could easily see that I did not know what I wanted to be, and advised me to meet their student counsellor, who could help steer students in the right direction. She looked at my diploma and said that I needed to study the Swedish language for her to accept me, and that I'd need to study English, chemistry and mathematics for Chalmers.

"But let's go to see if our student counsellor is available." She could not have been more understanding and helpful.

She made a copy of my diploma, and put my original in an envelope and gave it to me. She took me down a long corridor to meet the counsellor, but she was not in her room. She asked me to wait while she tried to find her. A few minutes later, they came back together. Irja shook hands with me and said, "You know where my office is. Feel free to contact me at any time if you need something."

All this seemed so surreal to me. Was it possible for a principal to act this way, to be so utterly polite, down-to-earth and helpful? *She'd* set aside time to ask me about myself, made a copy of my diploma, looked for the counsellor and asked her to help me immediately! The contrast with what would happen in my home country was so great that I wondered if I was dreaming.

After a long talk, the counsellor asked me to rethink what I wanted to study. She gave me some practical information, and a lot of brochures.

After that day, my decision was made. I would study in Gothenburg and not continue my trip to Santa Claus Country. I would return to Greece and arrange what I must, so I could come back to this wonderful place as soon as possible. I would apply for permanent deferment of my military service — which to this day remains compulsory for men of age 19–45 — on the grounds that I was studying abroad.

After leaving the school, I went strolling around the city to get oriented and see if I could find a job. I needed to make some connections, get some pointers and secure an income.

My starting point was the statue of Poseidon at Götaplatsen. There was a restaurant there, and I went in to ask about work. They said no immediately, without even asking what kind of job I wanted. I started walking down the street and dropped in at all the restaurants there. One after another, they all said, "No, we have nothing for you."

I was hungry and stopped outside a pizzeria to look at their menu and prices. The pizza looked delicious, and big enough that I would not need to eat more that day. I went in, and a waiter gave me a table. I asked him if all their pizzas were made the same size.

"No," he said. "We have a smaller size for kids. Are you alone?"

"Yes, I'm alone. I want the large pizza."

The place was very crowded, with waiters running everywhere. And then, to my surprise, I heard someone utter two words in my native tongue: "Vre malaka." (You arsehole.) My ears pricked up and I looked around for where these Greek words had come from. I saw a tall waiter who was a couple of years older than me, with black hair, aggressively talking to another waiter. He saw that I'd understand what he'd said and walked over to me. "Ellinas ise?" (Are you Greek?) I said yes and stood up, extending my hand.

He introduced himself. "I'm Pantelakis." He asked if I wanted something to drink and I said, "Water, please."

"Water? Don't you want milk or something with your food?"

I looked around and on most of the tables were either Coke or big glasses of milk. I said, "Milk, please, like the others."

He returned with a huge glass and asked, "Are you new here?"

I explained that I planned to study at university and was trying to make some connections and hopefully find work.

"I'm busy now," he said, "but come back at 5 PM. I'll have a break, so we can talk."

My pizza came and it was delicious — a proper, satisfying meal after everything I had been through. I also liked the milk. It reminded me of when Savvas decided I needed to grow, and every day gave me a litre of milk to drink, free of charge.

After lunch I began to walk again. I could not believe my eyes. What beautiful things I saw, even if it was far too cold for April. And there was a sense of harmony in the air. There was no stress, and everything was well organized. I started to look at the beautiful girls. I had never seen so many blonde girls with blue eyes. The only one I remembered from Greece was a famous actress. I looked at their lovely faces. Maybe the cold weather kept their skin so radiant. "One day I'll have a girl like this," I thought.

At 5 PM, I returned to the pizzeria and Pantelakis was sitting at a table, eating. "Sit down," he said. "Do you want to have another pizza?" I immediately said no, so my parents would not be disappointed. But it had been a few hours since I'd eaten; I'd walked far and wide in the brisk air, and I was hungry again. He looked at my face and ordered a pizza for me. Pantelakis could read my hunger.

"Why are you in such bad shape?" he asked. "Do you have money to eat?"

I said that I did have a little. More questions followed. "What do you want to study here?"

"I'm not sure yet," I told him, "but I think the money is in engineering."

He laughed. "I've heard that many times before, and I'd planned to study at university myself, but look at me now. I'm carrying pizza around. I've met so many students from Greece, but very few finish their studies."

He continued: "You look like you've come from poor parents, so do not waste your family's money. If you want to finish your studies, stay away from drugs, from Greeks, and do not run after blonde girls all the time. We have plenty of them, so you'll have enough time to have as many as you want."

It was then my turn to ask the questions, and over the next hour I asked so many that Pantelakis eventually had to cut me off. "You have to go now. I'm already tired of all these questions, and my break is over. But I'm here every day, so just come by and I'll give you free pizza."

The following day, I started my trip back to Greece with a head full of impressions and information. Along the way, I felt that the train was moving too slowly. I had a lot of time to plan what I should do when I got back.

MY FAMILY WAS EXCITED to see me again. Mum's first reaction was that I looked skinny. I had indeed lost weight, even though I didn't have much to begin with. They did not ask much about what I had seen, only if everything was well with me.

This is something I do with my own children or their friends. They will tell their stories if they feel like it, so I never ask more than to see if they are OK. In my adult years, some have interpreted this as my being uninterested in their lives, and that I was some sort of egotist. Far from it. In fact, I'm very much the opposite. I don't ask because maybe there are things they just don't want to share.

I told my parents that I needed to arrange some documents with the bank so they could transfer a sum of money to my account in Sweden each month, which would allow me to get enrolled at university there. I needed to change some currency into dollars again, and pack more clothes in preparation for heading back to Gothenburg as soon as I could. All my documents had to be translated into Swedish or English, so I could present my Greek work experience as I applied for positions there.

My parents were very understanding, as usual, and sent no negative signals or asked too many questions.

Two weeks later, at the beginning of May 1977, I was ready to travel back to Sweden. This time I would fly, for the first time in my life. Pantelakis had recommended another Greek man who could help me with a room for a few days.

I arrived in Sweden, and this time it was even more beautiful. It was now late spring, the trees had leaves, and everything was colourful and alive. There were so many flowers that it was a paradise for my eyes.

I stayed in a small room, courtesy of Pantelakis's acquaintance, for the first few weeks. I went to the university to meet the counsellor, who helped me arrange documents to submit to the police and the bank.

I would first study Swedish, as a matter of practicality. The money I was getting from my account in Greece via the local Swedish bank wasn't enough to survive on, but enough to give me permission to stay in Sweden. At the time, we were not allowed to transfer money without clear documentation outlining the reasons. I needed a job, although officially, at this point, I wasn't allowed to work in Sweden, and I could barely speak the language.

I tried to meet a lot of people, and visited the Greek associations. There were two: one for people on the left, and one for people on the right. Each hated the other.

I visited both, and the vibe was not welcoming. Nevertheless, one had bean soup and other food for just 5 kronor, with a lot of bread at no extra charge. And so, I had to go there, at least to eat. Some older people approached me and wanted to know who I was and why I'd come to Sweden. I got along with one older man, Lefteris, from Rhodes. He invited me to his house to meet his big family and to eat. He had been in Sweden since 1950, when early immigrants from Greece first arrived in significant numbers, and he and his wife worked as bakers.

Going to his house, joining his family and enjoying home-made food was medicinal. Lefteris told me how many other students who had came to Sweden had destroyed their own lives and wasted their families' money. Many visited the Greek association, played cards, smoked and used drugs. "The only diploma they got was one in how to live a bad life, and they never became what they set out to be," he said. "So, listen to me. We are your family. Come to us and eat with us. Do not go to the association. I can give you bread every day. I have free bread and it's more than enough for my family. Do not stick with other Greeks — just get into Swedish society and study. Make your parents proud and make yourself proud. Do not waste your time. In Sweden there are so many new things for you, and they'll steal away your attention."

His warning reminded me of the *sirines*, the sirens of Greek mythology. They were mentioned for the first time in Homer's *Odyssey*, living on an island in the Tyrrhenian Sea, in the western Mediterranean. Circe had warned Odysseus of their charming song, which lured sailors to their death. He ordered his crew to put candles in their ears, so they wouldn't hear the sweet singing as they sailed past. He asked to be tied to the mast, so he could hear the sirens' song but not be seduced by their charm.

Lefteris was right — I had to be wary of temptation, and remember why I'd come to Sweden. That had to be my sole focus. Meeting Lefteris and his family was a gift from God. To have a family when you might find yourself in a struggle — not just any kind, but an unfair one — is invaluable.

But why did all the Greeks warn me to stay away from Greeks? I could see during this time that some Greeks had become very successful in different businesses, such as small restaurants. The biggest textile trading company was run by a Greek with no more than six years' basic education. How could I go up to a Swedish stranger, with just cursory command of his language, and ask for advice or help? I could do that with my Greeks — we had the empathy to invest in others, and of course a common tongue — but I was in a foreign land.

My priority was to find a job under the radar. I started walking up and down the avenue where most of the restaurants were. On the morning of my first day I had rejections from nine places. It was 12:30 PM and they were all busy serving lunch. It wasn't a good time to disturb them, and most of the managers were irritated when I did. But I wanted to ask at ten places before stopping. I went to the last one and saw waiters running around like antelopes, and heard angry voices. There was a smart, elegantly dressed man of 35 or so up front, looking very upset. I knew that he had to be the boss.

I went straight up to him and asked if he had a job for me. "I'm good with cleaning and washing, and can help in the kitchen."

He looked at me as though I had just fallen out of the sky. "You can wash plates?"

"Yes, I've done it since I was seven years old."

"Can you do it now?"

"Yes."

"Then start!"

He took me to a room to change, giving me some trousers, a T-shirt and heavy black sandals. "It's urgent," he said. "Our dishwashing machine is broken and we must wash everything by hand." He took a couple of minutes to explain what I should do, and I saw that three others there already doing the same.

I started washing quickly and the manager stood next to us and watched. Two of the others left to wait tables, so there were only two of us left. I was quite fast, and within a few minutes they had enough clean plates to keep serving people. Two hours later, it was all over.

The boss in the elegant suit asked me to follow him to his office. "My name is Stefan," he said. "I must say, you were good and fast. Can you work a few hours a week during lunchtimes? You'd start at 10:30 in the morning and work until 2 in the afternoon ... sometimes maybe to 3."

"Of course," I replied, enthusiastically. "I can do that."

"Write down your address and phone number." He passed me a sheet of paper and a pen. "Do you have a work permit?"

"No," I whispered, "but I will soon."

"Oĸ, come again tomorrow and we will see how things work out."

He offered me 8 kronor per hour under the table, but said that if something happened, I must deny that I was working there. "Do not talk to others; just work."

I was thankful to have found a job so quickly, even if it was just for a few hours a week. About a month later, Stefan asked if I could help in another restaurant they had, because the dishwashing machine had broken down there as well. I said yes, of course. This restaurant was one of the most famous at the time, and quite expensive. It was located on the Götaplatsen, a public square on Gothenburg's main avenue. I laid into the job and they liked my efficiency. They started calling me the Greek *sifounas* (tornado).

I was happy and worked there for a few months while I studied. But, unfortunately, it would come to an unpleasant end.

They prepared the food in the basement, and sometimes the chef would ask me to go down there and peel potatoes. This was on top of my regular duties, but I didn't care. I liked to show that I could do everything, so they would allow me to work more. One slow afternoon, I thought they would either send me home or ask me to do something else. The chef told me to follow him to the basement, saying he'd show me what to do.

I followed him but immediately got a strange feeling. He started to act nervously and a little angry, but I did nothing. He was using foul words when he talked to me, calling me *malaka* (arsehole) and *tzatziki* (the sauce, but he was essentially putting me down and calling me an idiot). I never reacted. As my mother said, *"Ase na to pari to potami."* (Let the river take it.)

The chef now moved closer to me, and was soon on me like a wasp. I tried to keep my focus on the potatoes, but he stretched out his hand and grabbed my genitals. I dropped the potatoes and turned to run up the spiral staircase. He ran after me and shouted, "You're working illegally and you're trying to stay illegally in Sweden! I'm going to call the police!"

I still had the potato-peeling knife in my hand. I spun around, stopped and put the knife to on his throat and said, "One more time and you are dead ..."

I could not finish my sentence, as he screamed like a wild, cornered pig. I slowly removed the knife from his throat and stepped back as other staff came running down to see what was happening.

A few minutes later, Stefan said, "Do not come here again, or any other place around here." He did not pay me for the week, and I did not ask him to. It was around 7 PM, on a rainy day in August. I was scared, and thought of going to Lefteris's family, but felt that I was a criminal, and if the police were to catch me, I did not want to bother them. I didn't want to go to the room I had rented, as the police could have that address. I went to the train station, and walked around without looking anyone in the face.

I found a quiet corner to sit and wait. By midnight I was alone, save for a homeless man a few metres away. I was nervous that the police would come at any moment. I edged closer to the homeless man, breathed deeply and felt calmer.

By morning — still sitting there in the station — I was in a bad shape and didn't know what to do. Pantelakis was an option, but the pizzeria where he worked was only a few hundred metres from the restaurant where I'd had the trouble. By now, everyone on the street probably knew what had happened, so it wasn't a good idea to go there. I decided to go home. I stayed there for two days, waiting for the police to come. There was no telephone to call my parents, to ask for their advice.

Suddenly, there was a knock on the door. I did not answer, but Pantelakis opened the letterbox flap and shouted, *"Anikse!"* (Open the door!)

I opened it, and he stood there looking very angry. *"Vre malaka ti ekanes?"* (Hey arsehole, did you do it?) I explained what had happened and he said, *"Tha ton gamiso ton pousti ksero etsi kani ki me allous!"* (I will fuck his arse because he has done this to others, too!) "But why did you use the knife and let others see you?"

"Listen to me," I said. "I'm 19 years old and until today I've never been in any trouble with anyone! I even jump when I see an ant so I don't step on it! I can't explain it. Sorry."

"Come," he said, "you can stay with me for a few days."

I put a few things into a plastic bag to take with me. Pantelakis drove, swearing all the way, and we arrived at his apartment in Vågmästarplatsen. When he opened the door, a huge, friendly dog came running up to me. Pantelakis showed me where I would sleep and where his food was. He told me to stay inside. He left for a few hours and came back to take the dog out. He discreetly checked on whether the restaurant had called the police. They hadn't, so after two days he drove me back to my room again.

PANTELAKIS WAS A MENTOR, a brother, and an angel who had been sent to me. He had nothing to gain from helping me. He was just a nice guy from Cyprus. He worked hard and had a lot of friends.

One day while I'd been laying low at his house, he asked me to stay in my room. His girlfriend came over and they began smoking marijuana.

The next morning, he said to me: "Look at me, I'm destroying my life with this shit. Don't you dare try drugs or I'll kill you with my bare hands. Most of you who come here to study just find your solutions in drugs and running after blonde girls. Don't you dare — I'll be checking on you daily!"

It was the same advice he'd given me at the pizza place, the first time we'd met, and precisely what Lefteris had told me earlier, at the Greek social club.

Whatever I needed, I could call on my friend Pantelakis and ask for help. Any time. I always wondered why.

He could be rude, using coarse language and sounding very impolite when he spoke to others. I asked him once why he protected me and cared about me. He just stared at me angrily with his big, dark eyes. "Don't use fucking drugs," was all he would say. "Stay away from that shit!"

A few years later, on one of my trips to Athens, I opened a newspaper and learned that he had committed suicide in a hotel room in the centre of the city. He hung himself from the ceiling. They published a photo of him and mentioned that it was drug-related. That explained his 'angel role' to me: drugs had got the better of him and he could not free himself from their grip. I suppose he could see some of himself in me, where he once was, and that made him both sad and angry.

STENA LINE is a Sweden-based international shipping company and one of the biggest ferry operators in Europe, with a huge terminal hub in Gothenburg. I managed to get a job there as a dishwasher, with my shift starting at 6 AM. That meant I had to leave my apartment at 5 each morning to catch the first train. Stena Line was, and remains, a huge company, so there were ample career opportunities. Every morning I would arrive at 5:30 at the latest, because the next train was at 6:00, and I couldn't risk of being late.

I would begin by washing the gigantic saucepan, and then the dishes, from the evening before. That's not a bad work strategy: tackle the one that takes the most space — physically or mentally — if you know that the effort will be similar to what's required for some of the smaller items. You just feel that much freer when you get the biggest piece out of the way, as I did each day.

The chef was a Yugoslavian man who was hostile toward me from day one. He called me *malaka* all the time. It seemed that 'arsehole' was the only Greek word they all learned. He made it a point to make my work torture each day.

One morning, I tried to clean a huge industrial cooking pot. These are the size of barrels, and are used to prepare meals for hundreds. It was so large that I could not reach the bottom without climbing onto a stool and stretching my body and arms. The chef came up behind me and pushed me into it, and I landed in a pool of dirty water and food from the night before. He laughed loudly. When I said I wanted to change my clothes, he wouldn't let me.

What could I do? I could go to the manager and tell him what happened on a daily basis, but keeping my job was more important.

I felt alone in the huge room with all the dishes, often with food still caked onto them, as though they wanted to make my life harder. The chef and his assistants were typically 10–20 metres away. I would sing my favourite songs in Greek very quietly to myself until the others came near.

One day, the foreman asked me to accompany him to the company doctor. I followed him without question. The doctor, in his white frock, was quite polite, and asked me to sit down. He spoke slowly because he knew my Swedish and English were at a beginner's level. He asked me how I felt about my work.

"Everything is great here," I replied, deciding to play it safe. "Why?"

"You've been making a lot of hustle and bustle in the early morning."

I was shocked, because I had done nothing other than work fast. Wasn't that a plus, in any workplace?

"You sing every morning, and when there's too much to do, you make a lot of noises," he continued.

I tried to explain. "When I sing, it is so quietly that even I can barely hear it. When we have too much work, I work faster than anyone else. Please check with my supervisor." She had told me many times that I was working as well as two people combined, and she actually moved one to another department.

What had happened? It seems that I was working too quickly, and basically doing too good a job, and my colleagues had complained. However, nothing happened following that trip to the doctor. A few weeks later I asked if I could transfer to working on the ships, where for every two days you worked, you would get two days off, and the job paid more. They said yes, and I got my promotion. It was a lesson about envy, where the kitchen staff could not deal with one person working harder and making them feel inadequate. **I got out of a sticky situation, thanks to hard work.**

I DIDN'T EXACTLY HAVE SEA LEGS. I almost drowned on three occasions as a little kid and had to be brought back to life. There was the octopus incident. The other two times were when I'd stood on a bridge as my friends were jumping into the water and swimming. I didn't jump because I couldn't swim, so they just pulled me in to the deep water.

To this day I have a fear of water and the sea.

At age 19, working for a shipping company, I still swam like an old woman who didn't want to put her head underwater for fear of ruining her hair. But now, I had a job on the water so I could make more money and work fewer days each month. I had to get over this phobia.

In those days, people had big parties on cruise lines, there was a lot of drunkenness, and it was easy to pick someone up after work.

I worked behind the bar, collecting empty glasses and stocking the refrigerators. Most of the staff drank, but I didn't want to. I already had a hard time when it was windy and there were swells outside, and drinking certainly wouldn't have helped. And, I couldn't sleep easily when I shared a cabin with others. The barman used to joke with me, calling me *malaka* or some other epithet, trying to get me to down a few drinks.

One day, I saw that the supervisor made some money on the black market by stealing alcohol from the company. Sweden's liquor trade was, and still is, tightly regulated, so there was a lot of underground trade. I saw him sharing the proceeds with some of the staff. When they noticed that I was behind them, still cleaning, they jokingly (I think!) threatened to throw me overboard.

I was so surprised to see my boss do something illegal, in plain sight, and everyone go along with it. I couldn't believe that no one took any responsibility over this.

Things got particularly strange one Midsummer, Sweden's biggest holiday. People would get together to celebrate and drink a lot. By 11 PM, hardly anyone on the ship could stand up and walk straight, including some of the staff. We closed the bar at around 3 AM, and I went down to my cabin. Outside one small corridor I bumped into one of the senior crew — either the first or second officer, as I recall — stark naked and trying to find his cabin. I was shocked, as his cabin would not have been on the lowest floor but on the top.

I entered my cabin, which I shared with a colleague, to find him having sex with three girls. Being a foreigner was an advantage in those days, especially when people got drunk — I could get away with being 'different,' and not taking part in some of the more unsavoury activities.

A few weeks later, I found another job and left the cruise line, but see-ing this part of life wasn't something I'd expected of my new country.

Years later, I read that the company discovered there had been staff thefts. We weren't talking about a small percentage; it had accounted for the majority of the company's turnover! People who worked there said it had been going on for years, and no one bothered, so they got greedier and stole more and more. **It's a lesson for all businesses: don't let the rot set in, because when it does, it will surely spread.**

4
Inside Swedish society

THOSE FIRST YEARS in Sweden were difficult in every way. The winters were extremely cold, with the temperature dropping to −20°C (−4°F) for long periods. I had no money to buy the right clothes, and my Greek winter jackets could not protect me. I had never experienced such cold, and my body literally stung.

The food did not suit me, and I couldn't stand the sight of some of the dishes. Fried herring with lingonberries — that was fish with jam! There were big pork chops ringed with a thick band of fat, which they happily devoured! Someone explained that it was important to eat fatty foods ... otherwise you would freeze.

For the first time in my life, I became aware of how important my hair colour was. *Svartskalle* (black skulls) was the derogatory name for those who came from southern Europe, or non-European people. Finnish immigrants were not popular either. It wasn't safe for a dark-haired person to walk through town alone late at night. People would shout, "Go home, black skull!" or even attack you. Some immigrant boys went to the city in groups, looking for Swedish guys to fight.

It wasn't ordinary Swedes who openly hated foreigners, but there were various nationalist leagues that mounted racist attacks and organized riots. Yet, even regular young guys, when they had a bit to drink, could spit out condescending words. We quickly learned from the more experienced immigrants how we should act in the city to avoid being beaten.

If you wanted to go to a nightclub, there was less chance of getting in if you went in a group of more than two black skulls. The bouncers would let in a certain number of foreigners, and then stop. The 'ordinary' Swedes would stop going if there were too many black skulls.

The Finns had their nightclubs, which were exclusively Finnish in theory, but you could see a few other nationalities who dared to go. The Greeks had Zorba, a nightclub owned by two Greek brothers, but all sorts of nationalities were present. No Swedish guys would go, but there were plenty of Swedish girls. When you went home by bus at night, there was a chance you'd encounter some of the local thugs, and if you were alone, you could get beaten up.

Learning the language opened up opportunities, and you could meet others in the same boat, but there wasn't much chance of a black skull actually meeting someone Swedish. You seldom saw Swedes hanging out with an immigrant. If you did, they would attract a lot of attention. Swedish girls dating a black skull got dirty looks, and they'd hear some colourful language directed their way.

One sunny day, I was on Avenyn, a long avenue in the middle of Gothenburg, walking with Pantelakis. Two blonde girls walked past and gave us a glance. The more petite one whispered something to her friend and gave a big, happy smile. I only noticed some of this, but Pantelakis, with his more experienced eyes, signalled to me, "Say something, *malaka!*"

Before I could get a word out, he advanced quickly toward them and grabbed one by the arm. I stood still and tried to look away. He had managed to convince both of them to come back toward me, and said to them, "This is my friend Panos. Give him a kiss." He hadn't even finished his sentence when the girls jointly hugged me, one kissing me from the left and the other from the right. I couldn't move. Pantelakis began talking to them in Swedish, which I could barely follow, though I noticed they kept looking at me and smiling.

Pantelakis took us to the nearest café and said to me in his angry tone, "*Malaka*, take the chance now! She wants you! Don't you get it?" I was speechless. One of the girls looked me up and down and I turned red as a beetroot. "Are you not a man?" Pantelakis asked.

This angel had the lightest blue eyes I'd ever seen. I felt so indescribably inferior. What would everyone say about the black skull who had such a beautiful blonde girl? She would not want me when she found out I had no home, job or food for the day. What kind of man was I for a gorgeous creature like this?

Pantelakis was in command, and before long he was having coffee with one of the girls. A few minutes later he got up and said, "Now we're going to my place." And then, in Greek: *"Ela malaka pes kati stin gomena!"* (Come on, arsehole, say something to the girl!)

We got into a taxi. He sat next to the driver and put me between the two blondes. They laughed, and pinched me on the cheek, and the petite one — who I now learned was called Yvonne — was busy with her hands. I did not think this was particularly funny and felt even more insecure.

When we arrived at Pantelakis's, he took out a bottle of wine and then started hugging his new girl. He thought I was getting in the way with my angry face, and said, "Take her for a walk, but don't come back too quickly."

I did, and the evening ended quietly enough for me, but Yvonne wanted to meet again and again. We did so almost every day, and with my limited English, I explained some of my worries. A few days later, she invited me to her parents' home for dinner. The whole family was there. I was not ready for this, thinking it would be just her Mum and Dad. But along with them there was a little sister, and a big sister, and the big sister's husband and their children. I got really nervous when they started asking questions. I didn't understand much, and did not want to tell them everything.

The dinner dragged on. Time passed, but they were still sitting at the table. I tried to whisper to Yvonne that it was time for me to leave, because the last bus would soon come. She replied that her parents wanted me to sleep over! I'd never imagined that one could do that. To my great surprise, her mother went and made a nice bed for us, and I accepted the offer. The next morning, her mother was the first to knock on the door and say that breakfast was served.

At one point, I had been waiting for monthly funds from home, but they did not come as usual. To be allowed to stay and study in Sweden, money would have to come from your home country every month, via bank transfer. I don't remember the exact amount, but it would have been in the vicinity of $400 per month. Calling my parents was not the easiest thing. I would sometimes head to the pay phone and put in the crowns, though the phone was particularly hungry on international calls, and my stack of coins would vanish in a flash. It would eat the coins regardless of whether I managed to converse with them or not — the phone required a lot just to make an international connection. This time, I called the petrol station 500 metres from their home and asked someone there to tell them I would call soon. They would find someone who had the time to run to my parents' house and pass the message on. My parents couldn't call me, since I didn't have my own phone. The idea was to catch them at home to do the call as speedily as possible, before the money ran out.

After a few tries, I got through. I managed to talk to my mother, who told me that the police had visited, and that I must return within a few days since my application for deferring my military service had been rejected. The bank had stopped doing the transfers as a matter of course.

I kept inserting coins, but my allotted time came to an end. I stood there with a dead line, trying to understand what on earth had happened.

Afterwards, I looked to the principal at the university for help. I asked her to write a certificate saying I had been admitted to the university, but that I must study Swedish for one year as a prerequisite. She agreed and gave me a document stating this, but did not know how it would be translated, and how it would go down with the Greek consulate.

My money had run out, and I went to the Greek association to find a compatriot who needed money in Greece. We could then help each other, with me accessing their local funds and they accessing mine in Greece. That succeeded, but the problem was not solved.

I had to then go to the police to get a residence permit and prove that the bank transfers had been made. I got back in touch with my parents to get an update, but they shared some additional bad news with me: the military's deadline had passed and I would be sentenced by the court for evading my service, with an automatic sentence of three years in prison. I could hear the hopelessness that parents feel when they are powerless, and cannot help their own children. They did not ask what I would do, but my mother said, "Fight if you can." I could feel her soft cheeks, even though she was thousands of miles away. She remained calm but sounded troubled, knowing that her son was alone in a foreign country and in trouble. She felt inadequate, which is a horrible feeling.

My principal, my Irja, was my lifeline. Every time I found myself in deep water, I ran to her. She always stood up and welcomed me with her calm manner and friendly smile. It is impossible to describe just how incredible this was. She was the oasis from which hope sprung. Where would I have been if I had not met such a person, who had changed the direction of my life?

Several times a month she would write another certificate with different words, in the hope that the military would eventually get tired and leave me alone.

My preparatory studies in Swedish became urgent, demanding my attention if I were to get into university within the semester. But this was not possible, because they required me to have done at least three semesters in chemistry, mathematics and English, as well as Swedish. I studied around the clock and asked all those around me for help. My life was at stake here. Doing the work and getting through it was my sole focus. I changed my Swedish studies to evening courses so I could do the other subjects in the morning, and then work at the restaurant in the afternoon.

The Swedish language class was at 6–9 PM, three evenings a week. In that group there were different nationalities. During the breaks I would put my head between my arms on the table and close my eyes for a while. It was not that I was tired from running around since 7 AM, but the thoughts swirling around in my head, and the uncertainty, were tormenting me.

One night, I was feeling particularly drained, mentally and physically. I felt I had burdened so many other people with my problems, but there was still no light at the end of the tunnel. I lay my head down on the desk for a while, and this time I dozed off. I was woken by a kiss on the neck. I imagined it must have been a classmate, a pretty Colombian girl classmate who was fond of me and constantly flirting. I got up gently and tried to get her face off my neck, only to discover that it was my teacher, Tomas! I was paralysed. How could my teacher — a man — do that? What was wrong with me?

The next day, I visited the student counsellor and asked to change my days so that I could avoid him. It created a great deal of anxiety and uncertainty in me. I dared not tell anyone what had happened, not even Pantelakis.

The new course leader was a woman, but a few weeks later she had to go on maternity leave, and her replacement was a male teacher, a man of 45 or 50 with a thick moustache. It was unusual at that time for a Swedish man to look like a farmer from the Mediterranean.

After class, I would walk to the station to take the bus home, and he would do the same. One night, he caught me before I left, and very politely asked a few questions about Greece. He said he was a Graecophile and planned to travel there, and wondered if we could help each other. He offered to help me with Swedish if I were to help him with Greek.

We continued chatting on the walk to the station, which was about ten minutes away. During this time, he relayed how he had sucked Greek soldiers' cocks when he'd travelled to Kos and stayed outside military bases. This was the next big shock for me. I did not know what to say and chose silence. Should I change class again now? Would this even be possible? What would I give as a reason?

I chose to stay and complete the class. In the days ahead, though, some other students and I noticed that he stared at me, and his gaze often stopped on the lower part of my body.

It continued, and a few days later I had to change class again.

Several years later, I understood why these people applied to work in such environments. We were desperate and had problems just surviving.

We were vulnerable. You see this daily when you read of UN staff in African countries sexually exploiting young children who are desperate for food. This is going on openly, and no one will do anything, even in the 2020s. In that tangled bureaucracy, these disgusting monsters can only be moved to the next country, where they continue their predatory criminal acts.

I received another 'no' from Greece regarding my military deferral, and things began to look really dark for me. Soon my passport would expire and I wouldn't be allowed to study or stay in Sweden. Yvonne met me for a walk, and I told her I had no options left that I could think of. I had a few weeks left on the original pass, and was beyond worried.

I said we should visit her parents, as I wanted to tell them something. We went straight to them. I explained everything that had happened, and added, "I just wanted to say goodbye. I am so grateful for all the love you have shown me."

Her mother immediately grabbed my hand and said, "You stay with us. No one is going to deport you. You're going to marry my daughter and you'll stay here! We have a custom that everyone in this family gets married on the Midsummer holiday weekend, and there are only a few weeks left until then. We have time!"

And so it was. Pantelakis was my best man and Lefteris's family stood in for my own. But the happiness with Yvonne did not last long. My problems remained and tormented me. In Greece, I was a wanted man, and the threatened punishment increased with every year that passed. I constantly felt persecuted by them. It was a horrible existence, living in constant anxiety and fear. Not being able to see your own family, not being able to return to where you grew up, living as a stranger in a strange country, threatened with years in prison. Only those friends of mine who had been through something similar could fully understand it.

Yvonne and I were only 19 years old. Neither of us had an understanding of anything, nor had we lived alone or with someone else outside of our own families. The cultural clash became too great. Suddenly, our innocent, youthful love wasn't so sweet any more. I talked to my in-laws about this and they immediately decided that she should move home and leave me alone. They promised that on paper we would remain married, to help ensure my Swedish residency, and that I would always be welcome at their table.

Twice a year, I had to go to the police station to be interviewed about the relationship. If they were convinced that I remained legitimately married to a Swede, they would extend the residence permit for another six months. Yvonne refused to come, and her mother or father took her place instead on three occasions, telling the authorities that everything was in order and Yvonne simply wasn't able to take time off work.

IN 1978, I became an accredited foreign correspondent for *Avriani*, a well-known daily newspaper in Greece. It was the second or third largest at the time. I was lucky enough to have met the owners, brothers Makis and Giorgos Kouris, before I had gone to Sweden. The paper was popular, because it harshly criticized the system and the rampant corruption of that era. They wrote in ordinary Greek, so the working class could understand everything and feel that someone spoke for them.

The brothers were loved by some and hated by others. They uncovered many scandals and had published some popular articles I submitted to them. Before I went to Sweden, they had showed me around their offices in person. This led to them asking if I could keep them up to date on what was happening in Sweden.

I called at the beginning of '78, and Giorgos himself answered the phone. "Of course I remember you," he said. "How are you doing in Sweden?"

I told him I wanted to become a correspondent, and that I didn't want to be paid for anything they might decide to publish. Giorgos was a gentleman who acted quickly, and I appreciated that. He prepared papers that would allow me to register with the Ministry of Foreign Affairs in Stockholm. After a few days, I was formally accredited as one of the Greek journalists living in Sweden.

I got invited to the Ministry of Foreign Affairs, visited Parliament, and met with some ministers. This was huge for me at the time, but there was a big problem. Being visible was very important for networking, and working as a journalist in general, but I did not have the money to go to Stockholm or stay in a hotel. My clothes were not suitable in that environment either. And, I had so many black marks against my name: the Greek authorities were after me, I had worked illegally in Sweden, and I was married only on paper, so I was actually staying illegally in the country.

And so, I chose to keep a very low profile. I wrote only positive articles about Sweden, and not many. It was enough that I was on the foreign ministry's list and had a press card. It came in handy, because I didn't have a passport, and the few times I was stopped by the police I showed them the press card and all was well. That card was my most important lifeline. I did not want to make the slightest mistake that would take it from me. It was like when my mother managed to find the money we lacked to finally get electricity in the little house. Mum always had an extra lifeline and saved us, and I was going to hold this one near and dear to me.

In 1979, the poet and essayist Odysseas Elytis was awarded the Nobel Prize in Literature. He was the first Greek winner of the coveted distinction. Shortly after the announcement, I received an invitation to the award ceremony. I could not believe it — it was a once-in-a-lifetime opportunity — but decided to decline. I told this to Pantelakis and he stared at me with his big eyes.

"Re malaka," he said, "you're going. We'll rent clothes for you and I'll buy train tickets. There is a friend of mine who you will stay with. Do you understand how big this is?"

He took me to a second-hand shop that rented formal wear, but it wasn't easy to find my size. Most Swedes were much taller than me. We managed to find a suit that fit fairly well, but it would still need to be altered. Next, we discovered that nobody rented size 41 shoes, which were quite small by Swedish standards, so we had to find some cheap ones elsewhere and buy them instead.

"You will be the youngest and most beautiful there," Pantelakis assured me. "Nobody will see your shoes!" I could see how happy he was for me, his friend. It was like he was going to the ceremony himself!

I cannot say that I was entirely happy with the experience. There were so many beautiful, accomplished people, such wonderful clothes, so much elegance, and everything was so perfectly organized. I was mesmerized by how the attendees moved, greeted each other, addressed each other — it was a fabulous experience on so many levels. Yet, I had an uncomfortable feeling. There was a nagging worry deep inside me that I couldn't quite put my finger on.

My second great experience thanks to the press card was when Andreas Papandreou, the prime minister of Greece, met with his Swedish counterpart, Olof Palme, on a state visit to Stockholm. Both were great personalities in my mind, and I was asked to attend an official dinner at Palme's residence.

Visiting the home of Sweden's prime minister, who was a respected international personality, was great. I remember the friendly, relaxed atmosphere when I entered the residence. I had read that Palme believed that the Swedish ideal was based on everyone being equal, and he appealed to people from all backgrounds and walks of life. But that nagging feeling remained.

My first impression when I met Palme: he was like all the rest of us ... but not as tall as I thought he'd be. We of course form our own 'pictures' of how those important, famous people are in real life. In the next room, Papandreou was among some of his ministers and a handful of Swedish journalists. I stood to the side and waited for everyone to arrive, observing everything. Even though he had so many people around, Palme spotted me, turned around with half a step and stretched out his hand. I shook hands with him and he asked if I was new to his security detail. I took it as a compliment, as neither my physique nor height justified his question.

IN THOSE EARLY YEARS, I was endlessly curious about Swedish society. I had heard so much about the fine democracy and social system, which was a dream for many other countries. For a small, elongated nation with just 8 million people in the '70s, it was famous worldwide. There was no internet, but people living in the most remote corners of the globe knew about this special place. You also saw it in their Volvo cars, which placed human safety above everything else. The same was true with Saab. You knew there was plenty of brilliant, independent thinking going on here. You also saw it in tourist photos of the country, where everything was orderly and neat, none of it staged. By this point, the pop group ABBA had risen to prominence, and the quartet had a comfortable, tidy wholesomeness that could only have come from such a squared-away place.

I really wanted to get within the system, and see and experience all of this first hand. I had seen so much injustice in Greece, with so many of the government agencies not working, and a healthcare system that only a few had access to. Even when death came, you risked not being buried if you hadn't saved enough to pay the priest for your own funeral. It was a corrupt system, with a whole society built on running around, making pay offs and stamping paper just to get a birth certificate.

I also remember how difficult it was for retirees to get their pension. I had helped a number of older workers apply for their pension during my time in the factory. You had to go through a lawyer if you wanted any chance of getting a decent amount. You also needed a lawyer if you wanted the employer to pay within the first two years after you'd stopped working ... and the lawyer would take most of the first year's pension.

It touched me a great deal when I saw poor, worn-out workers whose bodies had been consumed by a lifetime of hard labour. By age 65 they were so ground down that they could hardly wait for Charos to take them away. But they would fight to get their hard-earned pension. It hurt to see that.

Sweden was known for taking care of its citizens. No matter who you were, you were treated with respect. Palme rode a bicycle to work at the Riksdag, the Swedish legislature. He could move among mortals because he was one of them. Healthcare was for everyone, as was the right to an education. Although taxes were high, there was a social contract that everyone understood. This could only be achieved when the government was not corrupt and siphoning off revenue at every turn. Everything Sweden took, it gave back in one way or another to ensure that everyone was looked after. The citizenry could trust the government. No wonder it was frequently cited as a democratic model to follow.

For me, coming from a country that only created chaos, fear and dread, it was impossible to describe the feeling of relief and possibility here.

SOMEWHERE IN MY BRAIN was a hidden wish, one that was growing slowly. Every time I saw a positive thing in Sweden, I thought of my own dreams and my home country. It was that vague notion I'd sensed deep within me, but could not quite grasp, during the dinner at the prime minister's residence. Day by day, this secret gradually revealed itself to me, and started to play on my soul.

My thoughts returned to the hard times in Greece. Even though I was now far away from it all, it wasn't easy to forget that earlier life and focus on new opportunities. It was actually painful to know I had escaped the chaos of my home country and was living this privileged new life, in such a wonderful new place. Every immigrant must feel this at some stage: you leave for a better life elsewhere, but part of you dwells on the past, and all those who still lived there. I might have found myself in a safe country, but mentally, I hadn't fully left. I'd find myself in the library, reading Greek newspapers that were weeks old. You couldn't really cut the ties.

Each development in my new life only created a greater sadness about the old one. Sweden and Greece were equally on my mind, and that affected me all the time. People told me to stop following the news from Greece, but that would have been like shutting your eyes — you can still hear and you can still feel. Cutting off the news didn't work for me.

One sleepless night, feeling I was too far away from my family, from everything, my thoughts ran back to my childhood dreams. What did I want? I thought about the theatre production I put on. I felt guilty, as though I had betrayed everyone, turning my back on them and giving up the fight, so that I, and I alone, could have a better life. But what could I do? No one in that dreadful, dust-choked old neighbourhood had *my* back when I needed it. When they had a chance to stand with me, they all said no, and turned their backs. "It's not the right time," they said. "We have to think about our jobs."

I paced around my 22-square-metre flat, like a fish in a bowl, all night. Is it possible to have a happy future? How can I be happy if those closest to me are so far away? That's not possible. When I was 11 or 12, I asked in geography class how it was conceivable that the Earth was round. That time, too, I said, "That's not possible." The teacher, a woman with long, dark hair, who was thinner than the others, was nice enough, but I didn't like her voice. She looked at me angrily and said, "Tomorrow, you can have an extra examination," and gave me additional pages to study.

The next morning, as soon as she came into the classroom, she asked me to stand up in front of the others. She started her questions, and I could answer most of them, but she was still angry with me. She asked, "Why did you question the shape of the Earth?"

"If the Earth is round," I replied, "why do we believe in maps and why do we act, in our decisions, as though it was flat? Why do we behave as though a decision taken on one part of the map only affects that part? If the Earth is round, then any one decision affects all of us. That's why I said that."

And now, pacing around my flat in Sweden, something happened inside me. The window was open, and outside was a park. Everything there was perfect: the lawn had been mowed with precision, and there was such harmony between the trees, bushes and the light in the sky. It was only 4 AM, but during the Swedish summer there's almost constant light in the sky. In June, it simply never gets dark. I was stunned with this perfection and a smile came across my face. It was a smile of hope, and at that moment a new dream began.

I knew that I wanted to be a politician, and that one day, not far off, I wanted to be Sweden's prime minister. I wanted to take full advantage of my new country and inspire my native country. I stopped pacing and made my small plan: I was determined to immerse myself into Swedish society as deeply as possible.

Every time I had a chance to get a new job, I took it. Being able to work in different institutions was the only way to see if the system functioned properly. I decided that I would try my hand at all sorts of jobs involving people and the state. I had the advantage in these early years, through my

newspaper work, of meeting Swedish political leaders and other personalities who put me in the mood to keep dreaming.

Socialdemokraterna (the Social Democrats) had already approached
me in my first year in Sweden, but I followed my father's advice: "Do not
get coloured before you are ready to go for it! Do not be impressed by a
leader: look around him, at his party!" I'd concluded that their only interest in me was to get a black skull in there — it was just tokenism.

In 1979, the Miljöpartiet (the Green Party) was just starting out. I was
interested in the environment, and the green movement was something
I wanted to be involved in. They approached me to be part of a team
that would begin exploring environmental policy. That was a fantastic
opportunity to get involved on the ground floor, and I participated in
some meetings held with small groups in members' homes. We had one
common goal: respecting the environment. Unfortunately, we couldn't
see eye to eye on anything else. The others seemed to have tunnel vision
— they could only see 'the environment.' "Yes," I argued, "but the environment does not exist in a vacuum." There are human beings, cars, societal
structures. Let's put things in context! But they didn't want to hear me
out, and I decided not to continue on with them.

That experience made me more curious about politics, but at the same
time, I could see that no party could be 100% attractive to me. I was even
approached by the Communist Party, even though I wasn't a communist.

IN 1980, I applied for a temporary position as a guard at Härlanda Prison
in Gothenburg. I had only been in Sweden for three years, so my command of the language was not the best, and that was a big disadvantage.
My hair was brownish black, and it was clear that I was an outsider — a
svartskalle — who had less merit than other candidates. In the interview
room sat three people with their light blue shirts, name tags on their
chests, and lots of keys hanging from their belts. Typical prison guards.

They asked lots of questions, and I felt comfortable answering them. I
just wanted the job, and they could not surprise me with their questions
... but I could surprise them. I was going to have that job!

One of my interrogators was an older man who looked constantly into
my eyes, and took in all my movements. I was normally quite fidgety,
but for seemingly the first time in my adult life, I barely moved. My legs
stayed perfectly still throughout the conversation. I barely touched my
lips or used my hands. I turned my eyes to the older gentleman often, and
finally asked him, "Mr Sven, is there something you want to ask me?"

He did not answer; he just continued to stare at me. I offered up a small smile.

The other two finished their questions and turned to Mr Sven.

He said that most of the positions were already filled, but there was an opening in the psychiatric ward, which housed the more erratic, dangerous prisoners. "It can be very messy, and it is extra-sensitive. A small mistake can have very serious consequences."

I did not respond, and he continued. "You are not Swedish, and too young, and this can create some problems. We've only had one foreigner work for us, and he came from Finland. It was not easy for him, you know."

"Mr Sven, this sounds like the perfect job for me," I told him. "And giving me a chance would be a good way for you to show that you believe in those of us who are not blond! You don't only have Swedes locked up, do you? I have had time to study behavioural science for three years, and worked in drug treatment for two summers." (More on that later.)

He asked me to leave the room. A few minutes later he opened the door with a big smile and asked me to come in.

I could see a look of relief on his face. Throughout the interview, he seemed very thoughtful, and my gut had said, "Now you will get your dream job!" And then, just like that, it happened! All three seemed comfortable with the big step they took in hiring an immigrant who spoke less-than-fluent Swedish and was not blond!

A few days later I started my in-processing and training, which lasted a week. I was impressed by their way of taking care of me, explaining things calmly and quietly. My new colleagues were curious about 'the Greek' who would be working alongside them.

I started reading around the clock about the Swedish legal system, devouring everything I could find out about prisons. I was also sensitive to whatever my colleagues would tell me. I did not want to make the slightest mistake. My dream was that one day I would find an area that I'd specialize in, and actually revolutionize through some sort of great change that would truly be of benefit to people.

The first weeks were really tough. Some prisoners disliked the idea that a black skull would be guarding them. The worst of them were from Finland, who believed that they weren't accepted in Sweden (even though, compared to me, they were). They were the most hostile toward other black-skulled foreigners. They tried to trick me a few times, or to get me off somewhere on my own, but I was on my guard. I showed great respect for the inmates, and day by day gained respect and sympathy from the older prisoners, who'd been there for a long time.

One night, when my partner on the shift had gone to the rest room, I thought about everything I had experienced over the previous few days. I had a hard time sitting still, and walked back and forth in the long corridor, working through my thoughts. I'd long realized that inspiration only comes to me when I move. Silence dominated the night, as everyone slept — even we guards were half-asleep in our quarters. I went slowly and quietly, and when I passed the cell of Pekka, a Finn who particularly hated me, I got a strange feeling. I stopped outside his cell door and heard a faint sound. It was a mumbled monologue. I carried on down the corridor, but something pulled me back. I decided to gently open the cell door, but when my hand pulled at it, I heard a scream from inside, so loud that I dropped my keys. I saw that Pekka's eye was hanging out of its socket, with blood spattered everywhere. I could not understand what had happened — his eye was literally hanging from his face. He cried, "My eye itches! Help me!"

I quickly opened the door, without thinking about alerting my colleague. Pekka, with his grotesquely dangling eyeball, suddenly attacked me. I summoned all my strength, and as if by magic managed to get him under control. My colleague heard his screaming, and our thrashing around, and ran to help.

We learned that Pekka had taken some drugs and thought he had something in his eye that was making it itch. He'd poked it out with a fork that had been hidden in the cell. When the ambulance arrived, he kept shouting that we should help him get the thing out of his eye! He kept yelling at me, "Please, fucking black skull, help me!"

Pekka was hospitalized for a while, was fitted with a porcelain eye, and eventually returned to the wing. I thought he would change after this, but I was wrong. His hatred for me never ended, but I was OK with that. I could see that his insults and threats were empty words. He was just a weak, unhappy person who had ended up on the wrong path.

Fifteen years later, I was at lunch, at a restaurant near my office, with one of my warehouse employees. I usually sit with my back against the wall. I just feel more secure like that. I began doing this in my first year in Sweden after experiencing some particularly unpleasant people. That day, however, I didn't sit my usual way, and my back was unprotected. I saw my employee's eyes widen, sending me warning signals, and he started to rise from his seat. Two hands grabbed my shoulders, and I spun round to face the strange man behind me. He shouted loudly, "Is that the fucking Greek?" It was momentarily frightening, but his tone was actually quite friendly. I instantly recognized the eye, and then the face, and memories of the attack in the prison cell came flooding back.

"It's Pekka," he said. "Do you remember me?" According to the rules, you should never do anything in the outside world to signal to others that someone had been in prison. So, I pretended not to recognize him. He spread his arms and wanted to give me a hug. I followed his movements, and as he embraced me he whispered loudly, so others would hear: "I liked you, you fucking Greek. You're a good guy." He patted me gently on the back. I tried to break from his hug but he wanted to hold me close. He stared into my face with what seemed to be some kind of respect, and pointed to his porcelain eye. "You remember it, don't you?! It was brave of you to come to my aid like that." He gave me one last squeeze, smiled and walked away through the crowd of startled diners.

During the time I worked in the prison, I tried to see and understand everything that happened there. Drugs came in easily: the inmates' wives or girlfriends visited two to three times a month, and always managed to bring something with them.

I started studying the statistics: what percentage of offenders came back again after serving their sentences, how much each prisoner cost society per day, what happens to them after their release. I also studied prison data from other countries, such as the US. It was clear that results were catastrophically bad, with large societal costs that hardly anyone knew of. The people who ended up imprisoned cost a great deal, but things actually got worse after they were released. The idea was to help people get back to life, not to make things worse. That was not how it ended up working, yet nothing changed. No country seems to have succeeded in coming up with a good solution.

I was asked by a couple of prisoners if I could become their probation officer, someone they could turn to and ask for help after release. I felt proud to be asked, and it showed they appreciated my personality. To them I wasn't a damned foreigner, but a person they could trust when needed.

I trained for this, and immediately started looking after two people after their release. One had been in prison for a financial crime and the other for drugs. There was little money in it, but it wasn't about the money. I wanted to see the whole process; to look deeply into the heart of this aspect of society, with my own eyes.

Drugs were a big problem in the '80s. I could see how established the mafia had become, and how passive and paralysed the whole legal system was. Of course I knew very little, but with the slightest interest you could observe the social trends, and the direction things were headed. You could feel it in the air. I wondered why the authorities did not act in the face of the drug scourge and the rise of organized crime. Surely, being proactive should be a matter of course?

I was looking for night work in a halfway house for drug addicts. This paid fairly well, and I could sleep there without doing much. It suited me, and I could have two jobs in parallel, while still being able to continue with my studies. Recovering addicts would go to these homes to be slowly reconnected with ordinary life.

There I learned that most of what society was doing to help people with such problems was meaningless. Much of this was due to political decisions that had not been properly implemented. Sweden had plenty of money, and wanted to show that it did a lot for its people, but many of these efforts yielded no results.

The following year, I applied to Lillhagen, one of the largest psychiatric hospitals in Gothenburg. After my first interview at Härlanda prison, I had developed such self-esteem that I knew I could get the job I wanted. I had nice references and a little extra something in my tone that could get through to an interviewer. Sure enough, the interview went well and I was hired by Lillhagen. I asked to be assigned to the toughest ward, where the difficult patients were, and my time there would be the most challenging experience of my life.

From the start, I could not fathom the idea of helpless people walking around like zombies, being fed a cocktail of powerful psychiatric drugs several times a day to keep them under control. Before I'd moved to Sweden, I once visited Dromokaikio, a similar hospital outside Athens, because an acquaintance had ended up there against his will. That really shook me up, but it was Greece, which lagged terribly in taking care of the mentally ill. My thoughts went back and forth to compare the two. It was strange that both systems abused the very people who needed their help. They usually say it's all about money, but Sweden had money, so why did they just shovel pills into these people's mouths?

I remembered that in Greece the atmosphere was actually warmer. The buildings were worn, and everything looked poor and unacceptable to my immature eyes then. But it was warmer in that you could hold someone's hand for a long time to calm them down. This, however, was human humiliation. I could not work there any more. I resigned after a few weeks and applied to a retirement home.

There, I could keep elderly people company and read the newspaper. It was located near Slottskogen, one of the finest parks in Gothenburg, where a lot of people gathered each day of the year. Summers were the best: people stretched out everywhere to sunbathe, or they would be exercising or playing. That retirement home was ideal in my eyes: it looked like a small hotel, with nice, homey rooms.

The person in charge showed me around and introduced me to the staff. Everyone who worked there was Swedish, and all the older residents were Swedes. Suddenly, again, I was in an environment where my black hair and brown eyes might create anxiety. It was quite comical when I read the paper to a couple of the residents, as I don't think they knew all the words, or had met an immigrant, or could understand my Greek accent. After a while, I stopped actually reading the paper, and just held it in front of me. I sat there, silently, and waited to see if they would react. They said nothing. There was no reaction at all. I put the newspaper down, took one older man's hand and asked, "Do you understand anything when I read?" He was 90 years old, could not walk, and needed help getting up and eating. Still, he was pretty clear in his head. He did not answer my question, but he held onto my hand.

I would read to the next person, and did the same thing after five minutes, stopping, and waiting for his reaction. He said nothing either.

I asked him, "Did you listen to what I read?"

He replied, "What did you read?"

I repeated this with different people and realized that the ritual that management had instructed us to carry out was an utter failure. That was not what the residents needed. Why would a nonagenarian who could hardly eat or go to the toilet without help want to know what a reporter had to say said about Vietnam? Instead, I tried to get them to tell me things. It was difficult at first, but they began to open up, little by little. Soon we'd be engaging in a legitimate, two-way dialogue. I was curious to hear the stories of their life — about their spouses, and their children — and this brought them to life! Some talked about love. I was given a strong reminder: we are all human. **Observe and listen, instead of dictating and imposing something that we think others want! I had this skill, and put it to use, throughout my life. Listen and analyse.** Whatever else may have gone dark inside, they had a great need for love and closeness. I saw how much they enjoyed my holding their hand; how hard could that be?

I applied for another gig in order to work with young people. I wanted to channel my energy into helping society flourish, and figured that if you could help young people bloom in the right way, you'd wind up with healthy citizens.

I managed to get a job as a substitute for a few days at a primary school where a friend worked as a teacher. I liked it a lot. I talked to the principal and managed to get a part-time job that suited me perfectly. I managed to read about pedagogy — the art of teaching — and that strengthened my ability and desire to do the work.

The school was located in Hisingen, a suburb outside Gothenburg. They had a bad reputation and low scores compared to the rest of the country. This was because they had many immigrant children who didn't do well on their exams. I saw a fantastic challenge and persuaded the principal to give me specific students with foreign backgrounds who had difficulty in school, regardless of the subject. I had an idea how to help them. After repeated requests, I was given two hours per week with each student, to coach them and help with their homework. I was incredibly happy for the assignment. At the outset, I decided to meet all five students at the same time, to get to know them together and see how they acted in groups. They came from different countries, and two were from Greece. Everyone had come to Sweden as small children, having completed a couple of years of schooling in their home country.

In the first hour I noticed that something was distracting them. They didn't seem all there. There was an aggression that led to small protests over anything that was said to them. They teased each other and said condescending things. Their way of asserting themselves was by arguing.

The day after, we met to go through the homework that they had a hard time understanding. I decided to ask them to put their books down and to go out and play football. They could not believe it! I started talking like they did: I adjusted my tone and shouted back as they shouted at each other. I used slang and swear words as they did. We split up and played football three-a-side. I could already feel which were the best players, and had them on my team.

When we started, the three on the opposite side felt I had cheated them, and started complaining that the players were not fairly distributed. I pretended not to hear. I summoned everything I could to keep possession of the ball, and we scored one goal after another. As you can imagine, my two players had a lot of fun, as the others became increasingly angry. They started swearing, and I dished out more of the same, but to an even greater degree. We played for a while, until they didn't want to continue.

It was time to go back to the classroom. They continued to quarrel all the way back. I split them up, one by one, and kept them far apart. I started talking to the easiest person and just focused on him. I just cared about him for the moment. When the hour was over, I asked how they liked our time together. Their faces showed confusion, and irritation, but at the same time, I caught a glimpse of something else. I sensed a feeling of liberation. The experience had been both heavy and lightening.

We would see each other again in a few days, and all five showed up on time. I noticed that they interacted differently this time. There was less aggression in the air. I asked how their school day had been, and everyone answered, "Pretty damned boring."

I said we would now play football again, and immediately I saw a stronger will on their faces.

One of the students on the previous week's losing side, Petros, said, "Yes, but it is unfair that you chose the best for your side, and you are good and older than us. I want your two players to be on the same team as me!"

"That's fine," I replied, "if you could explain why a little more." I said that the choices were either me deciding if they would be losers again, or them figuring out what they had to do to become the winning side. It didn't take long for the penny to drop, when they realized what I wanted to achieve. Instead of playing football, we chose to continue talking, in the classroom.

I wanted them to realize that even though it is tough to be in a new country — without knowing the language, without having support from home, and without having everything else the locals did — it was possible to surmount the gigantic lead others had and become something. But, they would need to spend that much more time training.

"Notice how people often lose to those that they underestimate? You see it every day in sports, and in most things," I told them. "Look at me. My Swedish is far from that of a teacher; I have none of the knowledge that ordinary Swedes have, but look at me now! I'm taking care of you. I don't think there are many immigrants who have come this far in such a short time."

During the conversation I noticed a change in their eyes. They became more curious and more interested in listening to what I was saying. "Do you remember when we first played football? What did you do? You swore to each other instead of supporting each other. You immediately saw that we were better, and you gave up and started complaining and splitting up. What would you do differently today?"

Petros said, "We thought about this, and that's why we wanted to form a new team against you. Then, I would have trained to kick far, so we wouldn't have to try to tackle you, because you're good at taking possession from us."

I got up and shouted in delight. "Don't you realize how smart you can be, and what you can do with your life other than just walking around and swearing? Let us promise each other that we will train so much that we will surprise everyone at school and, above all, surprise ourselves!"

But first, I said, I was going to say something that I wanted them to write down in capital letters, and have them in front of them all the time. I spoke slowly, deliberately and more than a little dramatically. *"I can because I want to, and it is I who decides the result!"*

I had the privilege of working with these five boys for two years, with fantastic results. They managed to calm down, developed nicely and performed well enough at school to no longer feel inferior. I wanted to see their after-school environment and meet their parents, so I arranged to visit their homes. It reminded me to some degree of my own upbringing, and my thoughts went to the millions of children who would not have that help, with nobody interested in them and setting them on the right path in their formative years. The school had its own routines for dealing with 'inferior' students, but they never yielded results and continued to waste money.

It was easy to end up on the wrong path as a 12-year-old. Drugs were already available, it's easy to start stealing and fighting, and see your life get rougher every day. The inevitable result was prison. We have laid the groundwork for a humanitarian atomic bomb.

I read 60 credits of pedagogy because they would qualify me to formally teach in a school. My plan was to apply for a principal's position at a city school where there were many problems. I got several part-time jobs in different schools for children and adult learners. I sought out opportunities to work on problems because it gave me a sense of self and security, and it provided a chance to be creative. I am a competitive person, and routine tasks just aren't for me. At all the schools, I found that the principals would become aware of my talent for leading classes and getting the students' commitment. I had all the necessary references and experience to become Sweden's first immigrant principal, and the youngest!

One day, I spotted an ad in a teachers' magazine for a principal's position. I called to schedule an interview. However, it was not that simple; they wanted applications submitted, and they would choose whom to meet. I called around to my old principals and asked them to write references, stating what they thought about my ability to do that job. They all said I was great, that they would support me, and they hoped I would get the position. I never did. I waited for another opportunity, but nothing came in the near term, and I let go of the idea of becoming an activist principal who could challenge the hidebound Swedish school system.

My thoughts about the education system have not improved since then. In fact, quite the opposite. The system is outdated, and the resources are distributed in the wrong way, because there are so many less-than-competent people who decide what one should and shouldn't do. My philosophy was that the best, most qualified educators should be teaching three- to six-year-olds. There should be higher status given to teachers in the early grades, and they should be better paid than their colleagues in the higher grades. To be involved in shaping children in the beginning requires a different type of teacher. You build sound foundations for the students in their first years. Few families have the knowledge or the time to provide this. I think any educator can teach maths or chemistry, but it takes someone special in those early grades.

Our entire modern society is based on the state shaping its citizens, but the result is easy to see: millions of unhappy, unmotivated young people who are uninterested in most things around them. Some are cynical about life; others live a shallow existence. There were also many who feel left out when their lives don't match up to what they see on social media.

By now, I had held jobs in diverse fields and started comparing what I had learned about Sweden with what I'd seen in my home country. I realized that all systems have their weaknesses, and the idyllic image of Sweden and all its advantages were pure myths. True, there is a well functioning, highly organized state, but people paid a high price on the human side to get there. I think again of when I was about to leave Greece and was stopped by the police because they suspected I had more money than was allowed. And how, on the boat, I wasn't allowed to substitute French fries for mashed potatoes. These institutions were built to handle people and they functioned as a modern 'factory,' all robotized down to the smallest detail. No one had thought of holding the hands of the elderly in the nursing home. It had been decreed that newspapers would be read, and that day's paper was in place every morning, regardless of the weather. That, at least, came on time.

I grew increasingly frustrated with all the passivity. Everyone saw things that didn't work, but they walked on by, closing their eyes and saying, "That's not my responsibility." In school, when the time came to select a student union president, hardly anyone stood for election. Had it been Greece, everyone would have wanted that position! These were such different worlds, yet the same on so many levels.

THE THIRD YEAR'S INTERVIEW with the police was the most important. Afterwards, I could get a permanent residence permit, and my troubles with the Greek military would almost be gone.

It was important that Yvonne would come along this time, and not her parents, but she refused. She had even threatened on several occasions to call the police and tell them the truth. I walked with my worries, around the clock. Would the police pick me up? Everything I had managed to do so far would be wasted. I was ready for the worst, and I already knew what the prisons were like, but I also knew I would not allow it to happen to me.

The call to set the appointment came and there was one week left. My in-laws had not managed to persuade Yvonne to help me through the ordeal.

I had one card left to play. Earlier in 1980, in January, I met a female police officer at the New Yaki nightclub in central Gothenburg. I had already made some contacts at the club, so I could bypass the queues and didn't have to pay to get in. I worked at the prison until 10:00 that night, and then went straight there. I was wearing the same clothes — blue pants and light blue shirt — but left my name tag in the car.

I was still a shy guy, and quite insecure about venturing on to the dance floor. I guess I'm among the few Greeks who do not dance! At that time, John Travolta was all the rage, and most of the men exaggerated their disco dance moves to attract women, like peacocks showing their feathers.

I stood at the bar and had a soft drink. A tall, handsome blonde in her mid-20s, dressed in a low-key way, came up and asked if we were going to dance. I declined. She smiled, introduced herself as Lotta and insisted on talking to me. While we chatted, a motley bunch came in and shook hands with me. I knew a few of them, but the others thought I was someone special: they had seen how I slipped past the queue and into the club. I never said much in such situations; it wasn't a good look to be working as a prison guard and run off to the nightclub right afterwards.

You never knew who you might suddenly meet. Whenever I was asked where I worked, I used to tell them that I was a Greek teacher or an interpreter.

There were some drugs, a lot of drinking and all sorts of commotion in the clubs every night. People could get into brutal quarrels because they were high or drunk, but I felt quite safe in the bar with my back to the road. I rarely drank and never touched any drugs, and as soon as someone in my vicinity used them, I excused myself from their company. Nonetheless, there were still a few drug users who came and pretended to be friends with me.

Lotta showed great interest in me, but also in topics I wasn't familiar with. She asked if this new mob were my friends, but I didn't answer.

The night was getting on, and the club would soon close. They played the last song, a slow one, and I couldn't say no to Lotta. It wasn't difficult to dance to something like that, because you just hold each other and sway, and no one could tell I had no dancing talent.

We left the club and decided to continue at my place. I was amazed at how easy it was to get her to come with me. When we were going to the car, it was so damned cold — 25°C below zero (−13°F) — that it wouldn't start. She suggested I leave my car and use hers. She was parked nearby and we were at my apartment on Redbergsplatsen in less than five minutes.

En route, I was in a good mood and finally opened up a bit and began talking. I watched her drive and enjoyed it. She was self-confident, and a highly experienced driver. Back then, I had rarely seen a young woman drive like that.

When we got inside, I noticed her eyes scanned the apartment while I made tea. I did not want anything to drink, and she stressed that she was only coming for a quick cup, and then leaving. She started asking some questions, and I responded with my 'Greek humour.'

"Do you live alone?"

"Well, it depends."

She kept probing. "How can you afford such a big apartment?" As she asked more questions and examined the surroundings, I became more interested in her. She had taken off her cardigan, and suddenly I could see her long, beautiful body, fine skin and classic Nordic face. I went closer to her and reached out to take her hand, but she was quick, and avoided me. "Get my tea," she said.

I tried again, with different compliments, but she remained cool toward me. She got up to go and I followed her to the door. She looked straight into my eyes for the first time during the evening. She gave me a hug and left. I took her hand and said, "Wait a minute, give me your phone number!"

"Give me your number instead," she replied.

A few days later she called and asked if we could go to the cinema. She chose the movie, and this time she was much prettier. It was evident that she had spent time on her hair. During the film, I held out my hand and she took it. We held hands through the whole film.

When the lights came up she let go. I figured she didn't want anyone to see us holding hands. The contrast was too great: a black skull with a nice blonde who was at least 10 cm taller.

I invited her back to my place for a bowl of Greek soup that I had made. This time she was not as curious about the apartment and my things. The small talk of her last visit was replaced with loving looks and vibes. She often locked her eyes with mine and seemed to enjoy it. I felt that she liked me.

We ended up in bed, and while she hovered over me and began taking off my sweater, she stopped, with the sweater over my face. I poked my head out and saw her staring at a book lying on the bedside table. She picked it up and asked in a really angry voice asked if it was mine. "Yes," I said, "it's my book."

Her face became more serious. "Are you a communist?"

The book, on Karl Marx's theories, was part of my studies.

I started laughing. "So you'd sleep with a communist — what's wrong with that?" She became furious, like a bull seeing red. She got up in a flash and started to put on her clothes. I kept laughing and goaded her on. "Come on, you may as well try sleeping with a communist at some point." She gave me a real earful and I quickly apologized, saying that I was joking, and it was all a big misunderstanding. It was no use — she left quickly without saying another word.

I lay there, wondering what had just happened. She seemed attracted to me, and we obviously hit it off. She had climbed into my bed! But Karl Marx and his beard scared her away.

The next morning, she called and wondered if I had seen any keys in the apartment. They were lying on the floor, having wound up there when we started hugging and throwing off our clothes. "Yes, they're here."

She went silent. It took some time before she said, "Can you go to your balcony and throw down the keys to me in five minutes?"

"Of course," I said, but I chose to go down and wait for her instead. I wanted to ask what had happened. I went to a store down the block and bought some bread for breakfast. As I came out, a police car stopped just down from the shop and Lotta got out. She was in plain clothes and walked briskly toward my door. Her uniformed colleague stayed in the car. I followed her, and when she stopped and looked up at my balcony, I came from behind her and said hello.

She was unpleasantly surprised, and said, "I told you to throw them down from the balcony. Why are you down here?" I gave her the keys. She appeared really angry, but said she would call me later.

The police car rolled slowly toward us. She got in and they left.

The next day, she called and wanted to see me briefly. I then found out what had happened and why she had acted so strangely.

That night at the club, she became interested in me because she thought I might be a drug dealer. She then picked up on who I was, and her curiosity grew because I worked in a prison.

The next day, everything became clear to her. I was too green to be a dealer. She felt it would be all right to meet me privately, but as it happened, hanging out with someone who read Marx would never be OK for Lotta.

We saw each other for a few weeks after that, but she felt uncomfortable about it, and believed I wouldn't be accepted by her family or friends. One day, as we were about to go to the cinema, she said to me that we could not see each other any more and wished me luck.

I was now down to two days before the interview for my permanent residence permit. I came to the conclusion that despite what had transpired between us, Lotta was my last lifeline. I went to the police station and asked for her. After an hour of waiting, she appeared. I asked if we could go outside the police station so we could talk without being disturbed.

"Please," I said, "there's something important that I want to tell you." I explained exactly what had happened, and what was coming up in two days. She stared at me, annoyed, but at the same time there was a spark of kindness in her eyes. "What do you want me to do? I don't work with immigrant issues. You shouldn't have told me any of this! Now, I have to ...'

She went silent.

After composing herself, she asked, "Who are you going to meet?" I showed her the summons. "You have no chance," she said right away. "The older lady who's interviewing you will do it properly."

"What should I do now?" I asked.

"Do not keep the appointment with her. You need to make up an excuse about getting hurt or sick. Go to the emergency room. Get them to call and cancel the appointment for you. But do not come here again. I'm risking my job now. Why the hell did I meet you? I'll call you in a couple of days, but make sure you do not see her for this interview."

I followed Lotta's advice and managed to cancel the appointment. A few days later, I received a new summons, indicating that a policeman would interrogate my wife Yvonne and me. But Yvonne still would not come.

Lotta called and we met in town. She read the summons and said, "The man is kind, but you have to get your wife to come. Otherwise, it's not going to work. If she does not come, you won't be able to stay in Sweden."

"Help me," I begged. I told her that I kept imagining the authorities coming, knocking on the door, and escorting me to the airport. The thought of this had haunted me every day for three years.

Lotta listened quietly and thought. Then she asked, "Do you know any girls who are Yvonne's age, and who are Swedish?"

I replied that I had met a girl, but she did not look like my actual wife. "She is Swedish and blonde, but she has a Finnish first name and a Swedish last name."

"Does she speak good Swedish?"

"Yes, she was born in Sweden and doesn't even speak Finnish."

"Can you check with her if she can come instead, and pretend she's your current wife? She'd need to know a bit about Yvonne, her parents, their addresses, what she does, and her social security number."

I checked with the girl and she did not know what to say. She liked me, and she had seen some of my difficulties and worries. She had empathy and understanding, despite her age. She decided that she'd do it, and tried to calm me by saying it would be fun and go well.

The new date approached and my worries grew. Everything hung on such a small thread. I had a hard time sleeping, and my anxiety was so great that I could not get any food down. I had constant stomach pains and lost several kilos, weight I could ill afford to lose.

The night before was one of the most painful in my life. I could be facing deportation or imprisonment the next day and the uncertainty was palpable.

Lotta offered to give us some help, saying she would meet us at the entrance and accompany us to the interrogator, so he could see that she knew us. She said this would make him forget to zero in on my wife's identification.

We arrived at the police station and my 'wife' was quite calm and held my hand. She had borrowed my mother's ring and reminded me to have mine on the correct finger. She had rehearsed what she was going to say about her work, her hobbies, her personal habits, and everything else she might get asked. Lotta was waiting at the station as promised, and greeted my new Yvonne. She was not as stiff as when I'd last met with her. She was more relaxed and even hugged us, putting her hand on my shoulder as she led us to the interview room. The door was open and a nice-looking elderly gentleman with a warm and sympathetic face welcomed us. I immediately thought that he could not be a policeman! Lotta gave Yvonne II a hug and said, "Yvonne, I look forward to hearing from you later!"

Seeing Lotta's act helped relieve my stomach cramps. Her last words confirmed to the policeman that this was who we said it was — my wife Yvonne. The interview lasted only a few minutes. I started to show my grades from the university and the principal's certificate verifying that I had completed 2½ years of study in two years. He seemed quite interested in this and, incredibly, did not ask any other questions. He said he was satisfied and wished us luck in life.

My pretend wife shook hands with him, and when it was my turn he took my hand and held it for a few seconds. He looked straight into my eyes and said, "Do not be so nervous! You have kind eyes and things will go well in life for you. Good luck to you!"

As soon as we got outside the police station I got cramps all over my body. I thought my heart had stopped. I started vomiting and my whole body shook. My legs could no longer handle my weight. I couldn't help wondering why I subjected myself to such ordeals. Why?!

I HAD ORIGINALLY EMBARKED on studying engineering, but had to ask myself if that was what I really wanted. It felt totally wrong, and every part of me knew that I needed to change my course of study.

I looked at sociology. I visited the university's counsellor, and she confirmed that I should change my major to behavioural science.

In 1983, during my national economic studies, I wrote my dissertation on the sociological and economic aspects of family structure in the past and present, connecting this to my own experiences. I had already seen so much of it first-hand, and had personally been through such upheaval and turmoil.

That was when I had my first big breakthrough in the media. As part of my postgraduate work as a social scientist, I chose to examine night-life at the disco and the importance of clothing in that milieu. I chose a research method that was quite demanding: participatory observation! In other words, I immersed myself into the field study, instead of the traditional academic approach of asking questions and collecting answers and statistics at arm's length. My teachers warned that this would be difficult, and the risk of failure was high. They also stressed that if I succeeded with this, I would be among a very exclusive club. That was exactly the encouragement I needed.

My degree presentation attracted examiners from other disciplines, as well as fellow students who were curious. There had already been considerable chatter about this, and some were certain it would be a failure, and I'd have to redo everything and lose six months of study. However, it proved to be a success, and the examiners were impressed. This quickly created media interest. The next morning, I was on the front page of the biggest newspapers in Sweden: the man who knows everything about disco life!

The state TV channels' news programmes at the time were very conservative in what they featured. Yet, I was interviewed about my research on the prime-time broadcasts. This continued for months, and different media wanted to interview me on-site at different nightclubs. Each time, I chose the club we would go to, and made sure that the managers organized my VIP access and let the bouncers know. The publicity had a negative side: there were some who disliked everything about this, and all the attention I got at the clubs.

I looked at some of the people there and sensed that they would have been quite happy to knock me down a notch or two. Some girls spilled beer on me while I sat, for no apparent reason. That was not something I'd expected. Nor did I expect that this would be Sweden's biggest news for several months. I had to go with friends who could act as bodyguards, and the nightclubs themselves would assign me one of their security personnel to look after me during the evening.

One night, I needed to pee and there was a long queue at the gents. The security guard waved me to the front of the line and stretched his arms out to protect me. I followed him, and at the urinals were a couple of guys who were disturbed by this. They made room for me, but I was not able to go. Not a single drop. I felt stressed that the guard was hovering behind me. I told him, "I can't concentrate. I'm going to take a shit now." He answered loudly, "Take your time! Shit in there."

The guy next to me gave me a dirty look, and the guard got angry, lifting him up by the neck a few centimetres off the floor, and carried him out as he urinated, so that he sprayed others. There was big commotion and several other guards came running in.

I *definitely* could not get a drop out after this.

All the attention was new to me. A black skull could walk past all the queues while blond guys stood in the cold, waiting for hours. Suddenly, plenty of people wanted to get to know me. They all wanted to be my friend. I was the centre of attention. Even the girls would now stand in line to talk to me. The guards kept them away no matter who they were — they just waited for me to nod that it was OK to let them near me.

I was the main attraction, but it did not help me meet the right friends or the right girl. I was a 'target' in different ways. The girls were crazy about me and managed to create inner, emotional turmoil. My friends and acquaintances were jealous of all the attention I was getting, especially from the girls.

Some evenings, it was impossible to resist the temptation, and I started to get used to how easy it was to pick up a new girl every night. No one was bothered about it. The girls themselves were content with one night, and the next day you could see them pick up a new guy. Sometimes we guys started competing to see how many we could pick up in one night. There were some who even changed girls two to three times during the evening, if they had the opportunity. The girls were particularly drawn to them. The more interested the girls, the longer the queue became.

There were some evenings where I was bored and passive, and the girl would call me a coward or gay. I had dreams about my love life, but it was hard to make it work.

I chose to walk away after a while. I didn't want to see any girls for a long time. My studies had been priority number one, but even though they were completed, I wanted to read a little more. In 1984, I graduated with a degree in behavioural science, after having studied pedagogy, clinical sexology, economics and a basic course in law. I felt ready to set new goals in life. My 240 academic credits corresponded to six years' full-time university education, but I managed to finish it in 4½ years, while working to support myself.

I was dead tired, body and soul. Things eventually calmed down with the military in Greece. I managed to get myself a good lawyer soon after, and through a series of legal dealings too convoluted to share here, I was let off the hook after several more deferments. Greece had joined the European Community in 1981 and everything began to change. Hope came back, for me and all Greeks. It was time to head back.

There was a lot of tumult within me and I chose to seek peace in Agio Oros. This translates to holy mountain. The Holy Community of Mt Athos, as it is officially known, is a male monastic society, located on a peninsula in northern Greece. It is accessible only by sea, and only men are allowed, a tradition it has followed for more than 1,000 years. It has its own administrative system, as an autonomous state within Greece.

I got a written permit to stay among the monks for two weeks. You hear virtually nothing there, just the hollowness that comes with complete silence. The monks themselves are barely visible; you only see them when they gather to eat. I chose to isolate and ate only when I could no longer cope with hunger. The stress from all that happened during those years in Sweden dissipated. I wanted to find myself again. I had lost sight of who I was. On the surface, I was a hungry immigrant who was now a well-educated immigrant with a black skull who'd gained acceptance in a clean, well-ordered society.

The days went by very slowly. It felt like I was there for several months. On a few occasions I talked to a big, gentle young monk about life. I had a hard time understanding why he would spend the rest of his life alone, far away from 'life.' I wanted to talk about man and woman, and the love between us, something he had chosen to shun. I was stubborn, and asked how we'd continue to exist if we didn't associate with women and reproduce. He would not answer. That was the end of our conversation, and from then on he chose to leave me alone.

I HAD DONE MANY JOBS, and studied different disciplines, in preparation for my next big step … into the world of politics. Yet, the closer I came to it, I felt something holding me back. I couldn't see myself in any of the political parties. There were still none that I agreed with 100%, or even close. In my mind, you would have to be a strange caricature of a person to agree with every single policy that a party promoted. Surely, most of us agree with some ideas here, other ideas elsewhere. When we vote, we look at who comes closest to promising what we find most important, but being beholden to one party, based on some overriding, blanket ideology, was a foreign notion to me. Getting a job as a school principal would have been a better way to show how things could be done, and use that as a successful model.

There was also something inherently wrong with the system. Some of our politicians, in Sweden and elsewhere, just haven't had life experiences — certainly not the way I have. I always said I had four eyes through which I saw everything: two Greek and two Swedish. Maybe six, in fact, with my own unique point of view. I could show people my vision, and explain what it was. Yet, we have some political leaders who simply joined the party and rose through the ranks. They hadn't even studied politics at university.

And, I didn't have much money. Politics is driven by it. You couldn't run a campaign without a lot of cash, and I couldn't get the sort of platform that reflected who I really was, and the big dreams I had. And assuming you raised the money, would those dreams still be pure? Or, would they be influenced by the donors and what they wanted?

I had to be Panos, and I could never compromise on that. I would have loved to have been prime minister, if it would help my people, but in reality, that wouldn't have been possible. I couldn't be tied to a party line, an ideology. I would have to do something where I could take charge, act as I felt was right, and inspire as many people as I could. Politics could not offer me that satisfaction.

5
Starting Panos Emporio

ONE SUNNY DAY, I was with some friends at Långedrag beach, just outside Gothenburg. There were too many people, and we felt packed together like sardines in a can. Still, I enjoyed seeing so many blonde women. It was a paradise garden, with so many different flowers for my eyes, and I could not stop looking around.

My friends jumped into the water, but I didn't share their enthusiasm. Everything around me was grey: the rocky beach, the sand, the stones, and even the seawater. I went closer to the water and put my feet in carefully, but it was too cold for me. "The water looks dirty," I told my friends.

They laughed, and continued to swim.

I went a little higher to observe the view. My thoughts kept stopping at the grey colour that dominated. I saw a field of grey ... and these gorgeous blonde bodies. I started to look at the dark swimsuits, and couldn't understand why these beautiful people wore something — any old thing, it seemed — just not to be naked. Many ladies were topless. Some of them passed me and gave me a smile, and said a few words, but I did not understand. I was too shy to look at them, and turned to face in another direction.

Come late afternoon, as the sun began going down and people started to pack up, I thought to myself: "Imagine if you could make these beaches, with all these dazzling bodies, more colourful." I didn't think of being a designer. I just wanted to put some colour on that dull, monochromatic beach.

Swimwear was seldom in our thoughts or our daily vocabulary in the early '80s, especially in Sweden, where the summers were short and sunny days were few. The total swimwear industry was inconsequential.

It was 1984, and I was working as a planning assistant for healthcare in Gothenburg, a municipal job with nice colleagues and no stress.

I enjoyed my first months, but when hard matters surfaced, I realized I could never work under politicians and their way of thinking. In my opinion, the directors of different hospitals tried to seize more power by having more patients, justifying an increase in the size of their facilities. In one meeting, I said, "Let's promote the hospitals and the staff who act proactively, so there'd be fewer patients," but this ran counter to the prevailing thinking.

There were statistics that showed that many women developed breast cancer because the system failed to detect it early. It was too slow to act, and women had to wait too long. I came up with an idea not to change the curtains as planned, and instead invest the money in a new X-ray machine, in order to speed up diagnoses. "Drop it," I was told. "These are from different budgets, so we can't do it." I tried to explain that rules are made to be broken, if that contributed to the greater good, and what could be more important to a hospital than saving lives? The hospital wouldn't budge. Preserving the bureaucracy and risking lives for the sake of growing patient numbers — and, apparently, new curtains — seemed to take priority.

You cannot imagine how infuriated and disappointed I was. I could not face my conscience if I continued to sit there and accept the status quo. I knew something was still missing. Plus, it was boring.

I thought back to Tolis Voskopoulos, the Greek singer and actor who had been my childhood idol. His life's values touched me. I wasn't consciously aware of it happening then, but when I look back, he had shaped my personality. To think that someone in our lives, even someone far away from us, connected to us in only the most abstract way, can affect our lives' journeys.

I was 26 when I made the decision to start my own brand. I had already tried many jobs and legally worked in Sweden for many years by then. Unofficially, it had actually been 16 years. I was old for my age. I had six years' tertiary education and a hundred dreams, but one of my main dreams was very clear.

Most of my jobs had been good, but they were never enough to stimulate my mind, my soul, my sense of self. I loved to learn new things; trying something new stirred my soul. I always took the harder path, because it stimulated my creativity and made me happy. I'm a born fighter and I would get bored quickly if my life wasn't full of rich possibilities and tough challenges. Maybe I need to prove to myself how good I can be.

No risks, no history.

Don't think I'm someone who loves to take risks just for the sake of it. I don't jump from aeroplanes or climb high mountains. I would never put myself in physical danger. Was it the same with my soul? I can't answer this yet — maybe in my next book. But inside me was the instinct of a survivor, the same boy who had an overwhelming desire to take another breath when the octopus dragged him under. **The secret to success is knowing that you want to take that next breath, so you fight to get to the surface.** You can't lose this fight.

I could see how unlucky, and downright miserable, others were because they didn't love what they did for a living. Many of us obsessed over money, but money is important only to a point.

Money comes when we do the things we love, because they are the right things. We have to choose if we are to do the things we *love*, or do the things we *should*.

The latter is a recipe for misery, killing our personality, even our humanity. If only we could get the right guidance at an early age, with an education system that helps identify and stimulate our true life's purpose, we would have a more harmonious, happy world.

Open your wardrobe and look at your clothes. You have plenty of garments hanging there. Most you'll never wear, and some you'll wear once or twice. There are just a few that you're happy with. There should be at least one garment in there that makes you feel *amazing* when you wear it. You can't explain why, but you feel comfortable, beautiful and relaxed. This is the one that makes you feel fantastic!

I needed to find my life garment, one I could wear that made me feel amazing. It had to have ingredients from Voskopoulos's life. I wanted to be on stage, but I didn't have a strong enough voice to be a singer. I had never become that guitar hero. An actor, yes, but I couldn't do that when I needed to eat. My career had to be one where I could spread love and respect, and inspire others. I wanted to be on stage, even though I'm painfully shy. I love to create. I like to push the limits. I had also worked out that materialistic things were not luxuries for me. **My luxury is my freedom.**

I never asked myself, "Do you have a business plan?" "How big is the market?" "Who are your competitors?" "Do you have enough start-up capital?" "Will you incorporate the business?" "Do you need other directors?" "What happens if this fails?" I did the complete opposite. There was no strategic analysis. When I look back to the age of eight or nine, I already had the talent of being able to process everything and know what would drive others crazy. Like that crocodile belt.

To decide to start a swimwear brand in a very cold country with barely any summer might have seemed like commercial suicide. Rationally, it probably was. But, that was the challenge. I was a born entrepreneur acting with my heart and passion. I never planned or thought about the risks. I must have innately analysed everything already, and the answers were deep in my soul. The way to uncover them was to do it. So often in my life I would act first, and the realizations would then come.

It was never about the swimwear, anyway. *The only thing that came to my mind was the life I wanted with my work.* It might have seemed impossible, but if I succeeded, I would have my stage, my freedom to communicate my life's philosophies and values, to travel the world, to deal with people, and, above all, have no limits to my creativity.

I made the decision very quickly and got on with the show.

During the evenings, I began to plan how to create my own brand, to inject some colour onto the beaches. I said nothing to anyone. I had no knowledge or experience in this area, and knew no one who could advise and lead me. There was no internet to turn to for research, and there were certainly no companies that would part with their internal knowledge.

A year later, my small collection took shape, but not before I did plenty of informal, word-of-mouth sociological market research. There was no room for failure. I couldn't have something with a success rate of 75%. I didn't have the money to risk. It had to be 100% successful and achieve great acclaim. There was no other option. I spoke with as many women of different ages as I could, asking what they felt was missing, or what disappointed them when it came to swimwear. Initially, it was tough getting answers, but I changed my methodology and began asking how many swimsuits they bought each year, and how often. One of the first women said, "I try to buy something every year, but I'm tired of trying them on all the time and finding that nothing fits me." That was the insight I needed: there was room for something on the market that women would find was comfortable and fit them perfectly, right off the bat. I found the weak points in the swimwear space. **I knew the market would open up to me if I listened, and responded, and gave people what they dreamed of. No one else at that time had listened. And, I have to say that not much has changed today.**

I PRODUCED a small quantity of my first collection in Sweden, and I was ready to sell through the shops. I packed everything into my $300 car and drove around, knocking on retailers' doors.

I was surprised at how conservative the market was. And, as a foreigner, it seemed no one could handle my name. I started to get upset after having to spell my name, Panos, again and again at each meeting. No one could pronounce Panos even after I wrote it down. They'd call me Partos, Paros, Anos and more! Even after all that, they apparently didn't have time to talk further, and asked that I come back next year. I was shocked that they weren't even curious enough to take a look. In some places, it wasn't even possible to see anyone to begin with.

I had thoroughly prepared how I would sell my creations, and had got it down to a 30-second pitch outlining all the advantages, and how easy it would be for them to sell my products. But no one was interested.

By the late evening, after driving around all day, I returned to my small apartment, which was filled with cartons of bathing suits — around my bed, under my bed, and in the corridor. I was lucky that I was so skinny and could squeeze through all the boxes. All my savings, and thousands borrowed from friends — the one and only time I'd ever taken a loan — rested in those boxes, yet I couldn't get anyone to look at them. Now I was running low on money for petrol, so I had to be sure that every kilometre I drove would net some results.

I went outside the city to find a telephone booth that had a directory and Yellow Pages, so I could find some shops and take the time to schedule meetings before randomly driving around again. Unfortunately, I kept bumping up against difficulties with my name. The Swedish shop owners were all stumped when I said, "Panos," even after I tried to spell it out.

An older friend suggested that I use a Swedish name. He and others had done so with some success, especially those from countries that didn't have such a good reputation there. But I said, "No way!" Soon, one day, they would all use my name like balsam in their mouths.

You couldn't take my name from me. It would be like taking away my soul, my heart, my history. My Dad called me Panos and my Mum called me Panagiotis. Mum did that, and never used my shorter nickname, Panos, because the priest gave me this name when I was so close to death. For her, the name meant a lot. It was a positive thing for her to say "Panagiotis," partly because it brought back the moments in those early weeks of my life when I was saved after the priest blessed me, and partly because its literal meaning gave her comfort and a connection with God.

Instead, I decided to make a few calls without using my name at all. That helped. I made an appointment for the following day to show my collection, and that shop turned out to be my first client. Two nice ladies, each around 50 years old, ran the store together. They never asked me my name, and they liked the collection.

One of them said, "Hmm, you're on to something, because customers had brought this up. Why did you put draping on this swimsuit?" When I told them why, they looked at each other with a big smile. "You're going to be successful," the other woman said. "Most swimwear sellers and producers are men who make women's clothes, but they never listen to women."

I explained how difficult it had been to show the collection and how people would stop once I mentioned my name, Panos. They offered me coffee and I wound up staying quite a long time chatting, all the while getting more valuable information from them. I learned a lot in that single meeting.

They told me that they typically bought from suppliers they already knew. It seemed that it would have surprised and confused a lot of retailers when I turned up with a bag, asking them to buy without knowing who I was. It simply wasn't going to happen. But when I called, I apparently sounded so enthusiastic, and they'd argued about whether they should let me come and see them or not. Obviously, things turned out my way.

This is a good lesson in life. Whenever you do something, you're going to get nos. When you are young and you want to start your journey, there will always be a naysayer, raining on your parade. A lot of people will inevitably say no — that was certainly my experience. **But at this point, my sole focus was on the one positive moment when someone could see something in my idea. In an instant, I forgot all the rejections and latched on to the *yes*. I thought, "This is nice," and put all my energies into going with that positive moment.** If you don't do this, you're going to feel like the world's piling on top of you. Revel in those triumphs; they'll provide the encouragement to keep pushing forward. Don't stop the journey because others just don't get it. Someone will, and from that point on, you can build on small successes and keep getting stronger.

Before I left, I asked, "Can you please recommend another shop that you have a good relationship with, so I can visit them and say that I'm coming with your endorsement?"

They suggested I call a good businessman, Pelle, who knew all the shop owners and had good relationships with them. "We'll call and ask him to help you with a few contacts," the ladies said.

They were as good as their word. The day after, I called Pelle. "Yes, I know the story," he said. "Come tomorrow morning at 9 to the Park Hotel, but don't bring anything with you. I have my own collections there, but I'll connect you with some buyers."

For me, that was a miracle. The boxes in my apartment had begun to loom angrily over me, because I had friends who were waiting to get their loan money back, and I only had a few days left to keep my promises.

At 9:00 sharp, I knocked timidly on Pelle's door and waited. Nobody answered the door, and now I was really nervous. Maybe it had all been a joke. Had I got the time of our appointment wrong? Maybe he changed his mind. I only knew his first name, Pelle, so maybe I was at the wrong room!

I knocked one more time, very gently, and no one answered. I stood there and waited, feeling increasingly uncomfortable.

Just then, three happy-looking women of around 40 came down the hallway, chatting away. They walked up to me and I moved aside. One of them asked if I was visiting Pelle. I said I was, and before I knew it, she knocked loudly on the door — a lot more forcefully than I had. The door opened, and there stood an elegant man of around 60, wearing a bathrobe that was slightly open in the front so you could easily make out that he was not wearing any underwear.

The women pounced on him, one of them asking, "Are you ready for your bath? Let's help!" and they laughed loudly.

He looked at me, and said, "Come in. What was your name again?" I began, "Panos, P-A ..." but he said, "Never mind, just come in and sit there."

Inside there were already two other ladies having breakfast and champagne. The new trio seemed to know them well and joined them with ease. I was sitting a little distance from them, and Pelle asked me to come closer. He gave me a glass of champagne, and when I politely declined he looked at me strangely. "Are you Muslim? What's your name again?" He gave me a huge smile. "I'm just joking. Just relax and I'll be with you shortly." The ladies continued loudly chatting, and that helped, because I didn't have to say much at all.

Pelle kept his bathrobe on and they made a lot of jokes, but I didn't understand too much. It was obvious that they liked their champagne. In the meantime, he showed his clothing collection. It was easy for him to write their orders down since he had forms at the ready. "I'm putting down ten pieces of … no, no, this is a good style, you must buy 20 in each size!"

It was the first time I saw how one could present a collection to buyers while actually telling them how many to order and in what styles. All of them were too happy to agree with everything he suggested!

Around lunchtime, they left and some new buyers were about to come up to the room. Pelle asked me what kind of help I needed. "I'm having trouble booking appointments," I said. "Buyers refuse to meet me and look at my collection."

"Yes, I understand," he said. "They don't know you, so it's not easy to get in. I can call three big stores on your behalf. They also have locations in other cities, and they can connect you with all of them. Let's do it now, and you can go to them directly from here."

On the first call, he talked to a buyer who seemed to be his best friend in the world. Within a minute, Pelle had made an appointment for me, and then asked his friend how many pieces he'd like to buy. He held his hand over the phone and asked me, "How much did you say these normally cost? The item in your sales' book, the first one."

"Thirty kronor," I told him.

He said, "It costs 30, plus five. Call so-and-so and tell them to meet him. What's his name again? Never mind … he's Greek."

On the way out, I asked him, "What do you mean, 30 plus five?"

Pelle stopped for a second and looked at me. "You said 30, but you have to pay five to the buyer."

"I don't understand. Can you explain?"

"You write 30 on the invoice, and for every piece he buys, you give him 5kr in an envelope." Before he finished, his next appointment knocked on the door and he escorted me out.

I tried to find out more about the 'plus five' angle. One friend, who worked outside the textile industry, told me the terms they used. She said it was very common to give a percentage back to the buyers. "You need to give him 5kr from your pocket," she said. Kickbacks were something that the Swedes learned from Hong Kong during their visits there. In Hong Kong, they didn't need to use kickbacks because taxes were so low, and back then they had confidence in their government, but in Sweden, taxes were so high that people tried to get a bit back.

From the beginning, I was lucky to have people with some great values to inspire me. A friend, Ronnie, helped me with financial advice. He used to say, **"Any single krona you make as profit after tax, you invest back**

into your company. This will help you." I asked him about the 'plus five.' He said, **"Stay clean.** Do not do it even once, because then you'll always have to do it afterwards."

A few days later, I visited the first shop that Pelle had put me in touch with. Everything went really well! The buyer asked me to deliver as soon as I could. In the room were two other women from the store, so I didn't want to ask him what 'plus five' meant in practice. I asked if he could show me the premises, so I could get a feel for the place, and if I could meet some of his staff, to say hello and explain the features and benefits of my collection. He laughed and said, "This is unusual, but let's see if we can do it." He walked around the store and pointed out where my items would be. As we walked and talked, I casually mentioned that I had heard talk of "30 plus five," but that my price was only 30kr.

"Yes, yes," he calmly said, "if it's 30, it's 30." He understood that I did not want to pay a kickback. Before I left his office, I asked if he could kindly call colleagues in three other cities and enquire if they would buy the same quantities that he had. I had to see how he would react. "Let's make those calls right now," he said. He called them in my presence, and two of them bought the same orders without my having to visit them. "It only costs 30kr and looks very nice and trendy," he explained. "Maybe too colourful for you, but the Greek insists they're going to be a good seller. Let's try them out."

After I left, I kept wondering why he didn't bother with those 5kr, and nonetheless helped me sell to the others. I never asked him, and we kept doing very good business together for a few years. He was one of my biggest customers in those early days. Thirty years later, I bumped into him at a café, but it took me a little while to recognize him. He said to me, "You must be the Greek, Panos, who visited me 30 years ago!"

We sat down and talked for a while. I said, "I need to ask you something, because you're not involved in business any more. Do you remember Pelle?"

"Yes, of course!" he responded. "He was a legend, and a very generous gentleman."

I told him about my problem with the 'plus five' arrangement. I said I never wanted to get something I didn't deserve, so for me it was a matter of ethics. I asked why he had accepted my terms.

He was silent for a few moments, and then said that he could see in my eyes that I wouldn't like giving a kickback. "I loved your products and felt your passion and energy, and knew I would be safe investing in your collection.

So, it was just good business for us to do it that way." He finished by saying he was proud of me and my journey so far, but also pleased with himself because he took a punt on a new talent … and made money from it!

Even in an industry where kickbacks and illegal payments were rife — even the norm — I discovered it was possible to remain true to my ethics and who I was. If you stick to your principles, act calmly and do not judge others, people will accept you, even if you don't play their game.

SHORTLY AFTER the deliveries were made, I went to the retailers to see how my designs had sold, and to see their staffs' reactions. I was pleasantly surprised at how well it had gone in just a few days, and was told the big deals that drew in a lot of customers would be the following week. **That day, I learned how important follow-up was. If I wanted to sell more, I had to be the one to contact the retailers, and to remind them how good my products were, so they would buy more.**

The big retailers wanted to add to their orders: they could see the business was ripe for the taking. The smaller ones were happy with what they'd sold, but didn't jump at the chance to stock more. To me this was completely illogical. You should want more of what you had sold, but they weren't convinced.

Nevertheless, I had a tailwind, thanks to Pelle's contacts who'd dared to try my products. They then became my ambassadors, helping to open other doors. I had gained momentum and was able to tell new retailers how well the others were selling my products.

In a short time, I managed to get about 30 retailers on board, small and large. In the first month I had already learned a few things that would go on to characterize my whole business life. It was a pleasure to work with retailers who wanted to develop their own business, retailers who did not fuss about payment terms, retailers who saw opportunities in my collection, and retailers who paid on time.

Yet, in that first month, there were already a number of problems, including getting paid for goods that had been delivered. And which ones were usually the culprits? The smaller ones, who from the very first meeting demonstrated a general sense of laziness. When I visited their stores to see how they displayed my products, I was disappointed that they were left in their warehouse for days. They could barely remember if they had received the delivery. You'd think that being small, they would be aware of every detail — especially new, potentially moneymaking products ready to put on the shelves — but it wasn't so.

After selling out at some places, I also started to have problems with deliveries. I did not have enough money to finance new production and buy fabrics; I had to wait until my existing customers had paid their invoices so I could start again. I asked the big retailers to pay as soon as possible after selling the goods. They asked why they would do this special thing for me, and I said I offered them better service and faster order fulfilment. Some agreed, and new production started.

However, the small customers continued to be my source of problems. They were late with everything, leading me to make an important, game-changing decision: **focus only on those who can pay their invoices on time and can sell in volume!**

I needed some small retailers to keep up the image, since you can have a decent retail presence at the better ones, but back then, volume sales could only really be found at the Swedish supermarket chains. They sold both food and clothing, and they had money and a large customer base.

I eventually got a number of big department stores across the country to carry my line without having to visit them. But come autumn, business stopped. No one wanted swimwear for winter, even if people still used swimming pools. I hadn't foreseen that, and decided to expand my product line in ways that would allow me to do business year-round.

I visited my biggest retailers, who were happy with our collections, and interviewed the managers. But before I got to them, I spoke with the floor staff and asked what sold best during the autumn, and what they didn't have, that customers asked for. After that, the ideas came, and I started to look at what I could easily produce. I went back to the department stores during the weekends, when they had the most customers, and observed their behaviour — how they looked at the clothes, what caught their attention, and what they said to each other. I dared to ask questions of the happiest-looking shoppers.

After a few days' observation, it was easy for me to decide on the next step. Consumers liked knitwear that was soft and washable. From my research, it was clear that most of such products on the market would get discoloured and, with hard washing, they shrunk. Most T-shirts in the shops had twisted seams after washing. Quality was the key word, and I would do with knit garments what I had done with my swimwear: make them colourful!

I went to various weaving mills and talked to technically knowledgeable staff. I realized that there was very little interest in creating high-quality products, because they thought there was no demand. They told me that they sold everything they made anyway, so why bother?

I applied to return to school, at Chalmers University of Technology in Gothenburg. They had a research department that tested the quality of various machines, manufacturing materials and medical devices. They also tested materials for fire safety. There I met an older woman who was responsible for soft materials, and she was aware of various shortcomings in what was on the market. There was some knowledge there, but few were interested.

I managed to come up with a specially adapted educational programme for my needs. At the same time, I connected with a good weaving mill in Greece that expressed interest in working with me, and a dyeing mill outside Gothenburg that had come a long way with the process. Hard, intensive work resulted in my producing a fine tricot material that did not twist in the wash or shrink more than 5%, and I could give a three-year guarantee on my sweatshirt.

I then tested them in the lab at Chalmers and was able to proudly show customers that I had the best material on the market. I was sure that this would be well received, and retailers would stand in line to buy my products. Unfortunately, that was not the case. Some appreciated the quality, but essentially didn't care. "We sell everything," they'd say. "We're happy with what we have!"

When the first run of knitwear was finished, I started calling my better retailers and persuaded them to buy a few boxes of my new mini-collection for immediate delivery. Everything was predetermined by me: each model was available in a specific range of colours, and there was a certain number of each size. In other words, the retailers were not allowed to choose. The size, colour and designs complemented each other, and shoppers would have to buy the five packaged-together female items, or the three packaged-together male ones. The stores summoned up the courage to invest in these, and as soon as the goods arrived, the phone began ringing.

The first call was from the Domus department store in Umeå, in the northern part of Sweden. "What the hell are you sending us?" they demanded. "We can't sell the short skirts and these bright colours!" I persuaded them to take these into the store, merchandise them properly, and wait a few days. They wanted to send back the 'scary' colours, but I told them, "You do not have to pay if you don't sell them! Keep them in the store for two weeks, and then get back in touch." After Umeå, it was Karlstad, who said the same thing, and soon it was the obs department store in Bäckebol, outside Gothenburg. To them I immediately said, "Don't send anything back. I'll be there in an hour. I'm on my way!"

I had invested all my money in developing these products without presenting the final collection to the buyers, but I was certain of success. Now, though, they didn't want any of it on their shelves and I risked souring the good relationships I had built with them.

I went directly to OBS in Bäckebol, going in via the regular entrance so I could talk to the store staff first, before meeting the manager to try and persuade him to keep the products. In the women's department, I looked for a younger woman I knew of there, Katarina, who was a little more fashion-forward and trendy. She said she had seen the products, but the manager told her they were sending them back. I asked what she thought personally, and she answered quickly: "They're different. We've never had anything like it, so it's hard to say, but they seem to have the good quality that our customers have asked for."

That steeled me, and I went straight to the boss. I persuaded him that we should take these onto the sales floor at once, and I would help hang them up. If he allowed, I could remain there with the displays to see how it went. He reluctantly gave the OK, and told the guard to give me a name tag so I could move freely between the warehouse and the store. Katarina helped with getting the stock out, and stood nearby in case she needed assistance with sales.

After a while, customers began flocking to the designs, attracted by the happy colours and interesting material. Katarina went and talked to them, and shortly after, the first garments were sold, one by one. What had not happened before was that the same customer would buy one of each style of garment, and in more than one colour! Katarina was very impressed. "Come on," she said. "We should go to the boss right away. He's got to know how good this is going to be!"

I asked the manager to call the department stores in Umeå and Karlstad, to calm them down and to tell them that the new products were selling well.

Word spread quickly between the different retailers: that Greek's collections with the strange colours are selling out quickly. No one seemed to be bothered that they could not choose the colours or sizes, because I sold them in these packs.

I was the first brand to sell everything packaged together like that, with predetermined colours and sizes. It was the smartest move I could have made, and it was an important contributor to the company's profitability from day one. Logistics! Planning for as little work as possible, focused on so few designs. Providing a small assortment of interesting pieces —

with reasonably different designs and colour languages, in fine materials — provided to be a resoundingly successful strategy.

It was now time to take on a big order from one of Sweden's largest department store chains. Word of my success had continued to spread, and that encouraged me to contact this major player. I presented two products. I wanted to get in there and take things up a notch. The buyer was positive and wrote the order that very day: 6,000 garments divided into two styles. This was big!

I had no choice but to shun the parental advice of never borrowing money so one could sleep at night. I had the physical order in my hand and visited SEB, the Scandinavian bank, at Redbergsplatsen. My customer was large and well established, with a solid reputation — a 100 percent safe bet. The fabric supplier wanted an advance, but the factory could give me credit for 30 days. The customer had a 30-day payment term and could not change that. I needed a loan of about 75,000kr to manage the financing.

At the bank I was told that they'd look into this and be back with me in a few weeks. "This is urgent," I said. "I need an answer in a day or two! I've secured most of the funding, but I need a little help for two to three weeks." The clerk I spoke with shook his head and answered coldly, "We'll get back to you in a few weeks."

I went home and tried to think about how I could solve the problem. The big buyers could help me go far! The retailer would be satisfied, and I would then get large orders, skipping over all the small businesses that gave me such headaches. Two days later, I went to the bank again, and the clerk was even more unpleasant. I was shocked when he said, "Are you from Greece?"

"Yes," I told him.

"Hmm. We had a Greek who borrowed money, and then went back to Greece, and we're still looking for him." He stared at me for a moment, looking quite hostile. "We will get back to you in a few weeks."

I said that I had been a small customer of the bank for several years, without any problems, and I'd worked hard to maintain an honourable account. Before I could finish, he sternly shook his head. He had made up his mind, and I knew that "in a few weeks" the loan would be disapproved. I used to call it the mentality of cowardice that so characterized some northern Europeans. They would not tell you things straight, out of a strange sense of 'diplomacy.' To a Greek, this is cowardice, plain and simple.

It was hard to handle being rejected just because you were Greek, and another Greek had cheated the bank. My thoughts went back to the school days when I needed to borrow someone else's encyclopaedia, and waited hours for them to open the door when you knocked.

That day, I made my next big decision: I would never again borrow a penny from anyone. I would plan my cash flow and grow at the pace I felt comfortable with. I had to let the deal slip. Since then, Panos Emporio has been a self-financed company, with absolutely stellar credit. This is how we were eventually designated one of the 20th century's 450 platinum-rated limited-liability companies in Sweden, a prestigious distinction I alluded to in Chapter 1.

This decision impressed many people, and retailers felt safe dealing with me. It actually opened the doors to the big chains. However, it wasn't as easy to bring in new, smaller suppliers. Some competitors wondered what I was really selling, because I came across as having so much more money than them. The rumour mill had it that the Greek probably packs 'other things' in his deliveries. Some whispered that he couldn't possibly rake in all those millions just from swimwear. Some day, they cackled, he's going to come undone.

I noticed that when I encountered competitors at trade fairs, they were so busy checking out what others were doing that they weren't focused on their own companies.

Years later, a neighbour commented to my five-year-old daughter, "I see that your Dad can afford a new car again." She replied, "But Dad is always at work, and you're always at home." It's little wonder that those who spent their time fretting over my success, instead of building their own, didn't survive when the next big financial crisis came.

My first three years were the hardest, working to build up capital and accumulate knowledge. It required that I worked in the evenings as a teacher, translator, and anything else I could do for money, to avoid taking a salary from my company. I realized that I lacked practical knowledge in importing, customs documents and bookkeeping. I had six years of academic studies, but that was not enough. I wanted to do the bookkeeping myself, to save money and have better daily control of my finances, so I went back to school. This time, I enrolled in Komvux, an adult-education institution, taking high school-level business economics, learning import and export document handling, and working up my own customs declarations. I could even prepare simple legal agreements, and manage their execution, thanks to basic legal training I received at the school.

As soon as I had the opportunity to visit the factories I worked with, I took extra days and got involved in production. I got to learn their jobs, and could see why there were so many quality problems. I started with raw material handling and moved on through all the manufacturing steps, down to the last finishing stages. I came to know the whole production process, to the smallest detail. My goals were clear, if unlikely to be achieved entirely: *zero quality problems, leading to no complaints, resulting in 100% customer satisfaction.* **I aimed to have consumers who were beyond satisfied — thrilled with the product and happy about everything else that came with the brand, so they could do word-of-mouth marketing for me. I did not have resources for a traditional marketing campaign, so my products themselves were the only means through which I could market my brand.**

Panos Emporio would be a winning proposition, year after year, yet my marketing budget remained close to zero. (We'll discuss how I did this later in the book.)

Over time, I would rely on continuing education, taking various short courses to master additional aspects of the business, stay on top of things and get a leg up on the competition.

My business philosophy was that I should lead and always be in first place.

Any way you look at it, if you're not in first place, you're stumbling around down there with the rest of the losers. To stay on top, I had to get better daily and never lose focus. I am driven by the idea of renewal, always looking to go to the next level. When difficulties arose, they sparked my creativity. I actually like it when things get tough and I face a big challenge.

To my employees I used to say: "We should have first place, and second and third should be empty! No one should even be so close to us, so they think they could ever take our place."

ON MY FIRST TRIP to Hong Kong, soon after the label was set up, I visited a supplier who was producing swimsuits for us. I was there to sign a HK$1 million contract with them, but I needed a far greater quantity going forward.

The first thing they asked when I arrived at the office was which hotel I was staying at. I knew the Hong Kong Chinese were impressed by status, so I was a bit embarrassed that I wasn't staying at a top hotel. "You're in a three-star hotel?" they asked in disbelief. I said it was my first time here, and I didn't know the city.

They then produced the contract. The boss took out his Montblanc pen to sign. I opened my small bag, took out my Bic biro and saw how stunned he was by the 10¢ plastic writing implement. I thought back to what my father and mother had taught me: be proud. I looked into his eyes, and said, "Look at my pen. You can be sure your million is very safe." This worked, since it appealed to his respect for frugality and entrepreneurship. At that time, a lot of Hong Kong business people had built their companies from nothing after fleeing mainland China following the revolution in 1949. Status impressed them, but so did thrift.

To this day, I still use basic pens. They do the same job, and an expensive one has no greater utility. In a broader sense, this approach still informs me today. I had no reason to play a game, to embellish who I was, to put on airs. I knew I was strong enough even when I was poor, and accepted who I was.

I asked him, "Do you trust me?"

"Yes," he replied, "I trust you."

"If you give me credit, to help me, you're going to have a nice, honest business on the other side," I assured him, and we went on to work successfully together for many years.

That served me better than I could have imagined. This manufacturer, for the first time ever on an international deal, extended credit. To me ... an unknown newcomer! For years, I was the only foreigner who got it from him. Normally, I would have had to open a letter of credit or arrange prepayment, but at the time I was a nobody in the business, and I had no money.

The lesson was that honesty and simplicity were important in business relationships, as was accepting who you are. Honest business people will always love honest partners and see great value in helping you develop your business. I always tried to connect with honest partners so we could focus on doing business, and not waste energy on suspicion. Our relationships were simple and straightforward, based on respect, understanding and trust.

When I looked back through old photos recently, I found some of me at a fashion show for my label in Bangkok, attended by the Thai royal family. I'd spent a lot of money on the show, installing Greek columns as part of the stage setting, and made it all quite sumptuous looking. Yet, there I was on the catwalk, wearing a T-shirt I'd bought at H&M for $9.

Years later, well after I was established as a designer, I was at the Eurovision contest finals in Latvia. I was behind the scenes, as a supporter of the Latvian entry, and I'd shown up wearing a T-shirt I had bought in Italy for $20. I remember the Latvian stage manager asking me, "You want to go on wearing this tonight?"

For years, I intentionally refused to put on something more 'suitable.' In hindsight, I came to understand some of the thinking behind this. I wanted to be seen as a person. I didn't want to be seen as 'a Greek.' I didn't want to be perceived to be trying too hard. I didn't want it to be my T-shirt that attracted you. I never wanted to be in the newspapers because you came to my house and I showed you how luxurious it was. I wanted to be seen as me, as Panos.

At celebrity parties, I always kept a low profile, because I envisaged how embarrassing it would be if someone came up to me and said, "Wow, what an amazing T-shirt! The colours!" or "What a nice jacket you have!" I dressed down, and purposely looked poorer than I really was, and this has been my practice my whole life. I still choose not to stay at luxury hotels, or even ask friends or associates to meet me at one to socialize in that sort of setting. It doesn't fit with my personality. I hate snobbery, so I would never stay somewhere that expressed that. I want to feel free, and I want to feel human.

I believe that living like this allowed me to grow far more as a person, because I didn't put shallow things first. It made my life more beautiful.

I also believe this is why my fans have followed me, some for 35–40 years now. Why do they feel connected to some schmuck who pieces fabric together? It's nothing in the grand scheme of things. **But they like my values. They might not have the complete picture — they may have caught something I said in the press, or seen me on television — but consumers want to be connected to the real thing.** They see my face, know I'm a nice guy, and that's why they want to be a fan.

GUT FEELINGS guided my designing, too. I often got asked how I almost always hit a home run. I'd go to an apparel industry fair with several thousand fabrics on display, and could pretty much close my eyes and pick the right one. For instance, one of the Greek factories took me to the fabric fair in Monte Carlo in the early days of my business, back in November of 1986. I knew that such a fabled place existed, with its casino, and its yachts, and its 'wild' Princess Stéphanie. I'd also read that the Greek shipping magnate Aristotle Onassis had tried to buy parts of Monaco, when he began acquiring shares of the Société des Bains de Mer (SBM), the group that controlled the casino. He faced opposition from Monaco's ruler,

HSH Prince Rainier III, who issued shares to dilute Onassis's holdings, so the principality would retain the majority.

I replied that I did not have the money to visit there yet — that it would be a couple of years before I could. The son of the factory owner, Filippas, replied, "Come with us. We'll sort out the accommodations and everything else. We can choose the fabrics together."

A few weeks later, I was in Monte Carlo, a dream place that I never could have imagined actually visiting. The first day we got there, I couldn't sleep. I walked and walked for hours, non-stop. It was fabulous. Clean, quiet, well organized, with beautiful cars, nice, well-dressed people, and a pleasant climate. It was 16°C (61°F) during the day, and I went in short sleeves, while I could see the elegant women wearing furs!

And all the luxury shops, lined up one after another. I dared not get closer than a few metres away to admire their window displays. I looked at the black-clad guards who stood outside the stores to let customers in. I wanted to get inside and see a Christian Dior garment or a Hermès bag up close — with no internet back then, not everybody could actually see such wonderful things — but I held back because my attire was so different from what the moneyed customers were wearing. I stood at a distance and watched.

At night, I walked around for hours outside these shops, pressing my face against the window glass. I tried to see as much as I could and catch any detail. I dreamed that one day I could go in and take a garment in my hands, feel how exclusive it was, and decide for myself if it was worth all the attention.

At the fair, we walked around the various fabric suppliers to see their new collections — so many thousands of fabrics and patterns. Each supplier had at least 500 different fabrics to present. I was quiet that day. I just wanted to see how it would go. Filippas and his father would spend a long time with each supplier, and talk and talk, and think and think about what was right.

The next day, I quickly made my choices. "They're daring and risky," Filippas said. "Couldn't you choose something more commercial?"

"No," I said. "They will make a difference. Trust me!"

"But you didn't look at all the fabrics. You just stretched out your hand and took out these," he argued. "You have to look properly and compare."

I told him that they had tired me out by staying so long and looking at everything. It seemed that they did so much looking just to have something to talk about.

My choices proved to be right. In fact, they were a resounding success. In the years ahead, when I went to Hong Kong, I had an uncanny ability to pick the right colour, design and pattern. All my factories used to pick up selections of fabrics and accessories so I could choose what would be right one to two years down the road.

Filippas asked several times why I was so confident in my choices, even though I was quite inexperienced. "It's my gut feeling," I'd tell him. At a deeper level, though, there were other factors at work.

Most people had the wrong attitude from the outset, convinced that certain of their choices would be right and others would be wrong. Nonetheless, everyone could still make money at that time because supply and demand were on the producers' side.

I did not have room to make mistakes, so I committed to doing things 100% right, each and every time. I did not *allow* myself to make mistakes. I quickly analysed everything and was goal-oriented. Everything that was uncertain, I put aside. I looked at what was important, without exaggerating about how it might perform. I had a clear picture of who would want that design, and at what price.

It was 1988. I sat at my hairdresser and waited for my turn. I noticed two women, in their late-30s, glancing over at me. They looked at their gossip magazine, and then back at me. One could not sit still and came up to me, showing me a photo of my friend Nikos and me at a party. "You look so nice, with your long hair, and I like your T-shirt," she said. I liked a Spanish brand called Custo, by the Barcelona designer Custo Dalmau, who did them with beautiful artistic motifs, made in soft, high-quality cotton. It felt custom-made for me, so comfortable, and with such a great fit.

On another day, I heard from several people who had seen me in a magazine. Intrigued, I bought a copy. It was the smallest, blurriest photo of me with a friend. Not a great shot, but I continued to get reactions from people who'd seen it for some time.

That same week, there was a multi-page feature about me in a fashion magazine, but I did not hear as many comments. It seemed that people were more impressed with a small, candid-looking shot from a party than four pages about my collection and me.

Realizing that, I decided I'd try to go to parties whenever someone would invite me. Getting an invitation to a big party wasn't easy. Thousands of 'celebrities' wanted to be seen, but only a select number were allowed to attend. The party 'fixers' chose the guests with great care, as it was important to them and their own brand. The more they managed to get publicity from a party, the more they would get paid for their next assignment.

And so, when the press started writing about me, the party planners took notice and started inviting me. I could not go to all these parties. For one thing, I was based in Gothenburg and all the action went down in Stockholm, 500 km away. Taking a flight was costly, as was a hotel room, so spending a couple of hours at a party would end up costing me hundreds of dollars. And, I'd lose a day and a half. I therefore decided to go to only a few each year, which made me even more interesting for photographers and the press. 'Here comes Panos!'

Early in the spring of 1990, I was invited to a movie première after-party. All the Swedish celebrities had gathered, and the film company had managed to get some international stars. I started to get used to going to that kind of exclusive affair.

Being visible at special events and large parties was a must for the brand. However, getting the full publicity pull out of them was not the easiest — magazines might take photos of 500 people, but only a dozen would be published. Most were of those in chic, colourful outfits, who made an extra effort in every way to be seen that evening. The press waiting on the red carpet were very experienced, and knew everything about everyone. Of course, they were looking for people who were extra-willing to talk about themselves, their love affairs, or show off their new partner. Newspapers peddled it and readers loved it!

I could not offer any of this commercial, audience-friendly behaviour. I offered no colourful clothes, no mischief on the red carpet, no hugs and kisses, no scandals. The press noticed this the first year: they took pictures of me, but I rarely ended up in print the next morning.

I used to walk around and chat with the few people I knew well, and depart after an hour or so. Some of the press saw this and asked why I left so early. I said I never drank at these parties. I've always disliked champagne, which was often served in abundance, to everyone else's great delight.

Their interest increased each time, and as soon as they began talking to me, their tone changed significantly. Suddenly, they were softer and not as annoying to me as they were to the others. It raised my hopes that I would soon be seen more in papers.

I often saw the same people going in and out of the parties, making repeated entrances on the red carpet. If the photographers didn't seem to see them or get shots of them, they tried again and again. It was comical to see the same desperate people fighting to be in a picture.

The party promoters had noticed me and continued to invite me to their big events. Some of them liked my low profile, and that I always honestly answered yes or no to their invitations. If something should happen that changed my plans, I had enough respect for their work that I always informed them well in advance. They appreciated this.

These fixers had great power, as the kings of the events. They could easily attract any celebrity to their parties. Even the Swedish royal family was on their list, even though they knew they'd never make an appearance ... but there was always hope. To my great surprise, many parties were extremely lavish. I always wondered what this gave back to the sponsors. They were often large companies with marketing budgets to match. I used to joke that marketing managers with big budgets had a problem spending it all, and didn't have time to see 'value for money,' so they threw it away on anything that would impress other marketing managers.

Going to these events was actually quite stressful. For many attendees it was all fun and games — a chance to see and be seen, grab another flute of champagne and party on. To my mind, though, if you were there to work, you simply could not drink. I was always sceptical of all those who indulged at these parties, from ministers and political party leaders to great artists and sports personalities. It was scary to see them, after a few drinks, let loose in front of the cameras. This made me even more cautious, strengthening my resolve to resist the social pressure and hold on to my principles.

It took a couple of years before the photographers started to see me as a valuable commodity, and my low profile started to slowly attract attention. Late one night, at one of the biggest events of the year, I stayed much longer than usual. One of the journalists and his photographer asked if they could take some extra pictures of me. "Of course," I answered. They placed me in front of the photo wall and took some pictures. Opposite me, two beautiful women stopped and watched, obviously wishing they could stand there and be photographed themselves. The photographer saw them, and in an instant he whisked them up next to me and started snapping away. One of those shots landed the top placement in the paper, and I had an idea: in the future, I would go to every event with two or more beautiful women!

I made my entrance on the next red carpet with two beauties … and showed up next time with two different women. The photographers loved this, and before long they would shout my name. "Panos, stand there!" "Hug them!" "Lean in, girls!" "Look here!" "And again now … not so stiff!"

In the beginning, the reporters ran up to the ladies and asked who they were, how they felt about me, and so on. But I'd taught my red carpet companions how to answer, so there would be no lurid headlines the next day. The journalists tried a few more times, but with our polite way of answering, they soon realized that they wouldn't get very far. They knew I wouldn't talk about anything private, so they took their photos but otherwise let me be.

My marketing philosophy was clear from day one: all publicity should focus on my work, my collections, but I would never give interviews about my private life or show my home. I turned down an incredible number of interviews with both national and international television channels that wanted that kind of coverage. Many people used to ask why. "All publicity is good publicity," they would say, but I didn't agree. I often read about my 'public' friends' romances in the press. At first, they were happy to be seen, but it did not take long for them to regret speculation about their divorce, or their finances, or their unsavoury habits.

That never aligned with my values. I was taught very early in life that you should have what you deserve, and leave everything else to others.

To me, working was not a way to get rich. One reason was that it was my life journey, and my way of living in the present. It was interesting, and it would bear fruit for survival at that moment. Thankfully, I had immense professional pride in everything I did. When I look back, my extreme self-discipline is something I am proud of. No one needed to push me to perform the best. This was built into me. I am a competitive person, and my fiercest opponents are inside me. They are my other self. The new me would compete against the old me: Panos versus Panos!

It would be plain humiliating to bullshit the press about my private life. Think of all the passion, the time I had spent to create something good and unique, something that people would love. Instead of just getting a little attention, for all the right reasons, it would be covered with dark clouds. These clouds might sweep you above the others for a time, but once it rains, you'll fall. That hurts, and it's difficult to lift yourself back up again. Then you take the next dark cloud that's rising, stronger than the first, which would also lift you up, a bit higher, and let you fall again, only this time it would hurt twice as much. The whole thing would continue until your tattered remains were scattered over the ground. By then, only vultures would be there for you ... circling, watching and waiting.

I stuck to my strategy of discouraging speculation about my private life. Every time I would make my entrance on the red carpet, the press looked closely at my two female companions, who were new and different every time. The pictures always got good placement in the media. And it wasn't just the press who liked this — other guests ate it up. They enjoyed the routine: my entrance with two ravishing women, my walking around a bit, my inevitable disappearance before the clock struck midnight. It generated a good deal of buzz among them. Deep down, they were dazzled by these ravishing women and were jealous of me! I often heard back over the years what they were saying: "How can he have so many beautiful girls?"

Men wanted to come forward and get to know me: the ladies were bait. But it wasn't only straight men who liked this; other women were also attracted by it. I embraced Onassis's saying: "Take with you to all important meetings a beautiful woman who will defend you against your opponents." It served me well, indeed.

A myth arose around me, but in a good way. Word got back to me of people saying they wanted to swap jobs with me. They wanted to be me! I remember hearing of several ultra-wealthy people, who had countless millions, who'd said this. I used to answer, "You should have thought so from the beginning, when you chose your profession! Did you want to work with industrial products or with beautiful ladies?"

The more beautiful women I brought with me to those parties, the more visibility I got from the press and all the other guests. The media landscape may have changed a great deal, but people and their interests have not.

6
Model behaviour

AFTER FOUR YEARS ON THE MARKET, I had learned a lot. I made valuable contacts and my designs sold well. In a very short time, consumers became loyal to my collections, returning year after year looking for the new designs. Word spread among retailers and new buyers began contacting us.

It was now 1990. I decided to dig a little deeper into why we were so good, and commissioned some qualitative market research. It was expensive for my small company at the time, but I wanted to know precisely what we were doing right. I could see that we were moving forward, and gaining momentum, but I wanted to know what consumers thought of my collections and why they chose our brand.

The results could be summed up in a few words: innovative design, good quality, affordable products, and the garments suited most bodies. You did not have to be a model to be able to wear Panos Emporio swimwear.

I thought about how we could be seen and heard more widely. Traditional advertising was quite expensive. I contacted fashion magazines and newspapers that were big at the time, but it was impossible for our small operation to buy ads. I flipped through the different fashion magazines and could see that our competitors had splashy ads in several of them. I examined their visibility, counted the number of pages they bought, and could see that their advertising budgets had to be at least ten times larger than my total turnover. Friends used to say, "Be happy! You are still the best-selling brand in some stores. Consumers love your products and you're increasing your sales every year."

My own thoughts swirled around. The more I analysed the market and our marketing, I realized it would be years before I would have the opportunity to advertise. I dreamed of seeing my beautiful creations in some of these fine fashion magazines. They were worth it, but the money just wasn't there. There was too wide a gap between the big players and us, and it would take too long to get to their size.

I WAS GOING to a small event one very windy night in Stockholm. It was February 1991, and half a metre of snow lay on the streets. A friend, Nikos, had been invited, and asked me to go with him, to be seen. I encountered some difficulties getting there. The train was delayed, and I would not be able to arrive on time. I was going to miss the soirée entirely. It felt like such a waste of time to travel five hours by train, pay for the hotel for a night, and then go back the next morning without really accomplishing anything. Nikos met me after the event and invited me to an Italian restaurant. He wanted me to forget the weather, the train delay and the missed event, the expense of it all, and think about something else.

We were at a small restaurant on Östermalm, where the well-heeled gathered. I did not think there was anything special about the place, but it was still packed. It was 11 PM, and most people had eaten and were talking over a bottle of wine. A few tables away, I saw the back of a beautiful girl, but I could not see her face. When she reached out to hug another guest, I got a special feeling. I wanted to walk past her table for a better look. I had to see her face. I am a shy person, and have never approached a woman and initiated small talk, but I had to see her from the front.

I walked around her table and looked straight into her eyes. I cannot describe the moment. Had I been a little braver, or had some Zorba in me, I would have screamed when I saw her! 'Eureka!' I went back to our table and asked my friend if he could approach her on my behalf, because I wanted to talk to her.

"What are you saying?" asked Nikos. "Do you know who she is?"

I saw that they were beginning to get up and said, "*Get her* before she leaves!"

"She is Sweden's most sought-after woman," Nikos gasped. "It's the tennis star Björn Borg's ex-girlfriend!"

"Just get her!"

She was there with a man, but for the first time in my life I wanted to overcome my natural shyness, take command, head up there and tell her I was dazzled by her. Or, with an impulse that was totally uncharacteristic of me, I would just think up something special when I faced her.

I went after her and tried to get her to stop for a second, but she completely ignored me, just like a superstar who avoids the fans who run after her. She barely needed to wave me away — she disappeared through the door in a flash. I don't know if I had been able to utter a word, but if I did, my words disappeared into the corridor and fell to the floor.

Nikos paid the bill and wanted to leave; he thought what I'd done was embarrassing. On the way to the hotel he told me the girl's name was Jannike Björling; she'd been with Borg for many years, and they had a son. "She is difficult, and everyone wants to get in touch with her," he said. "She and Borg are always in the paper, with articles about their lives, problems and quarrels." He was quite critical of her, and told me to forget about her. "She's impossible! Everyone's waiting for her, but they'll be waiting a long time!" As he told me this, he looked at me and burst out laughing. "You're naïve if you think you can get anywhere with her!"

I had been annoyed with myself that I had missed her, but a winning instinct suddenly surged through me. At that moment, I felt free to act with confidence, and pursue what I wanted. I didn't know why I wanted her, but I knew she would work with me on something. The next day, before I boarded the train, I went to a news stand and bought a pile of gossip rags, tabloid weeklies, fashion magazines and newspapers.

I sat down on the train and started flipping through the pages, and there Jannike was, in all the publications. There was something about her — her stories had the best placement, and she was on several covers.

She was in a paper every day, but I'd never focused on who she was. I always looked at the press for swimwear fashion, and while this fabulous woman would have been there in front of me every time, I'd somehow never taken notice.

An elderly couple sat in the seats facing me, staring at me and all the periodicals I was rapidly flipping through. I tore out clippings of all Jannike's pictures, and tried to analyse why they used essentially the same photo, again and again. There was little variation, but they were stunning nonetheless.

On the long ride home, after five hours observing me, the elderly woman asked, "Can you read Swedish?"

I managed to say, "I can speak a little Swedish," but I was completely entranced by the images of Jannike. I wondered why there was so much interest in her, since what they wrote lacked any substance. Every piece seemed to be speculation about her, or outright fabrications, with other publications taking what one had said and speculating further.

I enjoyed those five hours because I had hatched an idea. I wanted to shout it out, so the whole train could hear me. I knew how I could get through to someone that others had deemed inaccessible. And I knew that if I succeeded, literally anything was possible.

I did some detective work over the next few days to get her phone number or home address, and eventually found her number. Calling strangers was not difficult for me — I had been training to do this since I was a kid.

I called, remaining calm and confident about how I would handle her on the phone. No matter what she said, I wanted to meet her. I wasn't going to tell her any specifics on the phone.

The phone rang twice, and a man answered. "Tony." It was her husband.

"Hi, Tony," I answered quickly. "It's Panos! Is Jannike home?"

"Yes. Hang on … here she comes."

She took the phone. "Jannike."

"Hi, it's Panos."

"Who are you?"

"It's Panos, the designer. I have an idea that I think you'll like, and I'm going to be in Stockholm this weekend. Can we meet up on Saturday?"

She went quiet for a moment, and I heard her call out for her husband and hand the phone to him.

"What is this about?" Tony asked.

I managed to pique his curiosity and persuaded them to see me, at their house. They were laying low because the paparazzi harassed them all the time. For me, it was perfect: I would be able to talk to them in peace and quiet, in a place where they were comfortable. I was convinced that I knew how to get her to work with me, and meeting them both at their home was a dream scenario.

On Saturday afternoon, I knocked on their door at exactly 3:00, as arranged. Tony opened the door, and with a friendly voice welcomed me in. We sat in the living room, but Jannike was nowhere to be seen. My thoughts went to what Nikos had said: "Everyone's waiting for her, but they'll be waiting a long time!"

Tony was a famous photographer, and a pretty cool, calm guy. I took the opportunity to gauge the atmosphere. Tony told me that Jannike had received a lot of modelling offers, but she was not interested. She turned them all down.

Jannike soon joined us. I had packed some swimwear for her, and for Tony. I was spot on with her size, and Jannike's first reaction was, "Thank you, they look nice."

I asked her to try one on, and she did. She came back a short while after and said, "What a fit! How beautiful this is!"

We started talking a bit in general, but they were curious what I wanted from her. I only had one chance. If she were to say no, then it was over! I flashed back to some of my successful negotiations, to get into a positive frame of mind. I could not afford to fail. She had to say yes.

Top left: Showing a love of music from a young age. **Above:** With my siblings in 1966 — I'm eight years old in this photo. **Left:** Dressed as a cowboy — dreaming about playing other roles. **Below left:** As a boy scout on Greece's national day, one March 25. **Below:** Working at the foundry, age 17.

Top: With the singer Kostis Christou, a big name in the 1970s. **Left:** Picking grapes at home in our garden. **Above:** Literally my (Pakistani) brother from another mother, Khalid, with my parents in the early 1990s.

Above and left: Working as a guard in one of Gothenburg's toughest prisons. **Left:** Working as a foreign correspondent in Sweden. **Below left:** As a teacher in Gothenburg. **Below:** Studying engineering and textiles at Chalmers University of Technology.

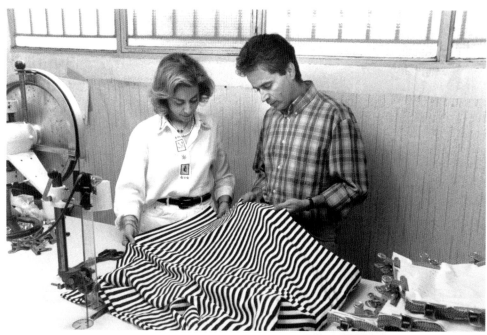

This page: Overseeing production and fitting at the factory with one of my first collections.

This page: Against all odds, I secured Jannike Björling to model for Panos Emporio.

Above: Triumphant at my 10th anniversary show in 1996. **Right:** Petra Hultgren modelling in 1996. **Far right:** Olympic wrestling champion Frank Andersson models Panos Emporio in 1994.

Above: Finnish model Janina Frostell, who later stood for parliament. She is wearing my Paillot design (specifically, the limited-edition Gold Paillot) in photos at top and left.

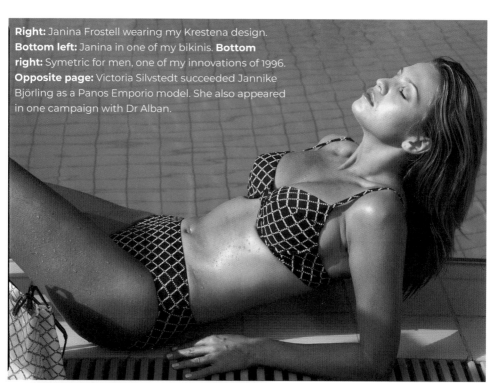

Right: Janina Frostell wearing my Krestena design.
Bottom left: Janina in one of my bikinis. **Bottom right:** Symetric for men, one of my innovations of 1996.
Opposite page: Victoria Silvstedt succeeded Jannike Björling as a Panos Emporio model. She also appeared in one campaign with Dr Alban.

PANOS EMPORIO

PE PANOS EMPORIO

PE PANOS EMPORIO

Top: An early publicity photo of me.
Top right: With Dr Alban on the catwalk at one of my shows. **Above and right:** Dr Alban modelling for Panos Emporio in Mykonos.
Opposite page, top: With Janina Frostell at my inaugural fashion show in Bangkok. **Centre row, left:** Janina Frostell flanked by male models. **Centre row, right:** With dignitaries and Princess Kokaew of Thailand. **Bottom:** A later show in Bangkok, and no less ambitious.

This page: *Baywatch*'s Traci Bingham photographed in Malibu, California.

Left: Rickard Engfors, then still doing his drag act, as my model for my *Unlimited Love* collection. **Below:** Actor José Solano, in a shoot where his father proved disruptive. **Bottom left:** With Traci Bingham after our 1999 shoot. **Bottom right:** The Lindqvist brothers, Joel and Henrik, from the Frölunda Indians hockey team, in a 2002 calendar shot.

PE PANOS EMPORIO

Above: Being presented to the Greek president, Karolos Papoulias, in the presence of HM King Carl XVI Gustaf. **Right:** The Bloody Cute design from my Poison by Panos range. **Below right:** My Kandia design, Scandinavia's biggest bikini hit.

This page: Celebrating 25 years of Panos Emporio.

Top: On location on a shoot in 2010. **Above left:**
Another bold print with the Hecate swimsuit,
2005. **Left:** Greek singer and Eurovision winner
Helena Paparizou modelling for Panos Emporio.
Above: Meander, the swimming trunk innovation
for which I won a silver prize in the Swedish Design
Awards in 2016.

I asked Jannike why she thought the swimwear she'd tried on was nice. "I liked the colour combination," she said. "It was a little different, and you feel happy when you look at it."

"You said something about the fit, too."

"Yes, they fit really well. They're very comfortable. You'd feel safe in it if you're going to jump in the sea or a pool."

I continued to ask simple questions about swimwear, what she liked and disliked, where she bought hers, and got Jannike to talk a bit. We chatted for half an hour about swimwear, and I told her about my dream and my vision. She listened and seemed genuinely interested. I had a good feeling that I could tell her why I had contacted her: I wanted her to be my model.

I struggled to find a way to structure the sentence. She interrupted my thoughts by saying, "Oκ, now that we've talked a bit, what did you want from me?"

I stared straight into her eyes and gave her a smile. "I have to say, you are so beautiful, and my creations will be so much more beautiful when you wear them. The whole earth will shake."

She didn't respond to what I said. There was no reaction at all. She was used to everyone liking her, so she asked the question again: "What do you want from me?"

I got up from my chair and said to her, "Tony, you and I are going to take the best pictures of you. You said you loved my swimwear. Let's get some cool shots of you wearing my designs. We'll go to Greece, and stay for a while. We'll take a couple of pictures a day, whenever we feel like it."

I had read in papers about her moods, how difficult she was to hang out with, that she wasn't great with scheduling, and that she wasn't a morning person. It was important for me to get her to see it as a holiday — a fun thing.

She had been under constant pressure in recent years, and I wanted to get her away from it all, so she wouldn't have to deal with another person making demands on her. She was very young when she'd met Borg. I'd read how she had to leave her adolescence and carefree partying, and suddenly move into high society, with the spotlight always on her.

Before she could answer, I continued, "You need to go on holiday, and Greece loves you. I think you would like Corfu. There are direct flights from Stockholm every Friday. I know the owner of Apollo Resor [the tour operator] and have already reserved four tickets, two for you and Tony and two extra, because I think you'd want to bring along your own make-up person and a friend." I had also read that she had her own hairdresser who she hung out with, and a friend who was always with her. I knew this would create a sense of comfort and security. I saw it as my strongest card now.

She looked at Tony. I could see she was starting to like the idea, but still hesitated.

I quickly took command again. "Would August be a good month to go?" She sat there quietly, and I didn't let go. "Let's decide, and I'll sort out all the practical details with Tony so you can focus on the fun stuff. I'll send over a number of swimsuits soon, so you can choose which ones you like."

I got a tentative-sounding "OK." It wasn't an enthusiastic yes, but it was enough for me. Now I had the opportunity to make the arrangements with Tony.

My negotiation tactics made it possible to get Sweden's most sought-after woman to meet me, and agree to model for me, without money getting in the way. She had never done a photo shoot before — she was not a model, but someone who had been propelled into celebrity because of her relationship. In Sweden, at least, this was unique. Many had tried to buy her endorsement, but she said no to everyone. These were giant companies, and she could have easily earned millions for each assignment, but it was a matter of principle for her. She would have liked the money, but I didn't have any with which to 'buy' her. Can you imagine getting such a well-known personality to show up more or less for free?

After a few days, we had figured out a plan for cooperation and the details were ready. Tony would take pictures of Jannike and I would get the rights. At that time, photographers had the rights to their images, and you were not allowed to do what you wanted with them without asking and paying extra. I already saw then how I wanted to handle the photos, even though I lacked knowledge and experience. I compensated by thinking innovatively, staying positive and envisioning the best possible outcome.

It was a revolutionary idea to get all photographers in the future to release the image rights to my company!

The team was ready to go according to my plans, destination Corfu. The tour company's owner organized everything he could, plus a little extra to take care of Jannike. She was a celebrity without parallel, but it was a shared charter. When you flew charter, there was no business class, but Apollo managed to place all four of them in the first seats up front, and chose who would sit behind them. The hotel was informed, as well as everyone else involved. I did not want her to feel uncomfortable or annoyed, because everything hinged on her not dropping out of the shoot.

We got some decent photos in the last few days, after things had moved quite slowly to begin with. We managed to get about 50 pictures, and some were really nice.

We developed the photos, and I sat for days and nights selecting the best ones, and then sent them out for retouching. The technology was not like it is today; everything cost a considerable amount of money and you would pay a lot per image to have it retouched. I didn't really know about that side of things, and the costs wound up being extremely high. The trip, too, cost much more than I had expected. It was my first photo shoot, and I had no experience with planning and budgeting to contain costs.

When the retouching had been done and the pictures were ready, I started plotting out my strategy to get the news out. I had never worked with the media or hired an advertising agency, and was aware that anything could happen. There was no money to hire consultants, and the agency that I'd contacted really scared me. **Their thoughts on what they could do, and the cost involved, reminded me of my parents' words: "Do not expect others to solve your problems!" You have the solution yourself. Use your knowledge and passion, decide where you want to aim, and then be decisive and act.**

I spread the best pictures all over the living room, and started sorting them into groups. Then, I added different messages for each group. Every night I studied the pictures carefully, and decided to choose only five to be presented to the press. Nothing else. I wanted only a few pictures in print, so everyone would see them and remember them.

Intentionally included among these five were two featuring swimwear designs that I had not managed to sell in any great quantity. Every year, it was difficult to sell a couple of releases that I believed in, but the stores didn't share my enthusiasm for. And so, they didn't push them. Now, I had a chance to test them directly with the public, and see what consumers would say.

After a few days of thought, I was ready to go to the media. I had 30 slides made of each image, and wrote some text that I wanted included in the articles. The story itself about why Jannike did it, for a start. It was important that she would come across as a superstar — that she was at her most beautiful and alluring — but of course my swimwear would need to get just as much attention. It was a critical balance that we had to get right. I could see how the press would handle the publicity by publishing fantastic shots of Jannike in a bikini, but it was not certain that my name would be seen as much.

I looked up a couple of journalists I had met as a foreign correspondent. I figured they could give me some insight into the thinking of the big newspapers.

I asked them if I could charge for my pictures. You could almost hear their eyes widening in bewilderment. "What do you mean?" one of them asked me. "*We pay you* to publish your photos and advertise your collections? We've never done anything like that."

That reaction steeled me. I decided that I should charge for our pictures.

My experience as a correspondent came in handy. I requested from the Ministry of Foreign Affairs lists of all media in Sweden. That was all the information I needed. The fax was the most immediate way to send out press releases in those days, and the lists I'd requested gave me all the right fax numbers.

I chose to reach out to all the major media channels. The largest were the evening newspapers. They were the most important of all; everybody read the evening papers and I wanted those readers! I called the editors in the morning to check on their interest. It was greater than I could have dreamed of.

I did not leave much info with them. I wanted to see their negotiating position. My original thought was that we would give them material that same day, for it to be published the next day. While talking to them, I changed my strategy on the fly, and said that I wanted it published on their best day of the week. Sundays sold best. We negotiated how the layout would look. I gave them the story with small, reprinted images in place of the originals, and sent that by fax. The quality of these crude, low-resolution copies was intentionally too poor for them to publish. They served as a teaser — as my bait. I realized what strength I had in these pictures.

They rewrote the words a bit and I had to approve the revisions. Late Saturday night, they sent their staff photographer to meet me so I could hand over the high-quality prints. The placement was crucial, especially the first time you release something. The space had been reserved: the middle spread and the front page. Getting them the photos at the last possible moment would discourage them from changing those positions because of some breaking news overnight, since they'd made the extra effort to acquire the images. I made the same deal with four major evening papers.

Through the evening and well into the night, I faxed releases to more than 300 additional media channels. I hit radio, television and the small local newspapers, which I'd learned from my journalist days were read by huge numbers of people outside the major cities. Everyone seemed to forget about the regional and local press in the big-time publicity hustle, but I did not. I gave them as much attention as the major players. However, there was a problem: how could I mass-distribute the high-resolution images, which was after all what this was all about? Email was around, but it was still primitive, and it would take prohibitively long to send photos that way. Even if I could email, scanning was not that easy yet, either. I could not get the same great publicity without crisp, clear pictures. I panicked that night, because the buzz was building and everyone wanted these shots.

I sat in the office all night, and one photographer after another came to pick up the pictures. I took a symbolic sum off each of them, not because I aimed to get rich off the exercise, but to bind the newspaper contractually to how the images would be handled. All photos would have the same tagline: "Copyright Panos Emporio." Every garment style was to be named, and the retail price would be listed.

That evening, one particular photographer had been commissioned by multiple newspapers for this assignment. The largest papers had full-time photographers, but the small local ones called around and found this solution — a reliable freelancer — to access the shots.

The next day, Sunday, 2 February 1992, I went to a news stand at the break of dawn and bought copies of each and every paper. By 11 AM, the first editions of the evening papers were hitting the street. I went to the central station, where there was a large newspaper kiosk that had most of the Swedish papers. Just outside the kiosk I saw that both the major evening newspapers had my material on their newsstand sheets! It appeared in the middle spread of the two largest papers, as we had agreed. I was overwhelmed.

That was a historic day. It was a great start to my marketing journey. The phone lines were burning up — buyers and individual consumers began calling, asking for swimwear. Everyone wanted to know where they could buy my designs It was very snowy and cold outside, but here was this incredible demand for swimwear.

Shops that normally wanted to take in stock in April saw the demand and were annoyed that I had run the news so early. They thought consumers would forget about it when the products hit their stores.

Some had warned me against acting so impulsively. The ad agencies were very critical of my approach. I had my own thoughts, and wanted to create demand so I could sell several products to the stores before the traditional summer season. I also wanted to take the pulse of the general public when it came to those hard-to-sell products, and I was absolutely right! The stores were inundated with requests for the two swimwear items that hardly anyone had previously bought.

The laws of nature say that when something has started, it gets bigger with time, like a tsunami. The more time passes, the stronger it gets. I knew that if the publicity was successful and the demand was high, it would not run out in two to three months. I had calculated that weekly and monthly publications would also write about this, so the effect would become more powerful as the weeks and months went by. It played out exactly that way: one outlet after another started writing, and the same pictures could be seen in all publications. My time was spent answering questions and requests for interviews, and I tried to keep Jannike away from the press. I wanted to handle them, to steer them toward my collections, and away from Jannike's private life. The press absolutely did not want to write about an apparel company, but I had Jannike in a bikini and they had no choice if they wanted to publish the photos. This was my strongest card, and I managed to negotiate satisfactorily without them feeling unduly coerced. Jannike had no desire to do interviews, and the press did not like that, but the symbiosis we'd struck would continue for a long time, and it was important for them to remain dignified.

The fashion press were quite critical. It seemed that Jannike didn't align with what they thought a model should look like. Some thought she was too short; others had their own petty critiques. I had expected that the fashion press would be interested, but all the major fashion magazines said no, they didn't want to publish the material. The private TV channels ran features but state TV was not interested. That also took me by surprise.

Nevertheless, every week I saw an increase in publicity and interest. Soon it was impossible for me to handle it alone. I collaborated with a photo agency, which would handle the images on the same terms: everyone should pay for them, and the accompanying information — especially the Panos Emporio name — must be mentioned in the text. The images could only be used for editorial purposes and the article had to be about Panos Emporio, directly or indirectly. If the photos were to accompany a piece about Jannike's private life, then the licensing price would be quite high, or we could opt not to sell at all.

The media had money at the time, so charging for pictures was not that difficult. I felt proud that we were able to do it as a small brand. This helped me move forward with the press. They got good info and nice pictures, and sold newspapers with them. Every day my contacts with the media became more crucial, for both sides. I was always polite and helpful, and made sure they got what they needed on time. Thanks to my journalistic knowledge, I had an insider's understanding of how to act towards the media community.

Our cooperation with Jannike went on for five years. It was unheard of to pick a celebrity who was not a model, to get this sort of publicity, and have her represent a brand for such a long time. One paper after another featured her, and the centre spread became a matter of course. The tsunami grew stronger every day. The media outlets that had turned me down soon got in touch and tried to persuade me to get Jannike to do interviews. Even the state TV channel and the fashion magazines that had refused to run our press release changed their tune. The fashion mags now wanted to do photo shoots with her, after having dismissed her for not being a 'real model.' After several false starts, the state TV channel came to us with another interview request and I decided to arrange one.

My policy was to begin allow wider coverage, even by media that had been unfriendly to us for several years. But, there were conditions. No one could interview Jannike without me being physically present, and nothing would be published without me pre-approving the text. No newspapers had managed to get decent photographs of her themselves, so they had to use our photos!

One magazine, however, was less than ethical about this. They wanted Jannike on the cover, as she was hot property, but said they could not use a promotional photo up front because it was against editorial policy. I told them they could not do a shoot with her, especially if she wore something else. They asked if there were some photos I hadn't used that they might run with. No, I told them; we'd used everything we shot. So, they took one of our images and altered the colour of the swimsuit. It wasn't legal — it was by any interpretation a copyright violation — but I didn't pursue it. It just reinforced in my mind what influence I had in the media, even as a small designer, thanks to my connection to Jannike.

IN 1992, we came out with our first catalogue, with a print run of more than 300,000 copies. It was an eight-page, A4 format booklet, and Jannike appeared throughout. There was mayhem in the stores as soon as the catalogue was released. All our retailers sold out of our swimwear.

We did not have enough product to deliver. I learned to let the shortages happen, to keep my products exclusive. Consumers would have to wait a year until they could find them again.

The retailers did not like it, and didn't think that customers would return in a year. "They forget quickly," I was told. But I was sure of where I stood. **From the beginning, I had managed to connect with my customers, and they did indeed stay faithful to me, year after year.**

The catalogue became an event. Every year, people waited with excitement to get a copy, and then ran to the stores and made their purchases. Imagine if we had e-commerce back then!

Consumers kept our catalogues because they cherished the swimwear inside. But Jannike was a big reason for that, too. The women liked her pictures, and how the swimwear fit her. Panos Emporio became known for fit, daring patterns and colour combinations, and being on-trend, and it was for everyone to wear.

We distributed the catalogues as a supplement in various fashion magazines. They were so popular that we could negotiate anything, and the magazines fought to be able to distribute them. It was always big news ahead of the summer, with competitors wondering what the Greek had come up with this time.

Our biggest challenge was getting good geographic distribution across the country, with as broad a range of products as possible out there. Retailers tended to opt for a narrow range, and passed on the new releases. Every year, the catalogue's cover photo, and the biggest photos inside, were of the latest designs, but they were not my best sellers. The retailers just weren't receptive, and it annoyed them enormously that consumers wanted the very garments they dared not bring in!

Over time, these hard-to-sell designs became the biggest sellers for several years. I never removed a model I believed in. It might have at first sold so few copies that it was impractical to restart production, but I took the risk and produced and delivered what consumers kept asking for over the long term. The stores got the message, and these designs were largely profitable for us and for our retailers. My perseverance and determination paid off. Many of these models remained in the collection for more than 20 years, something my competitors could only dream of.

I WOULD VISIT MY PARENTS regularly. On one occasion, in the early 1990s, I called Mum to say I would be coming in a few days. She said that they were excited that I'd have a chance to meet my new 'extra brother.'

I knew my parents were too old to have had more kids, but I replied, "That sounds great."

On my arrival at their house, I saw a man of around 40 wearing a white thobe, the long robe worn by Muslim men, working in the garden. He saw me and ran to open the door. Mum came out at once — she always ran when she saw a taxi arriving — and welcomed me with a big smile and a look of contentment that could only come from the heart. Before the man could say a word, she said, "Come here, this is your new brother." He took my hand and wanted to give me a hug and a kiss on the face.

I had a warm feeling, deep down in my soul. I understood what had happened, and how he came to be my new brother. I said nothing, and walked into the house. Maybe he thought I was too dry. I'm like my father. "Words are for the poor people," he used to say.

During the dictatorship, and for years after, thousands of poor immigrants from Pakistan were brought to our area as workers, to drive down salaries. Greek people have a quality that's common in certain cultures: *filoxenia*. It might be translated as hospitality, which of course can be found in many places, but *filoxenia* was something more, something deeper. Racism had been supressed under the dictatorship, but it began to rise after Greece had become democratic.

These imported workers were struggling to put food on their families' tables, and now the locals were saying that the Pakistanis were here to take their food. You could feel the xenophobia in the air, with comments and hostility directed toward the newcomers.

My new brother, Khalid, had a hard time there. He helped my parents in the garden, and when they realized he didn't have enough food, and that he could be deported, they decided to help him. They went to the authorities and said they'd provide for Khalid's continued residency in Greece. It was exactly as I expected of my parents, with their big, generous hearts.

When I learned of his story, I had to wear dark sunglasses to hide my tears. He reminded me of my own life when I had emigrated, and the stories I knew of so many other people's lives.

OUR COOPERATION with Jannike ended a year after she was charged in November 1994 with buying and using a gram of cocaine. I was in Paris when I received a call advising me that it was the biggest news story in Sweden: Panos's model, Jannike, was caught with drugs.

I did not fire her immediately, because I felt I needed to find out all the facts. I particularly wanted to know if it had been for her personal use, or if she was part of the drug trade.

The press was hysterical, and there was one sensational headline after another. For us, it was a very serious situation.

As I have I said repeatedly here, I've never touched drugs, and I never will. I decided to issue a press release explaining why we didn't fire Jannike. We acknowledged that she had a problem with drugs, but as an employer, I had a moral responsibility to support her and encourage her to get the help she needed. The press disapproved of this, and the 'experts' wrote how wrong I was, and that my brand would be badly tarnished.

The media kept the Jannike drug story going daily, but I still chose to give her the support she needed to move ahead in life, extending our arrangement by one year in the midst of all the turbulence.

I was surprised that consumers who had read so much about the scandal still felt positively about her. The damage was not as serious as everyone expected. Personally, however, I suffered the consequences. Every time I travelled, and arrived at customs, I was stopped for an extensive search of my bags. Sometimes they commented, rather clumsily, "Hmm, you're Panos ... Jannike's boss."

This lasted for more than two years, until one day I couldn't take it any more. I sought out the chief customs officer at the airport to tell him that this was not OK. Some weeks before, they had stopped me after I'd been with my car in Copenhagen on a business trip. I guess they'd watched *The French Connection* too many times, because they wanted to dismantle the whole car to examine it. It was common knowledge, with all the press I had received, that I was anti-drug, not a drinker, and barely smoked a cigarette, let alone smuggled anything into the country. They thought it was fun to stop me, I suppose, but after I talked to the chief, I passed without any problems.

The big question for us was who would replace Jannike. We still published the catalogue every year. It was an event. The entire Swedish population was waiting for it. People talked about it at work, and it was in the public consciousness through the spring. The media began to speculate about what we'd do this time around, and every day I received calls from celebrities who wanted to take Jannike's place. We were hounded by artists, models, actors and athletes, known and unknown. The press heard about this and wondered what we'd do. They wanted to be the first to write about Jannike's successor, which gave me a huge bargaining tool.

THE MISS SWEDEN CONTEST (Fröken Sverige) was still a reasonably big thing at this stage, and Björn Borg's eponymous fashion label, which had underwear and swimwear, was a sponsor. Because I couldn't pay big money for my faces, I began to think that there was another way to get the winner of the pageant to model for me.

I called the current titleholder, and drafted an agreement for a half-day's photo shoot. I paid all of $500. The media got wind of this, and before you knew it, Panos Emporio and Miss Sweden were mentioned in the news together. Björn Borg had paid for sponsorship for years, and supplied the swimwear for the contest, but at that point the media made the mistake of crediting the swimwear in pageant photos to Panos Emporio. My brand was on everyone's minds — it didn't matter whose line you were actually wearing, they thought it was Panos Emporio. That was the case even though there was only one set of photos of Miss Sweden herself actually in Panos Emporio! People didn't believe their eyes, they only believed their imagination.

After a few years, Borg realized that he had paid all this money but I got all the publicity.

Something similar happened in Båstad, a resort town in the south of Sweden. Every July, the town hosted the Swedish Open, an international tennis tournament. For the week of the Open, the celebrity set from around Sweden and beyond, especially those connected to the world of tennis, would descend on Båstad. *Magazine Café*, a laddish men's publication published by Hachette Filipacchi, who also published *Elle*, would host a major party that attracted tennis stars, celebrities and the media. I was invited as a guest, and headed there, arriving somewhat late. I walked around and said hello to the other guests, and was surprised at how many people said, "Thank you for inviting us!" "Fantastic party, Mr Panos!" "I hope you can organize next year's as well!" I had to pinch myself. What was going on? Was I dreaming? I never said I would be hosting any party!

The event was really well organized. *Café* paid for everything as the sponsor, and it was top-notch. But all these people thought it was my doing! This was not lost on Fredrik Helmertz, who was *Café's* editor-in-chief, and later editorial director for Hachette Filipacchi in Sweden.

"Panos," he said, "we arranged everything here. But people think it's you!"

"I'm sorry," I told him, shaking my head, but with a big smile on my face. "I can't help it. It's the power of Panos!"

THE REALITY is that it works the other way around, too, when you don't necessarily desire the publicity. I was invited to join the secretive order of the Freemasons, in probably 1999 or 2000, and attended a couple of meetings over the course of a year. It was so boring that I never returned.

Many years later, a newspaper did a front-page story on the local Free-masons' lodge, and how its members had net worths in the billions. There was a picture of the Grand Hotel in Stockholm, along with other properties purportedly owned by its members. The top photo, of the most prominent member, was HM King Carl XVI Gustaf of Sweden. The second was of one of the country's most famous singer–songwriters, Lasse Berghagen. And the next one was ... me! Then there were a bunch of prominent people who had passed away, and one living former minister of defence.

I hadn't had anything to do with the group in 20 years, and even back then it wasn't much, but the newspaper wanted to publish faces who would help them sell issues, and they identified the most popular men in Sweden.

Why did they include me? I think the lodge itself had provided some names, even though one in particular (!) had only been to a couple of meeting and hadn't set foot in the place in decades.

7
The King of Swimwear

In 1996, we marked the tenth anniversary of Panos Emporio. I had two strong cards. I was completing work on a major innovation. It was in fact the world's first innovation in swimwear since 1946, when the bikini was invented by Louis Réard, a former automotive engineer who'd taken over his mother's lingerie business earlier that year. My breakthrough was a revolutionary design called the Paillot, a two-piece design that could be worn as a swimsuit, a top and miniskirt, or a top with a high-waist bottom. I was also about to finish a men's range called Symetric, since we men needed something that would help us, to use the old tailor's term, dress evenly. Regular trunks tended to stick to the skin when we came out of the water, and this alleviated that problem. It made sense to pay attention to how we looked as well on the beach. Both would lift the brand to new heights.

I decided I would I finally hold a catwalk show, at the 1996 Stockholm International Fashion Fair. I rented the largest hall, with a capacity of 1,500 people. The organizers laughed when they heard about my plans, and said that for my first show I should aim to have about a hundred guests. They could not persuade me: I'd already decided it would be the biggest show in the fair's long history, and a historic moment for me as a designer.

I persuaded them to give me a large, elongated corner stand measuring 150 square metres. The set quickly took shape. Looming behind the long, white catwalk was elegant, stylish Greek architecture, including 4-metre-high Ionic pillars. It was a stunning replica of the Acropolis that could be seen from anywhere across the venue. Everyone would be amazed! It was an obvious reference to my Greek heritage and culture; I wanted to make my origin clear. Maybe it was because after ten years in business people still had a hard time pronouncing my first name, Panos, which consists of only three consonants and two vowels. This would be the year when *all* Swedes would learn to pronounce my name. In retrospect, maybe the Greek imagery was because my homeland had hurt me, poisoned my childhood dreams, and forced me to flee. And then, I was looked down upon in my new country as a poor black skull. Now, I wanted to shout so loudly that the ancient Greek gods would hear that I existed, that I am Greek, and will always be Greek.

It was not enough for me that thousands of trade fair visitors would see my temporary Greek palace, or that those who came to the fashion show would experience it as well. I had decided that the next day I would dominate all media. I wanted the front page and centre spread in the most prominent papers ... and radio, TV and all the hottest fashion magazines. All the attention would be on my company, my new creations and my fashion show. No one else would have space.

I went back and forth in the hall, and sat at the back, to see how guests would experience the catwalk. There were some small details that weren't right, and at the last minute I asked them to raise the catwalk half a metre. It created chaos — craftsmen everywhere tried to figure out how to elevate the walkway, and build extra steps for the models who would come up. The pillars wound up higher. I remember that most of the crew wanted to give up, but their boss, who was a good stage builder and worked in TV production, saw what I was saying. He was determined to make it work, so everybody would get the same experience from the show. I had told him which famous faces would appear on the catwalk and how my new innovations would be presented. He acted as though it was his own production. He took it personally. He wanted to make a difference and wanted to succeed.

A few minutes before the show was due to begin, we cleaned away the construction debris and prepared to let in the press and then the other guests.

The fair's organizer had tried to get me to take the last slot of the week. There were a number of fashion shows from different designers scheduled every day. But I wanted to attract the most attention, and decided I had to be first. Being the first to headline could create a tidal wave of interest, and help draw people to our booth. I wanted everyone to talk about Panos Emporio and my innovations.

I planned for the most important media to have decent spots, particularly the national newspapers *Expressen*, *Aftonbladet*, *Dagens Nyheter*, and others that were read by millions of people. The largest dailies received exclusive material and the opportunity for interviews before the show, so they could offer their readers something special. One magazine was given an exclusive on the Symetric men's swimming trunks, and another got an exclusive on the women's Paillot design. That second one arranged to take extra photos with my models in the morning, and we had in-depth interviews. I was promised the front page and centre spread, but they didn't show up for the main event, which really disappointed me. I was sure I'd get the space that was promised, but I wished they could have experienced a show Panos's way. Feeling the vibes in the hall was important.

To get maximum coverage, I chose the most famous personalities of that year to walk the catwalk — people who were recognizable from TV, or famous artists and celebrities. Everyone was chosen with the utmost care. Among the invited guests you could see big-names entertainers and politicians, with a mix of all types of people and ages. It was such an unusually strong lineup that many wondered how I'd been able to attract them there.

When we let in all the press, my assistant ran behind the stage to inform me that more journalists than expected had signed up, and all the press kits had run out. About 50 reporters went without one.

This gave me extra energy, and I tried to pump everyone's mood up so the models could do their best on the catwalk. Several of them gently peeked through the curtains to see the audience and shouted with great joy. "It's a full house!" "There are so many people and so many photographers." "This is going to be fun!"

Once the show started, I stood backstage, swept up in the euphoria that spread through the hall. It was a magical feeling. When it was time for me to walk out and take my bow, my body was shaking and I was too weak to get up. The producer gave me a wave, motioning for me to get out there, but I was frozen in place. Two of the most experienced models saw what was happening, came up behind me and literally picked me up by the arms. They guided me a few steps forward, through the curtain and out onto the catwalk. My eyes scanned the audience, looking for familiar faces, seeking confirmation that everything had gone well … but it didn't work. All the lights were on the catwalk and the hall itself was pitch black. I did not like it, and since that day, in all my screenings and lectures, I demand that the audience be lighted so I can make eye contact. Without that, I lose inspiration and connection with the crowd.

The final song of the show was Greek, of course. My entrance, and my final bow, should always be to Greek music, no matter which country I'm in. It gives me extra power and joy, and feels like I am nourishing my roots.

Following the show, there was chaos as all 1,500 attendees rushed to visit our stand. Even more joined as they met their colleagues en route and told them where they were going. Our staff simply couldn't take care of all the interested visitors. It was just as chaotic through the remaining days of the fair. The buyers were impressed by the women's design innovation, although not as delighted by the men's innovation. To dare to do something new and different in men's fashion at that time was a step too far, and not welcome.

The following day, the phone started to ring at 6 AM and didn't stop. Friends and customers heard about my show on the radio and wanted to congratulate me. I went straight out to the news stand and bought all the papers. Everyone had at least half a page from the Panos show and little else from that day about my competitors. *Expressen* and *Aftonbladet* had kept their promise: both had given me fantastic centre spreads. This attention created even more traffic around our stand — it seemed that everybody at the fair wanted to come by and look at the collection. One fashion magazine after another wanted to write about us. Lots of different TV shows invited me on, both on the state channels and the private ones, to talk about Paillot and Symetric. I had to say no to many requests, and this was deeply disappointing to them, but I honestly didn't have time for everyone.

Several international buyers and agents were present and showed great interest. We were not ready to export to a multitude of countries, but we would choose a couple. They were Finland and Thailand.

The fair manager came by to congratulate me on how successfully we'd pulled everything off, which she said was unparalleled in her long career.

Some big-name fashion journalists had in the past called me *Baddräktskungen* (the "King of Swimwear"), but in 1996 I felt I had officially earned the title. The prestigious fashion magazine *Damernas Värld*, with distribution in in Sweden and Denmark, did a multi-page report headlined, "Oraklet på baddräktstronen" (the oracle on the swimsuit throne). Although 165 bathing suit providers had participated in that year's Stockholm International Fashion Fair, there could only be one king. After that, I'd hear, "It's no fun competing against you." "We just don't know how you do it." "You're so damned good at everything and you get all the attention!"

Indeed, to this day the Paillot design remains a staple of the Panos Emporio range.

170

AFTER THE STOCKHOLM EVENT, we had many new contacts who wanted the collection. I chose Finland as the first new market. I knew a lot about Finland through Markus, a Finnish Swede who was very insistent about wanting us to invest there. We met at the fair but there was no time to talk, so I asked him to come see me when the dust had settled. A few weeks later, he showed up at the office without an appointment. That was unusual, but he wouldn't take no for an answer.

I was in the office that day and received him. His perseverance, and his certainty that we would succeed in the Finnish market, aroused my interest. I decided to go there to get my own feeling for the place. With a trade fair happening in Helsinki, it was a good opportunity for me to formulate a sense of how we could move forward.

We walked around the fair and I could tell that they really wanted to follow Sweden, and to work with us. There was a distinct Eastern European feeling in the air — it was hard to explain, but it felt as though they had fallen behind Sweden in terms of how their fashion trends were progressing. That wasn't a surprise, since the entire Finnish fashion export industry had been focused on the old Soviet Union, where the countries' trade agreements gave Finnish textile companies an advantage. Many large apparel companies produced for their giant neighbour without having to make an effort to market or sell their products.

The Finnish textile industry was impacted severely when the Soviet Union fell in 1991, but traces of the cooperation remained present for a considerable time.

When we walked around the fair, Markus knew quite a lot of people, and most looked at me in a peculiar way. I jokingly asked him, "Am I the first Greek in Finland?"

"They've been talking about you," he said. "They have seen you on TV and in the papers." He also noted that the Swedish language is a must in all official information in Finland. It was on street signs, in restaurant menus, and if you wanted to work in municipal government or for the state, you had to know Swedish. This really aroused my interest, as all the marketing that we did in Sweden would be automatically usable in Finland as well.

That afternoon, we were invited to see a fashion show and were both seated in the front row, as VIPs.

When the show started, one model in particular caught my eye, and held all my attention. After the show, I told Markus I wanted to speak with her.

Face to face, I knew she was the woman I had long been looking for. Her name was Janina Frostell. Although I saw her on the catwalk, I knew she would excel as a photographic model and that I could get awesome pictures with her. She had once been Finland's representative to the Miss World competition and got as far as the semi-finals. She was affiliated with a modelling agency, and my policy from the beginning was to not go through agents, but to deal with the model directly. She wasn't someone I absolutely needed, but having her on board would allow me to create huge media attention in the Finnish market. I told Janina, "Negotiate with me directly, and then you tell your agency. This is no ordinary modelling assignment."

Janina was a nice girl, but she needed reassurance at this stage. When she felt safe, she would light up in a shoot, but her self-confidence was shaky, and that could pose problems for the photographers. I saw a weakness, but knew I could work around the extra inconvenience before each photo shoot. She was already attentive and I could give her a big push forward. By this time, people knew I could get things done quickly, in my own unique way.

It didn't take me long to figure out the Finnish female ideal. I noticed all the women who made it into articles were well endowed: the bigger the bust, the better the picture, regardless of whether the woman herself was all that interesting. Bust size was a big deal there. Finland had a completely different image of women than Sweden, where a large bust, even a natural one, wasn't something that would get you photographed in a fashion story. There is a strong feminist movement in Sweden, and breasts are considered a natural, maternal thing, associated with babies and wholesome motherhood. Breastfeeding is done openly in Sweden, a social movement that was really taking off at that time. Breasts weren't overly sexualized outside of certain men's magazines.

Every time I chose a female brand ambassador to shoot and collaborate with, it was a must that women would like her but straight men would love her. Janina met this requirement. When we chose a male model, it was only important that straight women would go crazy over him. It didn't matter what straight men thought because I knew back then — and this still applies today — we are greatly influenced by what our women say. A woman might say to her boyfriend that he would look good in a pair of swimming trunks, and that he should buy them, and that was practically always how we got sales from men.

The following day, we spoke again to Janina and I invited her to Sweden to tell her my thoughts on how we could collaborate.

I knew exactly what I wanted to create with her, and how I wanted it to play out. I had examined how the media worked in Finland and which outlets would be the most important to us. There was TV, of course, but it was a more difficult medium to get into. Back then, there were two major Finnish newspapers competing with each other, just as in Sweden. But Sweden had a lot of fashion magazines and other alternatives, something that wasn't present in the same way in Finland. All in all, it was a less interesting media landscape. There were the weekly tabloids, but they essentially covered what the big newspapers did.

During Janina's visit to Sweden, I prepared a mini-photo shoot in order to have some images ready for the press. I wanted her to pose in the Paillot, and for the logo to be included, regardless of whether the press chose to write about her or not. At least that would guarantee me a visual. The live-action Disney adaptation of 101 *Dalmatians* was hot at the time — the cinemas were packed and our spotted four-legged friends were very popular. I contacted the local Dalmatian club to come to the office with a number of puppies. I knew what the photos would be like: Janina in a black-and-white Paillot and a number of adorable little Dalmatian pups surrounding her.

I explained to Janina what it meant to work for Panos Emporio as a brand ambassador. It wasn't just about being beautiful in the photos, but that I wanted to create media buzz about our cooperation in Finland and in other markets. We would raise her profile to that of a superstar. However, she would never be allowed to speak directly to the newspapers. We would have control over what would be written. She absolutely could not pose for a picture for them independently. All images would go through us, and the image rights would reside with Panos Emporio. The newspapers would have to write our company name into their credits or captions. She would also participate in visits to the largest and most important business and purchasing meetings, and attend the industry fairs. I had prepared the pitch myself and was sure we would succeed.

Janina liked what she heard, and agreed to everything. She was ready to start with the first photo shoot the next day. The initial pictures, from our mini-shoot, were good, and I thought about how and when we would launch the collaboration.

Markus, my Finnish adviser, started calling his biggest customers to book meetings and present the collection, but they were less than enthusiastic. Time was against us: it was already September, and most customers used to set their budgets and finish their purchases by October.

I decided to conduct a press conference to present Paillot and Janina, but it yielded zero results. It looked as though we would have to wait until next year's sales to be able to get into the buyers' budgets. But, I didn't have the patience to wait a whole year before I could act again. What would Janina do in the meantime? The story was fresh, and it was now or never.

I thought about playing the last card: the two Finnish dailies that competed with each other for exclusive stories. Markus came up with a couple of reporters' names, for us to gauge their interest. Both were intrigued and wanted to know more. I got their contact details and arranged to speak to them … separately, of course.

During my conversations, I was 100% focused on quickly analysing their first sentence and their tone. In a short conversation I could decide who I would like to trust to break the news, and who would be my future media partner. It was a mutually beneficial scenario, and would develop into a symbiotic relationship.

My sociological marketing came in handy here as well. I was able to present what was best for the publication, and how they could increase their sales. I had great respect for their journalism and made sure to give them the right information, so they could publish a fantastic report that would attract new readers. I essentially did the preparation work for the journalist and made the story eminently marketable, so they could easily adapt it to their target readers. My job was to make them believe in the news and information I provided, and assure them that I would always keep my promises. No damn excuses, ever. The media became a partner with whom we had a common goal: many readers!

Iltalehti was the first newspaper I called. Markus had already filled the journalist in on who I was, and had shown her articles from Swedish newspapers. A nice, friendly voice answered my questions, though I still had to make an extra effort to explain who I was. I fell in love with her voice and thought about giving her the exclusive, so I wouldn't have to call the next paper. When the time came, I asked my big question: "If you and I come to an agreement, are you in a position to guarantee where the story will go, all the way through to publication?"

Her answer was a quiet, "Yes … but it depends." That left me unconvinced, and I decided I would have to call her back. She didn't try to persuade me to tell her more, or seem particularly excited about my proposition. She barely understood what the story was.

It was time to call *Ilta-Sanomat*, and a journalist who had a bit of a reputation. She was known to be tough. "She can get fucking angry," Markus told me. I didn't have anything to lose: if it didn't work out, I could always return to *Iltalehti*.

"Rita here," she answered. She sounded very determined, but not rude.

"Hi Rita. My name is Panos, and I …"

"I know who you are," she interrupted. "I've read about you. You're the King of Swimwear in Sweden." It was a marked contrast to the first journalist.

Rita continued, wanting to know what this was all about. I greatly appreciated that, and immediately got the feeling that she was right for the symbiotic relationship I sought. She was a powerful person who knew what she wanted and would surely keep her promise. We talked for a couple of minutes and it felt 100% right.

Rita chose to travel to Gothenburg to meet me and conduct our first interview. She still did not know about Janina and the collaboration I had with her. It was an urgent matter for me to get something published in Finland so that Markus could persuade one of the big chains to bring in the collection. A major article in the country's main newspaper would open the door.

It was strange that even though we weren't doing business in Finland yet, 30–40% of the population knew about us from Swedish media. It was an extremely conservative, cautious market, but it was high time their Eastern outlook changed, and they tried something new. I would give them the opportunity to move beyond the sort of stodgy old thinking, look and feel that no longer worked in Finland.

Rita arrived a few days later. She moved as fast as she spoke. "Let's get down to it. Show me what you have." She fell in love with the collection, and was impressed by the quality and all the details. She had fashion sense and an eye for detail. It felt so inspiring to host a serious, sceptical journalist who also happened to be knowledgeable about fashion, and have a discussion about trends and style and fit. She was not a fashion journalist, but she had travelled to the most important places in the world. Her specialty was interviewing those great personalities that others might have thought impossible to get. She'd had direct, face-to-face interaction with controversial politicians, rich celebrities, the biggest sporting stars, presidents, sheikhs and more. She was a strong-willed citizen of the world and could adapt to seemingly any scenario. No one could resist her.

A few days later, *Ilta-Sanomat* published a great article about my innovations and me. The newspaper had me on the front page and centre spread.

It all played out in exactly the way I'd wanted a symbiotic partner to or-chestrate things. Rita had told me the night before that I would be in the Sunday edition. I got a preview of part of the text to make sure everything was correct and there had been no misunderstandings.

On Monday morning, I called her to do my usual follow-up, something that is a hallmark of my working life.

"Thank you, Rita. It was a really nice article, and nicely laid out," I said, and asked if she'd received any feedback.

"It's a little early, but I'll check and call you in a couple of hours," she replied.

She called later to report that the issue had sold wonderfully, and they'd received very positive comments. I let out a sigh of relief. "You didn't think it was going to go differently, did you?" she asked.

The same day, Markus looked up the buyers to give them a last chance to work with us before we closed our orders. But first, he checked on whether they'd seen the big article. He then warned them that there would be a deluge of interest in the spring, and they'd have lines of cus-tomers stretching out of the door. We managed to get into the largest of the Finnish chains, and got them to reserve key shop windows and plan press and marketing activities.

After that, *Ilta-Sanomat* was the only Finnish paper to get exclusive news and interviews from us, and we carried this on for several years. Janina and Panos Emporio had the most front pages, as well as the great-est amount of press coverage, in the newspaper's long history. Every time we presented new swimwear, the paper broke sales records. By the spring and summer, Janina and Panos Emporio were splashed across their pages. As we moved into autumn, I wanted to entertain consumers so they wouldn't forget the brand. Since we are seasonal, we generated more news by saying that Janina would travel with me to a new market, and be willing to be part of television programmes outside Finland. *Ilta-Sanomat* accompanied us on some trips. The newspaper covered the story when Janina went with me to Bangkok to present new products and participate in a fashion show, and went behind the scenes on a photo shoot.

Television was also important at that time, but it was always more diffi-cult for a programme to be seen as often as a newspaper article. However, MTV3 in Finland realized the value of taking advantage of the great inter-est in Janina and Panos Emporio, and ran a couple of programmes that were successful in the ratings. They followed us to different places, such as Bangkok and Greece, and created episodes from there.

Both Panos Emporio and Janina were the most talked-about names for several years, and not only in Finland. Brand awareness was extremely high, from children as young as seven up to the elderly, and we created plenty of media buzz in Thailand, Greece and Sweden.

During that time, Janina became a national treasure in the media and the pride of the Finns. She became a symbol of beauty and international success. Political parties even tried to get her to run in parliamentary elections, and in 2019 she finally stood, as Janina Fry, her married name, for Finland's RKP political party (the Swedish People's Party) in the Uusimaa constituency. She was unsuccessful, though three of her party colleagues did take seats in the constituency under Finland's proportional representation system.

BACK HOME, there was growing buzz about who the model would be to launch Paillot for the tenth anniversary collection. Expectations were at a fever pitch, especially after we ended our business relationship with Jannike Björling. Speculation centred on several Miss Swedens, as well as various artists and celebrities.

I wanted to take things to the next level, so it was important to find someone who had a brilliant career ahead of her.

I closely followed the Miss Sweden competition each year, and among the 1993 finalists was a girl from the northern town of Bollnäs who caught my attention. Bollnäs is a very small place, which had around 25,000 inhabitants at the time. It had been a railway maintenance centre as the line extended northward, but in the 1990s that facility, the biggest employer in town, closed. To give you an idea of how small it is, its sister town is Shepton Mallet in Somerset, England. If you haven't heard of that, odds are you haven't heard of Bollnäs.

I could see something special in Victoria Silvstedt. I became increasingly curious and put her on my press watch list — I wanted to keep track of everything written about her. Victoria was soon chosen to represent Sweden at Miss World.

In the autumn of 1995, she and I wound up at the same movie première after-party. I noticed how she behaved that evening, and afterwards decided she would be my next star model. She had the potential to become big, not only in Sweden, but far beyond.

Victoria did not have a typical model's appearance, nor were modelling agencies after someone with her physique. The agencies wanted tall, slim girls with small breasts. This girl from the provinces was just the opposite:

she was tall and muscular. You could see that she was a skier. But I liked her charm, and I could see how good Victoria could look in the pictures and what energy she had!

The most difficult thing now was how to launch her. I had generated such great publicity with Jannike, and here was someone who would take her place. I couldn't afford to lose my momentum. I risked sabotaging everything I'd built if I made the wrong move. I couldn't afford to lose the publicity we'd received as anticipation mounted over who the next Panos Emporio face would be. It would be disastrous if we were to slip off the front page and wind up buried inside, with a few words of text and some random image. The launch had to be done differently — and exceedingly well — or the press would not be interested.

In the 1990s, *Magazine Café*, the Swedish men's fashion magazine, had a great reputation. When they wrote about someone, the newspapers would follow their lead. I had established good contacts with the editorial staff and treated them differently, getting news and photos to them in good time, since they had a tight, monthly publication cycle. That would allow them to come out with the news on the same day as the newspapers. They loved this, and our collaboration was built on great respect and trust.

I visited the editorial office and told them that I had a new girl in the wings who would have a brilliant career, and I'd be having her photographed in Miami in a month's time. I offered them the opportunity to be behind the scenes, interview her during the shoot, and be the first with the news.

They liked the idea. I suggested that if they wanted exclusivity, they could send a press release with images out to newspapers the night before their next issue hit the news stands. That way, I could ensure that the girl from Bollnäs would get good publicity.

It was another win–win, of the sort I loved to engineer. *Café* got an exclusive that would increase their visibility and help sell copies, and I got a partner who would take care of my publicity. Once again, **this symbiosis characterized my marketing strategy, and everyone benefited. I was respectful and kept my promise, as I'd been raised to do. Negotiating, understanding the other side and their needs and acting in good faith were key to making such collaborations work.**

It was important that we were able to assert ourselves and continue to get space in the media. There were many strong players in the Swedish market, including H&M, which hails from here, and competed with us for space in both fashion and general media. It was easy for them, since they

> ## Vägen till nordens populäraste baddräktmärke!
> ## Hemligt recept!
> ## All reklam är förbjudet!

Above: Text from one of my presentations. Translated, it reads: 'The road to the Nordic region's most popular swimsuit brand! Secret recipe! All advertising is prohibited!' When your advertising budget is nil, you're forced to be creative.

bought a lot of advertising and could request reciprocal press support, something that media claim they don't do, but always do. You would be surprised at how far they extend this accommodation.

I had zero budget for above-the-line advertising, and had set myself a rule of not putting a single dollar into it. It would have been impossible to compete directly with H&M for that space as traditional, paid-for visibility, but **I had my passion, my designs, my charisma and my reputation. All of that would help me connect in an even better way with the media**, and they would want to give me something I could not pay for. I knew that people loved to read about my collections, my models and me, and everyone wanted to browse the Panos Emporio catalogue. There was newsworthiness there, by all those measures, so the press saw value in it. Even here the symbiosis was valuable and favourable to both parties. So, all three parties — the press, the public and yours truly — had something to gain.

The *Café* journalist who interviewed Victoria was impressed with her, and this naturally made for a better article. In addition, they learned that she had a secret: she was on her way to shoot a photo spread for *Playboy*'s December 1996 issue.

On 23 November 1996, the story and photos hit. We got centre pages and appeared on the front pages of most newspapers. We had a strong new card to play, in our continuing symbiosis with media.

Many wondered why I released photos of swimwear in the autumn, when there was a metre of snow on the ground and it was −15°C (5°F) outside. "Are you crazy?" they used to ask.

There was considerable thought behind this. November is one of the darkest months in Sweden. It's windy, cold, there can be a lot of snow, and people do not look all that happy. Everyone is waiting for spring to come, when you start planning your holiday and see the future with positive eyes.

If I had released the photos during the summer, when everyone else did, we'd get lost in the clutter and the results wouldn't be great. My approach had a certain allure. Imagine flipping through a fashion magazine in November and seeing page after page of heavy winter clothes, in dark tones, against gloomy winter backdrops. Then, suddenly, your turn the page and there's a fantastic bikini picture in an exotic environment. You're going to remember that. It's the only bright image in there. You'll get swept up in the possibilities and feel energized starting to dream about summer.

I did receive a lot of resistance from some newspapers that didn't want to publish swimsuit photos in the autumn. They used to say, "That's not relevant right now. Come back next summer!" But once I'd managed to get my shots run in the autumn, and the publication could be the first with the news, they realized that the interest was greater and their sales actually went up.

My strategy was to be visible year-round and, above all, to create demand for Panos Emporio before everyone else started marketing their collections. The stores also disapproved. They thought they would lose autumn and winter clothing sales when consumers started asking for swimwear in November. And then, the summer collections wouldn't be appearing on their shelves until April at the earliest.

It might not seem that radical an idea, but placing the consumer first, before the products came out, was extremely successful! Our garments quickly sold out, and we managed to persuade the buyers to take stock much earlier than April. Eventually, we started delivering swimwear in November! This would not work in southern Europe, but it worked great in cold northern places because consumer psychology and behaviour are different.

Several years later, even the fashion magazines started publishing their swimwear reports early. The June stories shifted to March, and even earlier. They did the same thing as we did, starting early, and then beefing up their efforts considerably during the summer.

History repeated itself with Victoria, the new face of Panos Emporio. The fashion press had again chosen to take a negative view of my choice, refusing to put her on the cover. They argued that she was too big, she was too curvy, she didn't have 'a model's body.' I also heard a lot of weird comments about her. They apparently disliked the way she talked, because she somehow came across as 'too American,' and because she laughed a lot and was always happy. All this felt extremely unfair because most of those who criticized her hadn't even met her. And what's wrong with being happy? Some called her "bimbo" to her face at parties. That made me really angry. I shouted back at one insulting buffoon, "If a 25-year-old girl has become this successful in five years, with a fortune in the millions, and you call her a bimbo, what does that say about your IQ?"

In the second year, the fashion press started to show interest, and wanted to publish our pictures, but the third year was the best. It's impossible to describe how much publicity we were generating by then. Magazines that didn't usually write about swimwear started running our photos and wanted to interview Victoria. She was now appearing all over the world. Her career exploded, and those who'd criticized her a couple of years earlier suddenly found her interesting. I had managed to launch the career of another fascinating, in-demand public figure.

I cared most about what the Swedish people thought, and they had a positive image of Victoria. Many women liked our photos because they could see that she was well endowed and not a stick insect. If anyone was disturbed by her having had breast implants, they weren't our customers.

In 1997, several major magazines wrote along the lines of, "Finally, swimwear is made for us ordinary people," along with our photos of Victoria.

Victoria was a hit with us for three years and became one of the most successful models in our history.

We also had success with our menswear model, recording artist and producer Dr Alban. When the general-circulation press started reporting positively about him wearing our creations, that in turn helped us out with the more difficult fashion publications.

We had photographed Dr Alban, a cool and caring artist, with Victoria on Mykonos earlier in 1997. It was a strange time: hurricane winds prevented planes from taking off from Athens to Mykonos, and no boats could sail there either. Dr Alban was on a tour of Germany and had only one day for the shoot. My contacts, who were waiting for him in Athens, did everything to find a solution. They told me that they would risk trying to make it to the nearest island, and then try to hire a fast boat to Mykonos. "It's calm," Dr Alban told them. "Let's go! Panos is waiting for us!"

He arrived and we started working immediately. We only had four hours left. The gods were not on our side: the clouds were grey and menacing, and strong winds blew sand into his face. We got some shots, but they weren't what we had expected.

We were on the beach the next day, waiting for the sun and hoping we'd be able to get some good images. Initially, I was philosophical about it all, but then I got angry, having lost a day of photography after Dr Alban had risked his life to get there. And still, I didn't have any decent pictures! Victoria and Dr Alban tried to cheer me up, but it just wasn't going to come together. We'd have to take it on the chin, and reschedule another shoot, at another place and time.

Just before we packed it in, an old Greek fisherman walked past, and Victoria, in the white Paillot, started walking behind him. He continued at his slow pace without looking back at her. Victoria, the small-town Swedish girl, somehow pulled a Greek phrase out of thin air: *"Kalimera agapi mou!"* (Good morning, my love.)

The fisherman turned around, looked at her for a moment without changing his expression, and then continued on his way. Victoria kept following him, and I told the photographer, "Press the shutter!" As the old man got near his boat, which was bobbing at the edge of the water, I shouted to them, *"We're taking pictures of you!"*

Victoria was about to reach the boat, but the photographer wanted to check the light and take test shots with a Polaroid. "Who gives a shit about the Polaroid?" I shouted at him. "Press the fucking button, *now!*" The fisherman had a few metres left before he would reach his boat and climb aboard. Victoria turned to me, looking for direction. "Step on, too," I said. "We're going to get our shots!"

They were now both on the small boat, and I called out to the fisherman to ask if this was all right. He waved OK and said no more. Victoria started to pose in front of him as he weighed anchor and started rowing. She danced lightly. The fisherman got swept up in the moment, and suddenly groped her from behind. She shouted, *"Nej, nej, nej!"* (No, no, no!) but continued to dance in front of him. He made a second attempt, managed to pull the swimsuit down and his hands wound up on her breasts. Victoria shouted again, *"Nej! Nej! Nej!"* I was telling the fisherman off in Greek, but he shouted back, *"Ma ti nazia einai, 'Nai nai nai!'"* (But she's saying, "Yes, yes, yes!"). Incredibly enough, the Swedish word for 'no' is the same as the Greek for 'yes.'

He figured it was his turn to have some fun and started rowing toward deep water. I was in shock, but needed to compose myself to get Victoria back to shore. "Get off!" I shouted to her. She dove off and swam back … conveniently clothed at the time in a Panos Emporio swimsuit.

When she returned she carried on with the shoot. In hindsight, attitudes have changed dramatically since the 1990s, and a model would be much more looked after and protected today. Had we been there in 2022,

Victoria would never have got on to the boat, or pursued a total stranger like that, in the first place.

One of the photos of Victoria and the fisherman wound up in the centre spread of many magazines, but it had come at a cost.

Dr Alban surprised the press in the summer of 1997 when he appeared on our catwalk in swimming trunks and sang from his new album, which he'd released that day. It might have been unusual, but he is a consummate creative artist, who, like me, respects values.

He is one of ten children, hailing from Oguta in Nigeria. He originally came to Sweden to study, just as I had. To finance his studies, he took up DJing in Stockholm. His passion for music was incredible, and he would sing to the records he spun in his DJ sets. His stage name, Dr Alban, referenced the fact he was studying to become a dentist. He actually finished his studies and opened a dentistry practice, but so loved his music that he kept going with it. His songs and albums charted regularly in Europe in the '90s. The media were not always kind to him, so we had an understanding on this level as well. He is a terrific guy, a close friend, and we've always stood up for one another.

If I thought Jannike was a hard act to follow, it was nothing compared with her successor. Victoria Silvstedt was very difficult to replace.

As improbable as it seemed, I had someone in mind who would really make headlines: HSH Princess Stéphanie of Monaco.

At the time, she was a controversial figure, with a reputation as a wild party girl. I had seen her photographed a lot in bikinis, since she was based on the sunny Mediterranean in Monaco, and I was certain I'd be able to get her. I was used to succeeding.

The reason I didn't was that I could not talk to her directly, as I had done so persuasively with my previous models.

I wrote to her, and she replied to say that she would think about it. I tried again and again, but eventually gave up. In all these years, she was the one woman I could not get to model for me.

In the 1990s, *Baywatch* was the most talked-about TV series in the world. I used to watch it, and I was hooked on the actress Traci Bingham. There was a quality about her that I liked. It was probably her exotic, multinational look — her parents are both black, but her father had some Italian and Cherokee ancestry.

We managed to locate her manager, but I really didn't want to go through him. When it became apparent that I had no choice, I began negotiating with him. At first he was not interested, or maybe it was the American way of feigning disinterest to strengthen their bargaining position.

He asked what budget I had, which struck me as unusual. With my European way of negotiating, we would normally talk about her costing so much per day, making it easier to work out where you stood. I'd never been asked how much I could afford. He was quite determined and very dry; my attempts to lighten the mood yielded nothing.

I asked if I could get her address to send over some swimwear in the meantime, but he wanted those to go to his office.

I called everyone I could think of who might have her contact information, but came up short. Therefore, I decided to do as the ancient Greeks had with the Trojan Horse.

I packed lots of swimwear, with several designs in separate bags, with short, handwritten messages about styles and fit. I included my fax and phone numbers. Along with the most colourful, eye-catching garments — the ones I figured she'd really like — I wrote a clear message: "Call me. I have an important question, so I can bring you the right bra size."

From her body language on TV, I could see that Traci was proud of her figure, and how she looked was important to her.

I put the message on four different garments. It was unlikely that her manager would open every pack, look through them and actually see the notes. I've found that these people only think about their commission, and aren't nearly as tough as they try to appear.

A few days later, I called the manager and asked if Traci had received the samples. He replied that he had not found time to get them to her. I asked if he could please do so, so we'd know what size worked on her. Otherwise, I said, we couldn't go any further. "The samples are sized to a Nordic standard," I told him. I knew Traci was short, and wanted to make him worry that size might be a problem. I did not negotiate money at that point, letting him believe there was a budget.

I called a couple more times that week, until he finally answered, telling me he would leave the package with Traci over the weekend. That assured me that he hadn't seen my messages to her. He also had not commented on the Panos Emporio tenth anniversary book I had included in the packages, or the photos of me with previous models, including

Jannike and Victoria. I even made a collage with pictures of our previous models, captioned, "Now it's your turn to be with Europe's hottest brand and the world's foremost swimwear designer."

I was certain that would stoke her competitive instinct. When she sees me in these photos with all these beautiful women, of course she'd like to take their place. I sincerely hoped so, at least.

The days passed and I heard nothing from Traci. I called the manager again and asked if he'd given her the swimwear. "Yes," he answered. "She got it all a week ago."

"Can you ask her to try and come back with comments regarding the size of the swimsuits? This is important."

"Yeah, OK," he told me.

A couple of days later, Traci called. I suddenly lost my English. Her voice was warm, and she started telling me that she thought all my little notes hanging on the swimwear were cute. She said she'd planned to call but was busy filming.

She was impressed by the designs, and commented on my models. She wondered why I was interested in her when I was always surrounded by such fabulous girls.

I laughed, told her I thought she always looked fabulous, and asked if she had been to Sweden. She said she hadn't, but told me she thought it would be fun to go there.

I started to paint a picture of how a collaboration would work, telling her it wouldn't just be about doing a shoot and going our separate ways. It would be a win–win proposition, as it had been for my other models. I said I wanted her to come to Sweden for a big press conference, where I could present her and our collaboration.

"Wow," she said. "*Wow!*" We continued to talk for a good while, and I felt it was going well.

I wanted to discuss her fee, which agents always controlled, but we didn't get into it. But I did ask: "If we started doing this together, would you still want to be the face of Panos a couple of years from now? I only work with those who enjoy collaborating with me, love my designs, and want to be associated with us long-term."

She didn't hesitate. "That would be amazing!"

"There's only one problem," I said. "Your manager isn't one to ne-gotiate, and doesn't understand how it works in the European market. He's used to an American market of 300 million people, but we're only 8 million in Sweden, and 4 million in Denmark. They're small markets, but this could be a very interesting journey for you. So … can you ask him to stay out of this, so you and I can reach an agreement?"

"Panos," she began, "I would love to do this. Let me talk to him. This is something really different. I like your designs; I feel gorgeous when I put them on. My stylist also said how amazing they all were when she helped me try them on."

I told her I was thrilled that she loved my work, and ended the conversation by saying that I hoped we'd have a chance to make it all happen.

"Now, we don't want to wind up in difficult negotiations when you and I want to do the photography, so make sure he gives you the green light, and he can stay out of it."

"Write my number down and call me tomorrow night," she said. "I'm in LA, so check when it's night for me here and call then."

When I called her back, she seemed upbeat and happy. She said it went well with her manager, but he wanted to see all the photos. He wanted to be present for everything and have control over what we shot. And, we couldn't shoot more than five looks per day.

She said she would be able to schedule two days for the photo work there in California. I would either have to rent a house by the beach, as a base of operations, or book a large Airstream trailer for her. I'd also have to hire a couple of security personnel if we were shooting in a public area, though she would prefer not to be in one.

"Yes, I can take care of all that," I said. "But first, do you and I agree that this is a win–win on so many levels, and only a symbolic sum should be paid to you?"

"See if you can solve the practical things, and if the date is OK for me, then we can agree," she replied.

As soon as we hung up I started tracking down the editor-in-chief of a Swedish fashion magazine who'd done a lot of work in the US, and had many photographers and stylists as contacts there. I reached him, and told him that if he helped me out, I'd be able to provide him with some great material.

Until then, I had never set foot in America, and I didn't know how things worked there. But with the editor's help, we rented a nice big house in Malibu with a private beach. I hired a Swedish photographer so I could control the photography and have the rights to the pictures. The rest of the team was Traci's own, people she was used to working with.

A few months later, all was set, and I headed to Malibu. We would all stay at the hotel the first night and go to the rented house the next day.

We had agreed to meet at 3 PM in the hotel lobby. I got there and saw Traci and some people around her, including a well-dressed man in his 40s. I thought he must be her manager.

I went forward to greet them one by one the in the Swedish way, which I think is nice. You look them in the eye, shake hands and say your name. I then sat down opposite them, and it went quiet. They looked around for a while and asked nothing. I engaged in some small talk, but got some weird vibes. After a few minutes, Traci turned to me and asked, "When's Mr Panos coming?"

I was taken aback. "That's me," I said.

They looked at each other and smiled back. Then it went quiet again, and they whispered something to one another. I wondered if this was some kind of joke.

Then she repeated the same question: "When will Mr Panos arrive?"

I had no idea what had happened, but in the end, they agreed that I was indeed Mr Panos and started talking about details for the following day. They declined my invitation to have dinner together that night, saying they were busy. This made me anxious. What if they just disappeared from here? I had invested a lot of money in the travel, the house, security, the photographer, etc.

I lingered in the lobby to see if they would take their bags to their rooms or if they would just leave. Later that night I saw Traci go to her room. She just waved but said nothing.

We were set to leave at 8 AM but no one showed up. After half an hour, I went to reception and asked if they could call her room. There was no answer, and the receptionist did not want to answer my next question: were they were still in the hotel?

Shortly after 9 AM, I saw part of her team coming down to the lobby. I approached them and asked when we would be leaving. "We're getting ready," they said. "We'll be good to go soon."

We eventually departed together, arrived at the house, and it was a relief that Traci and the others liked the place. The private beach guaranteed that no one could disturb us, and we did not need permission to take photos.

We started sorting out the practical details, and at 1 PM we were finally ready to shoot. However, at the last moment Traci's manager came to me, saying he wanted me to read his contract and sign it. It had clauses on how the pictures could be used and a lot of rules. I tried to get him to wait until that evening, so we could start shooting immediately. The Southern California sun was growing stronger and the light was getting trickier.

"It's going to get too strong for Traci's skin, so we'd better get to work," I told him.

"That's right," he replied. "Glad you said that. She must not be in the full sun, so make sure the big beach umbrella covers her whole body, during the entire shoot."

I looked at a giant parasol they had brought along, and couldn't begin to imagine how that would work. We needed full-body shots with the sea behind her. We couldn't erase an entire parasol from the photos, and I certainly didn't want it in our shots.

I looked at him and saw that he meant business. Traci emerged wearing the first swimsuit, and she looked fantastic. Her assistant held the large parasol over her. I wondered what the hell this was all about. Did they shoot *Baywatch* — a weekly television series set entirely on the beaches of LA — with a gigantic flying umbrella?

I took Traci aside to explain what I thought about the pictures. I wanted her to tone down her lips to appeal more to the European audience.

I explained that sensuality and sexuality are two different things, and that I was all about the simple, natural and spontaneous look. The more relaxed you are, the more appealing you become. You want to look effortless; that was more attractive than someone who was trying too hard. You want others to make the effort to rise up to your level, and weed out those who are out of your league.

I managed to make her feel safe in my hands, so she could relax. We started taking photos as she sat down on the sand, with the parasol over her. It went slowly, but the whole team eventually became comfortable, and that was the most important thing I needed to achieve.

Her manager sat and stared as things got under way. I saw that even he began feeling safe, but noticed that it was getting hot for him in his suit. After taking a call, he came up to us and said, "See you tonight at dinner. Make sure Traci takes a break soon."

We had the time to take many nice photos, and Traci was fantastic to work with. She was very happy with how things were going and barely wanted to take a break. When I tried to remove the parasol, she explained that her skin turned black quickly, and because she had to look just so for other on-camera work, the umbrella had to stay.

I finally understood this, and said we would find a solution for the next day, so we wouldn't have to constantly manipulate an umbrella. Why had they not said anything about this from the beginning? I just thought they were being difficult when they raised it that afternoon.

During dinner, Traci said. "I want to apologize for what happened when we met."

"What do you mean?" I asked.

"Well, we didn't believe you were Mr Panos."

"It wasn't a problem. You'd never met me before."

"We got your pictures with the other models, but I guess I had another mental image of what a successful Greek designer would look like."

And with that, the others glanced over at her. Everyone wanted to know what she was thinking.

"I thought you would be very strong, with a big Greek belly, and smoke a thick cigar. So, my picture of you didn't match the real you. And then, you just seemed too polite to be this successful."

Everyone started laughing, and I wondered how many large, cigar-chomping Greeks she had met!

ON THE SECOND DAY, everyone was ready early and seemed to be in a good mood. Everything went quickly, and we decided to book a white horse so we could take the final shots at sunset, with Traci on the horse, wearing a red one-piece swimsuit featuring the Panos signature across the chest. She liked the idea, and her team agreed to make the arrangements.

We shot videos during the session, and she loved commenting on all the garments and everything that happened. Among the last group of photos we were going to do were close-ups of my new sunglasses collection. We struggled to get a good picture. The photographer then asked Traci to remove her bikini top, with her back to us, and turn her head a little toward the camera. She wanted more skin, without a nipple being visible.

Traci asked if her manager was in the house. Her assistant said that he wasn't.

"Then let's do it!" she said.

She threw off her bikini top and found the right position. My photographer loved that moment: it's a joy to work with a model who relaxes and instinctively finds different poses. We had worked on the sunglasses pictures for a few minutes when a police helicopter approached. Everyone tried to cover Traci and quickly put her bikini top back on her.

I asked why, and was told that you were not allowed to be topless, even on a private beach. The helicopter did a few passes and disappeared, and we started again.

I could not understand how they could have *Playboy*, but you couldn't be topless on a beach — a private beach at that! How unlike Sweden that was.

Time passed and the horse had not arrived. I asked the others to check and they were told that it was on its way, but the horse and handler had to take a longer, less direct route to get it to the beach.

The sun was setting quickly and I was in a hurry to get that last photo, as well as some video that I intended to cut into a commercial. In the distance, we spotted a man and a horse walking very slowly toward us. One of the team ran over to hurry them up a bit, but they continued coming at the same slow pace.

When they finally arrived, we barely had ten minutes left before the sun went altogether. The horse's handler explained that it was tired after walking so far on sand, which they hadn't expected. Traci was ready, and she apparently loved horses, but when she walked toward it to get to know it better, the horse reacted strangely.

"Stop," said the handler. "She cannot be photographed in this swimsuit!"

"Why?" I demanded. "We're in a hurry!"

"No, it's not possible. The horse reacts badly to red."

The horse had cost quite a lot of money — almost as much as Traci's fee — and now we weren't allowed to get our photos. We took some from a distance, but the horse was tired and closed its eyes. It was impossible to get any with its eyes open.

After the shoot, Traci wanted to head to a nightclub. She was energized by what she had experienced; she told me the collaboration was the most fun she'd ever had. A few of us went to a couple of clubs, and the night got long. She introduced me to some actors, and everyone was curious about me. She acted as my PR agent that night.

Some we met that night wondered why I hadn't invested in the US market. "You're the perfect person for us," they said. "Come here, and we'll help you grow!" By the end of the night, everyone in those clubs knew who I was! There is a big difference between little Sweden and how bold, brash Americans always act and think. When they see an opportunity, they want to push you forward. That's why they call it the 'Land of Opportunity.' In Sweden, on the other hand, people ask, "Why?" "How would that be possible?" "Who do you think you are?"

A lot of it stems from Americans' love of the independent spirit, and they're particularly attracted to the story of the self-made entrepreneur. Those who rock the boat, and disrupt the system, are praised and fêted. You can see this in how forward thinking they have been in so many areas, such as in film and high-tech. It's a far cry from *jantelagen*, the idea that no one should stand out, which forms a big part of Scandinavian culture and its belief in equality. There are aspects of American culture that remain foreign to me, but I really love the ambitious, forward-looking spirit.

ONE CELEBRITY SHOOT that was harder to do was with Traci's *Baywatch* co-star, José Solano. *YM* magazine called him their 'Man of the Year' and one of the world's most beautiful people in the mid-1990s. His manager was his father.

We quickly agreed to work together, but the shoot was not the easiest. Mr Solano senior had very narrow views on which garments José could be photographed in.

I had many nice innovations at the time. Men's swimwear was the most conservative category one could think of, especially in the US, where the only thing they knew were long, baggy surfing shorts.

I had a neon yellow brief and an apricot brief, and vests and swimming trunks in a stretch fabric. They were unique at the time, and we had innovated by having different colours on each side through the use of a special glue. When José's manager-father saw the garments he said, "No way! He can't be in that colour."

We took out a pair of regular trunks so we could get started, and asked José to get into the water up to his knees. Once again, his dad said no, because it was windy and he could slip and get hurt on some rocks. "Do you have special insurance for this?'" he asked.

José was cooperative, but it was one of those rare times for me where I was close to becoming really unpleasant to another person — his overbearing father.

José said something in Spanish to his father when he'd started complaining again. It seemed that José felt it was embarrassing for him to act like this all the time. He liked the designs and the colours.

The next item was the Symetric swimming trunks. But José's dad could not see the padding on the inside, and said no again. He went away for a short while, and José took them to try on. We started taking pictures of José, and his father came running in front of the camera, shouting, "No Speedos!"

"It's Panos Emporio!" I replied. "They aren't Speedos!" (Speedo is a brand name, not a generic term for a certain swimsuit style.)

He turned to José and said in Spanish that he should take them off.

People were not used to wearing smaller European-style swimming trunks in the US, and the father did not dare let his son be 'exposed' in them, or even seen in happy colours.

We managed to photograph some clothes with José, but it was unpleasant to have someone (someone unpleasant!) coming between us all the time.

ONE THAT WENT EVEN LESS SMOOTHLY was with the athlete Zlatan Ibrahimović. Even when he played for Malmö as a teenager, I knew he would become one of the greats of European football. By the time he was signed to a Dutch club and was starting to gain momentum in his career, we agreed that he should become one of my models. I contacted Sweden's two largest sports chains and gave them a great offer to carry my men's collection, with high margins, with Zlatan as the model. They declined!

As for Zlatan, I didn't hear from him until the day before the scheduled photo shoot. Even his agent hadn't been able to reach him for weeks beforehand. When he finally called, at the last minute, he assured me he'd be there, but he never showed up. I got angry, and when he called two days later to set a new time for the shoot, I said no.

COUNTLESS CELEBRITIES came knocking, asking if they could be the next Panos Emporio ambassador. Famous people even suggested their 13-year-old daughters, saying that in five years' time I could potentially have them represent my brand. Being the face of Panos Emporio became a dream job for so many. At the time, I truly had no idea of the influence I wielded: I was just trying to do a job, choosing the right models for my brand. What was remarkable was that I seldom paid massive fees to my ambassadors. People thought I must have paid tens of thousands — millions, even — but most of the models did it because they wanted to. **Our values aligned, and I could see that they had charisma, giving off good energy to other people. This was something you couldn't buy.**

8
The big league

DRIVING ALONG one autumn night in 1996, it seemed darker than usual. I had done a TV interview that hadn't gone particularly well. "What kind of car do you drive?" asked the host. "I drive a Merc," I said, and the look on his face said that it was somehow below my position. There should be no shame in driving a solid, respectable automobile. I'd worked hard for it. Couldn't we have talked about love, about humanity? Or politics, and how that could change our lives for the better? I had planned so carefully what I was going to say, but I'd retreated into my shell like a turtle.

Afterwards, on the drive home, I turned on the radio to take my mind off the uncomfortable interview. I wanted to just disconnect, chill out and listen to the sports news.

"And now," I heard, "the fabulous story of the little club that has written football history." They had accomplished some feat and marched straight from division five to the Allsvenskan, the top Swedish football league. Now, though, they'd run into financial difficulties and were looking for sponsors. I was intrigued. Why couldn't they find sponsors? Success breeds success; it's the law of nature. Why should it not apply here?

The next morning, a friend called me to catch up. Since I knew he was crazy about football, I asked about the club. "It is called Ljungskile SK (LSK) and is located near Uddevalla," he said. "Look online and you'll find a lot of information about them."

I found some great articles about the club. I felt the wings of history sweeping me back in time. It could just as easily have been a fairy tale from ancient Greece, part of my own Odyssey. The sun's rays had found their way into my office. My dreams were revived. Life was here at my doorstep again!

I printed the stories from the web and read them over and over. They touched me. All my irritations drained away now that I had something new and exciting that attracted my interest. I found their fax number and wrote, "I would like to congratulate you on your success and wish you good luck in the future. If you're going past Gothenburg, you are welcome to visit me. If there is something I can contribute, it would bring me great joy."

Three days later, a man who called himself the sponsorship manager for Ljungskile SK phoned. He had received my fax and wondered if I wanted to sponsor the club. He sounded dry and grey. I could picture him in front of me, a middle-aged man who rarely met people and lacked basic communication skills. I was bothered by his colourless manner on the phone. And they'd put him in charge of inspiring people to invest in the organization?

I replied that I had not thought that far. I tried to be diplomatic without showing my disappointment. He probably thought I was strange, writing to the club to offer my support, and then saying I didn't know if I wanted to. I guess I hadn't been clear, but it's weird how money always complicates life. Sponsorship means nothing to me. I see no value in it as marketing. Who cares what brand name is on a football player's chest? What you care about are the game, the results, the win or the loss.

The next day, a sponsorship package arrived in the mail. Totally uninteresting; it went into the rubbish. That evening I saw a report on the sports news about the club. I once again recognized what had filled me with brightness earlier in the week. They had done with their limited means what no one thought possible. It reminded me of when I came to Sweden and started working my way up. I knew how it felt to be constantly opposed, not get any bank loans, and find that no one believed in your ideas. I had managed to get here against all odds, and now I wanted to help others in the same situation.

A couple of days later, the sad sponsorship manager called again, trying to book a meeting. Despite my previous negativity, I agreed to meet them.

Two powerfully built gentlemen at the upper end of middle age arrived right on time. Which was the boring one who'd been so cold on the phone, I wondered? Neither appeared to be him. They actually both had a spark of personality and didn't seem nervous about meeting me. They were calm and spoke simply. They asked about my business and wanted to know who I was. They told me that my fax had not gone directly to the club, but apparently came through to a company in Ljungskile. Hence, the three-day delay in them following up with me.

The conversation became more interesting, and lasted longer than usual for me. The two had made a good impression. One was a visionary, free of the usual Swedish social hang-ups. The other was more considered, and listened intently.

They asked what the next steps were, but I explained that I saw no benefit in being the club's main sponsor.

The visionary, Bosse Fagerberg, was not happy with my answer. They changed their approach and focused on what I could do for the club. They talked about its future and the need to bring professionals on board, to move it forward. The whole discussion was now about the future and not about my sponsorship. I liked that. After getting to know these gentlemen a bit more, I felt they were genuine.

At the second meeting, we left the sponsorship talk behind and went more deeply into the idea of cooperation at a higher level. We talked about a personal commitment. When more facts came to light about the club's finances and achievements, and the business community's apathy about sponsoring it, I began to question myself. Why would such a club need to advertise for sponsors to survive? Why did they not want to sponsor such a success? Were they worried that the club would somehow drag them under overnight?

I became even more interested and read everything I could find. I realized that without an immediate lifeline, the history-making, which had done the impossible, could soon disappear. They needed money, and a lot of it.

The rebuilding of Skarsjövallen, Ljungskile's home arena, was happening in the midst of all this, and the work would soon grind to a halt without an infusion of cash. The team might never get to play in the premier league, and face these great teams they'd long dreamed of challenging.

I had learned through my company that, in business, money is everything. You will get nowhere if you cannot pay your suppliers, and no one will lend you any money if you can't provide complete security for the creditor. Not if you are small and honest.

Among my meetings with the club's representatives, they told me about another sponsor who would soon give his answer. Could I do something great for the club alongside him? He was bigger and stronger financially, but my name could draw audiences, additional sponsors and the media. The other sponsor knew how sports clubs worked, and the club had high hopes that he would eventually pitch in.

I decided not to view the possible investment in LSK as advertising. It had to be something that I wanted to do on a personal level, that would give me inner satisfaction and add a little colour to my life.

When I told my close friends, no one was positive about the idea. "It's too much money." "You don't have time to do it." "Think of your family, and your children, who don't know what you look like because you already work so hard." "How can you make time for that?" "It will be a money pit."

Deep down, though, I had made up my mind. It was like when someone advises you to stop liking a person because he or she is 'not the right one.' What happens? There's a chance you will like that person even more. Sometimes you even want to force it, to prove a point.

I can tune out the emotional static in dealing with things, given my long, often challenging life experience, and I can see things from many different points of view. As has so often happened, a series of coincidences led me to a decision. I didn't know if it was right or wrong. Maybe I could have invested the money in something else that created greater international interest, and ultimately made me happier. You can always speculate.

I slept little for the next two nights, but I was alert and in a positive frame of mind. The days were getting darker outside, but I did not notice. I called my legal adviser, who also sat on the board of my company.

"Well," he said, "have you thoroughly thought this through? Are you sure about what you're getting yourself into?"

"Yes. Let's make an appointment for us to arrange all the formalities," I told him.

I took a stand, and made my decision, and felt a great sense of relief. I'd also decided how I would respond to everyone's questions: it's my money, and I have the right to decide what it will be used for. I can afford to have an expensive extravagance once in a while. All I do is work; I don't have time to spend my money. It does no good sitting there as numbers in a bank statement. I wanted something else to think about, other than my work — something I sincerely wanted to care about.

There was a lot to think about after I'd decided to go in as the main sponsor, and many problems to solve. One dilemma was that a bank already had its logo across the chest on the players' shirts, but my top-line sponsorship would give me this space.

I explained that I would buy out the bank's commitment if they were not willing to renegotiate. The club's bank then learned of my involvement, and there was a leak to the press.

Journalists called in from all over the country. We were not prepared for such an onslaught. Tv and the papers presented their own speculative versions of what was happening, and it was not overwhelmingly positive. The most critical voices had not even attempted to contact the club or me.

And then, some of the club's board appeared in Tv interviews. I was disappointed, but I understood. As Andy Warhol said, "In the future, everyone will be world-famous for 15 minutes." The people of Ljungskile were now getting their 15 minutes, and most seemed to enjoy the attention. Their small town was on everyone's lips. The speculation became wilder, and out of fear that it would harm my company I scheduled a press conference for the next day. I hoped that I'd get someone from the club to state the facts and help set the record straight.

My legal adviser told me, "Do what feels good to you. Do as Panos always does!" The press conference would be characterized by my way of dealing with my fellow human beings. Do things the way I would like to be treated — that was my philosophy. That's why I'd always hated the notion of 'business as usual.' I do not recognize myself in such a cliché.

We would hold the press conference on our home turf, a complex that housed Panos Emporio and other labels. For the first time, we would host Sweden's leading sports journalists. I would give them the facts, since they didn't know anything about us. "Let them see who we are," I told my team. "Get started, and then make it a party." You do that before a wedding, right? And in a way, that's what this was. Dress in white clothes, set out some food and drink, play music in the background, and deliver some prepared remarks about the bride and groom.

"Decorate the whole house so that they feel welcome," I said. "Up with the Swedish flag, and put my giant Greek pillars around the entrance." The property owner agreed to everything.

At the appointed time, the reporters strolled in, one by one. They walked around, staring at everything suspiciously. I had gone all out on the refreshments, but most refused to take a cup of coffee or a sandwich, seemingly afraid that it could be perceived as bribery.

Someone from the press corps muttered that this luxury had nothing to do with football. This wound up in a number of newspapers, along with how the white marble in my showroom was at odds with the down-to-earth football culture. The most interesting point for them seemed to be how much money was involved.

The coverage was cynical, and I was furious. The reporter from TV4 tried to get a reaction from the people of Ljungskile. At a sausage kiosk, he asked, "Can I have a Panos with bread, please?" The man had no idea what he was talking about, and seemed embarrassed. "What would you say if your guys played in bikinis?" another sports reporter asked a group of retirees.

A really dirty smear campaign dominated the media in the weeks leading up to the football club's annual meeting. The Gothenburg and Stockholm papers were the ones that most clearly showed their disapproval.

Despite all the hostility, the "underwear salesman," as they called me, refused to sink to their level.

I decided that if there wasn't a unanimous vote of support at the meeting, I would decline the naming rights proposal and still fulfil my financial commitments. I did not want the club to suffer. I was personally proud enough to accept a defeat. It was not about prestige, it was about true love for the club.

I'm used to talking to large groups of people, but was extremely nervous the day of the big meeting. The media had made me a villain, a tyrant, a rich guy buying his way in. As I walked through the crowd, I dared not look people in the eye.

I felt a pat on my shoulder. It was an elderly man who wanted to show the press clippings he had collected in recent weeks. I did not know what to say.

I looked around. There were around 60 attendees, of all ages. That was exactly what I had wanted to see. Sport has no age. The room felt warm for the middle of the cold winter. Most people's eyes were on me. Many wanted eye contact and gave modest smiles. Some raised their hands in a gesture of victory. I felt calmer. Was it possible that people liked me? It seemed so. Maybe I was not the terrible monster I'd been made out to be, after all. The atmosphere calmed me down and I got a sense that things would work out just fine.

The meeting went quickly, with a unanimous decision that I would get naming rights, with the team henceforth being known as Panos Ljungskile. I would also be given a board seat.

Where were all the dissenters the media said would be there? *Göteborgs-Posten*'s columnist had said that the club had "sold its soul." The great irony is that the newspaper had received help from Panos Emporio on an award for sporting achievement. We had concluded a deal with the swimmer Louise Karlsson, and the paper had named her "Sports Achiever of the Year," without a single word about our collaboration with her.

The next day, I searched the news for coverage of the meeting. I dreamed of being able to read, "Panos unanimously elected to the board." It would have been wonderful to see, "Panos Ljungskile is the new name, selected after a unanimous annual meeting vote." I searched for something — anything — along the lines of, "We wish the club and the new sponsor good luck." I could find nothing of the sort. I had been naïve. They would continue to bully us, and instead of wishing the 'couple' good luck, we would be punished. It seemed that a poor foreign boy who became rich should not flirt with Sweden's sports life, and must pay a high price.

WE HAD SEEN UPSIDE POSSIBILITIES for both partners. The club would have a stronger position with suppliers and other sponsors. They could look for new players and attract a greater audience. They would have access to an innovative entrepreneur and become more businesslike.

One media outlet wrote, "Panos bought into the board." That was maybe partly true, but not entirely. The media were obsessed with my board seat, suggesting that I'd forced myself in. No one admired my courage for joining a heavily indebted association to turn it around. No one talked about the risks I took. No one wrote that I would do this without compensation.

I had spelled out certain requirements when I joined the club. I wanted the board seat, and an additional seat for a person I would appoint. I wanted to be able to influence things. I was not there as a decoration.

This took all my time and energy. I went to Ljungskile every week, sometimes several times a week, driving an hour or so each way. I rearranged everything to fit my own business trips in around the club's board meetings.

The unwarranted personal attacks on me only made the Swedish people more interested. They could see the benefits and praised my courage in investing and helping the small club. All sorts of people, including those not interested in football, wanted to follow its developments.

The train service changed the name of the small community's stop from Ljungskile to Panos Ljungskile. Passengers heard the conductor exclaim, "Next stop, Panos Ljungskile!" Many residents of Ljungskile work in Gothenburg, and excitedly told their colleagues about what was happening. From what I was told, there were many positive comments on the name change.

Not that that mattered to the press. For instance, this appeared in a paper in Borås on 1 February 1997: "There is a discussion going on about letting Ljungskile leave Uddevalla to form its own municipality. Perhaps a swimsuit could adorn the new municipal coat of arms."

I HAD a personalized number plate on my car, and when I was out driving, people honked and waved, and some flashed victory signs. Others stopped me in the middle of the street to thank me. People wanted to talk to me, and they wondered why the media was so hostile.

And yes, there were those who disapproved. "I do not want to buy your fucking swimwear to sponsor Ljungskile!" an angry retailer exclaimed. How can you hate someone who has helped in sports? That retailer was excluded from our register.

Another questioned my mental health. "Your boss isn't too wise, is he?" one person said to one of my employees. "Why doesn't he give that money to his staff instead?" The strange thing is that the guy had children who were active in sports.

One of my sales representatives met with enormous resistance in an area in Bohuslän. "We will lose a lot of customers," he said. "They don't like it at all."

My response was resolute. "I'll cover anything you lose," I told him, because he made commission on his sales. "Keep me informed about who gives you trouble because of this." I didn't want to sell to those people anyway.

I do not make products to make money. I put my soul into my designs, and get a lot of personal satisfaction from it. My profit comes when people wait for months for a new collection; when someone wants to wear a Panos garment. They love my way of shaping a product. It makes them feel good. They want to be associated with me, and I with them.

As the backlash continued, I was bewildered that this kind of hatred would exist. I'm naïve, childish perhaps. I treat myself to the luxury of being childish. Children cannot hate and be suspicious. I want to be like that.

WEEKS AFTER THE ANNOUNCEMENT, I was at a restaurant with a friend at Stureplan, a plaza in central Stockholm. Many celebrities were there, but my friend mentioned that we were receiving better treatment, than the others. I hadn't noticed. I was there to meet a potential sponsor for the football club. He was a wealthy, upper-class figure, and I was mentally going through my pitch.

I had carefully planned what we would offer. Not many people would donate thousands of kronor without getting something back, so this had to be good. Time passed, and the person did not show.

I motioned to our waiter. "The bill, please," I said dryly.

"It's on the house," he replied, "and we want to take this opportunity to wish you good luck with your club."

You can imagine my surprise. We were at a restaurant frequented by VIPs. And I had become a rather controversial figure of late. "This is courtesy of my boss ... and by the way, his wife wants you to know that she thinks you're a great designer."

Well, that was nice!

I made a follow-up appointment to see the man who'd skipped our meeting. I was welcomed by an intelligent, well-dressed gentleman —

clearly the type who drank expensive wine, smoked fine cigars and ate with different kinds of cutlery. In other words, he was the exact opposite of me.

The discussion started gently enough, but he quickly explained his disinterest. He had promised to sponsor a different football club, IFK Gothenburg, and they in turn would help him obtain various permits via the Municipality of Gothenburg to build a hotel. Ljungskile would be an obstacle.

I decided there was no point continuing. I have a hard time with such people. He knew why we had come — after standing us up at the restaurant — and that we'd travelled from Gothenburg. This was an insult. I thanked him and left, disappointed with myself. Why did I listen to the person who'd persuaded me that there was a saint in Stockholm ready to give hundreds of thousands to the club? Do not expect others to solve your problems. Each individual is responsible for his or her own life. As my parents had always said!

I TRIED TO RUN a fundraising gala, and hired the hottest artists at the time, to attract the widest audience possible: Lill-Babs (born Barbro Svensson) for the older fans, Dr Alban, who had not performed in Sweden for a while, and Martin for the youngsters. Barbro arrived with a bad cold and a hoarse voice. When I met her at the airport, and heard her, she could see the worry on my face. She tried to comfort me by saying, "Everything will go well."

On the day of the gala, the rain poured all morning, and I was hoping for a reprieve by the time the concert began at 5 PM.

Each performer did their sound check and I welled up with tears of gratitude that Sweden's top artists wanted to help me out. Barbro wasn't even interested in football, but she loved life. During her sound check, she spotted a man in a wheelchair and ran off-stage to guide him to another drier spot. Then she ran back up on stage as though nothing had happened. "Where are the others in this world who have such a big heart?" I wondered.

The rain did not ease up. Lill-Babs opened the show, and braved the rain. I looked at the audience, and there were 50 people at best. What a defeat, presenting Sweden's greatest artists for 50 people. A handful of others had gathered outside the fence, to listen without paying.

Barbro hugged me afterward and whispered, "This is nothing to worry about." But I became very angry with myself. The artists had volunteered their time and I had exposed them to such an embarrassing situation. To this day I am so thankful to each of them, especially Barbro, who is no longer with us.

SPORTS ARE CLOSE to my heart. And I like to win. I can't even play with my children because I have to win. A few days before LSK's first home game, I had a feeling we would win. It would be a gift to our fans.

A record audience was expected at Skarsjövallen, the local stadium. I had already printed a T-shirt that said, "Panos v. Press, 1–0." How sweet a victory it would be when the writers who had condemned my team and me were forced to report positively on it.

Some journalists had begun to wake up. They saw my commitment and my feelings. On a few occasions, they actually mentioned their surprise at all the criticism. Some female journalists said that this was how toxic things get when men dominate sports journalism.

On the day of the match, the sun shone and the people on the streets of Gothenburg seemed to be in a summer mood, but it was no more than 8°C (46°F) outside. I sat at a café on Avenyn, the main boulevard, with the Graaf sisters, two glamorous Swedish models who were fairly unknown at this point.

Soon it was time to leave for Ljungskile, where we'd be playing IFK Gothenburg. We were the underdog, but I'd planned a victory party for that evening. My companions would wear brightly coloured clothing from my 24 *Hours* collection to the match, Hannah in orange and Magdalena in yellow.

I did not even have time to park the car before everyone's eyes were on us. An older man cheered me on with a big smile as we stepped from the vehicle, which was enough for me to let go of my worries.

The sisters walked half a step behind me, as I had asked, and kept their eyes around my aura. They would not greet anyone. If I stopped, they stopped. If I started walking, they would start at the same pace.

We decided to walk from the VIP parking lot to the clubhouse through the press room. In the meantime, we would chat with each other to avoid people who wanted to exchange a few words.

All eyes were on the Graaf sisters, who created a buzz. Men and women, old and young, stopped cold and stared at them. People appeared on the left and right saying hello, trying to take my hand and cheering us on. When we got to the clubhouse, I tried to take the back door, so we wouldn't have to pass our players. If we lost, maybe someone would surely blame it on the sisters for distracting them!

We sat down for a few minutes, and then decided to continue on. This time, I told them we'd put a little strut in our step and dial up the energy level.

Into the press room, and all movement stopped. One guy almost dropped his camera, fumbling with it like a hot potato. Mouths gaped and eyes widened. I saw one journalist dribble coffee down his chin.

You could have heard a pin drop. We exchanged a few polite words, I gave them a wave and my gorgeous escorts followed me out.

WE WENT to the VIP stand and watched our guys warming up. People took out their cameras and tried to secretly take pictures of us. I could register their great pleasure, and pride, that their poor club in the middle of the forest had such prominent guests. **"Poverty is not shameful," my parents used to say. "It is shameful to sit with your hands crossed and complain. As long as you have hands you can influence everything. You can shape what you want, in your way."**

I was so focused on the match that I all but forgot about Magdalena on my left and Hannah on my right. They sometimes leaned in and asked why the referee always blew in the opposing team's favour.

"It's always like that," I explained. "Those who are already strong have the referee on their side. We must try to forget it and make sure we can score an extra goal to win the match. We're playing against 14 and we are only 11."

I realized that we had the match under control and IFK would leave Ljungskile without a win. The photographers should have had a lot to do with the action on the field, but most of their time was spent looking at the sisters.

During half-time, we did our walk again. In through the press room and out again.

This time some people had gathered around the front door and I met their gaze.

"*Gia sou!*" shouted one in Greek. (Hi!)

Those sisters could make people speak different languages!

I thought about Greek mythology and its stories about women. Without women, our lives, or at least my life, would have been meaningless. Two beautiful women could change the whole atmosphere in a second, and could spread so much joy and energy. Onassis was right.

The match was exciting and eventful. There were several goals. We won, but the referee gave it to IFK.

I had won the attention of the journalists, and with the sisters, I was able to control that. I also won the admiration of the people. They were pleased that I had two beautiful women with me. No one misinterpreted my motives, and many joked about it for a long time afterwards. We had something there that day that our opponents could not offer. We were unique in many ways.

WHEN IT CAME to the second round of the league, I thought about banning all journalists who would not use the team's correct name: Panos Ljungskile SK from Skarsjövallen. However, my board was cautious, and felt that could harm the brand. In hindsight, I should have done it, to start a debate on journalistic ethics.

The sports media had ridiculous excuses for why they wouldn't comply. *Expressen*'s sports director said that they followed 'popular speech' and the team was called Ljungskile. But why did they not identify all teams by the same criterion, and publish tables referencing *Bajen, Blåvitt, Makrillarna* and *Gnaget*? Other sports managers promised to investigate, but never followed up. The state TV channels also ignored it. Tv4's teletext editorial staff were the first to be consistent in using the real name, but only in teletext, not on the broadcast channel. It seemed that the real name was only used when it came to something negative, in headlines like, "Panos Ljungskile lose big!" Another printed, "Panos's financial problems." In the same paper, on another occasion: "Ljungskile had a cannonball match!" How curious that the same media were also quite happy to offer up positive, gushing coverage of sponsored events like the Scania Stockholm Open. They were controlled by giant corporations that the press didn't dare offend.

Every time the media were negative, my phone went white-hot. People famous and unknown wanted to offer me their support.

The straw that broke the camel's back was when Sveriges Television's *Västnytt* news programme made a montage of the club's brand with the headline, "Panos Emporio Ljungskile in economic crisis." Here was a television channel financed by our taxes, deliberately linking the Panos Emporio name to fake, negative news, to harm the company.

My employees tried to get access to material from *Västnytt*. The terse answer came from acting editor-in-chief Yngve Hansson: "We have no obligation to disclose statistics and do not intend to do so either ... and thus I consider the correspondence on this issue closed."

We referred them to the broadcasters' review board. The answer we received: "There was no reason to investigate in particular whether

Panos Ljungskile sk was linked to negative news stories, and Ljungskile sk to positive ones, by the *Västnytt* editorial staff." They also stated that the photomontage was in accordance with "the minimum requirements set out in the Radio and Television Act." My first reaction was to want to buy billboards all over Sweden to reveal Sveriges Television's abuse of power. I didn't, and after a while I calmed down.

The more they attacked, the more public interest grew. Some people, even a few associations in the Allsvenskan league, wanted to change their name to Panos, in solidarity. There were actually teams in other regions that wanted to do the same. I could have allowed two football clubs to change their names in 1997. So much for those PR experts who said I wouldn't get publicity. What would the directors of the multinational giants say about all that to their marketing managers?

I HAD BEEN MARRIED for about four months at this point, and the home phone rang one Wednesday at 1:20 AM.

"Am I disturbing you?" came the male voice.

"What do you mean, are you disturbing me? It's the middle of the night. What do you want?"

"I work in *Aftonbladet*'s sports editorial office, and we've received information that you have left Ljungskile."

"I've no idea what you're talking about."

"Are you still a sponsor at Ljungskile?"

"No. I do not know of any club called that."

The line went quiet. I simply wasn't going to respond if he insisted on getting the name of the team wrong. He mumbled a little, and then returned with, "Is your name Panos Papadoplos?"

Again, the ignorant insistence on getting my name wrong. What was it with these people?

"No, that's not my name. My name is Panos Papadopoulos, and my club is called Panos Ljungskile. What's this about?"

"I've received information that you are resigning as a sponsor," he said.

I denied it, but he repeated the rumour, pressing me for confirmation. I got annoyed, telling him it was rude to disturb us in the middle of the night. What was the reason for this? The answer was simple: it was a slow news day. Panos made for good copy. That was it. This was not the first time. Sometimes they had already decided what to write anyway, regardless of what I told them. When there's a lack of real news, they put ethics aside and resort to making things up.

IN BANGKOK, Sweden's King of Swimwear would have his first major fashion show in Asia. The interest was enormous, and journalists from all over Asia would be in attendance. A fashion company from the small, cold country had in a short time conquered the Thai market, becoming the most popular swimwear brand there.

Big names were on the VIP list, among them Princess Kokaew of Thailand. The Swedish ambassador, together with some of the Swedish companies in the region, knew how important this was for the country's image. A dozen TV stations covered the event, along with 95 active journalists and 60 photographers. Giant Greek pillars had been produced by Thai craftsmen with great care, fabrics and colours were specially developed, and the catwalk had been built according to my drawings, faxed from Sweden. Everything was in place.

Oddly enough, while there in that exotic tropical locale, I missed my countrymen from that cold, elongated land that extended above the Arctic Circle. Yes, there were a few Swedes there, but I truly missed the company of the Swedish people. I asked my Thai PR manager just before the show why there didn't seem to be any Swedish photographers or journalists present.

"They will come," he assured me. "The Swedish media have representatives here in town."

"But why aren't they here?"

He avoided answering my questions, diplomatically replying that he did not know.

"If you don't know something like that, as my PR lead, you won't be working for me."

He looked shaken. "There's just so much pressure," he said.

I took his arm and asked the question again: "Where are the Swedish media?"

"I do not know," he repeated. I could see in his eyes that he was lying.

The show began. The spotlight went on my two naked, live human statues, wearing body paint, in their role as Greek gods. The music began to play slowly and the Swedish ambassador made his way to the catwalk to give a speech.

The spotlights were aimed toward us, and I thought they were focused on the princess sitting next to me. The ambassador said something and the light was back on me again. My tears of disappointment over the Swedish press's absence were impossible to hold back. Soon, I would have to go behind the scenes to inspire and lead the show. But the inspiration never came.

Twenty-five minutes later it was all over, but I kept looking through the crowd to see if the Swedish media were there. "I'm not here doing this just for me," I thought. "I'm doing this for all of us." I felt completely deflated.

Afterwards, we headed to Bangkok's most popular nightclub with some famous people. Finnish MTV followed the entire evening and covered the scene inside the club. Everyone was in a partying mood ... except me.

I cornered my PR manager outside the restrooms and pressed him to tell me what he knew. I shouted at him to tell me the truth, becoming really angry, and he knew he could no longer lie.

"When the news reached a couple of evening papers in Sweden, the interest was huge, but when they heard who was running the fashion show, they said, 'No, not him again.'"

So, it had come to that.

AFTER HALF THE SEASON, PLSK were not doing well, and the odds were that we would leave the Allsvenskan. Despite all the fanfare, energy and optimism, we just weren't cutting it in the big league. I had to block out all the turbulence and chatter and do what I had to do.

During the summer holidays, the first thing was to get a sponsor for just over 150,000kr to finance personality tests for all my players and coaches. I wanted to know their strengths and weaknesses. I had a hard time understanding how sports clubs bought players for hundreds of thousands, or even millions, without any real knowledge of whether they'd fit in with the team.

If you could handle each player in the way best suited to him, you could deal with his shortcomings with the right training and guidance. The ancient Greeks said, "Physical and mental strength are intertwined."

I persuaded the head coach that we could do the tests en route to an away match in Örebro. We had a number of foreign players, and I arranged tests in different languages. The atmosphere was quite good in the bus as they filled in the test. However, when the tests were collected, we found that some had not filled theirs in. I did not say anything. I didn't want to create any overt hostility.

The coaches completed their tests a few days later, as did the masseur and everyone else who had contact with the players.

In Örebro that afternoon, I could see how a player with poor self-confidence made a bad penalty kick. We had a striker with fear of attacking. There was a defender who didn't dare to look a striker in the eye, and an insecure goalkeeper. I read the sports journalists' comments about which player was the best. Many times, I had a totally different opinion. I counted how many mistakes one of our key midfielders made during a match we lost. It turned out to be over 70%, yet all the newspapers gave him the highest rating.

The coach should have seen this. Some players were afraid to move and signalled that they wanted the ball. They were forever second on the ball, so insecure were they on the field.

Yet, they could be two metres tall when they met big teams like IFK Gothenburg or Halmstad. They outclassed both of them at home. They had shown that they could play and achieve results. Still, the press kept telling them how inadequate they were.

We did not place in the Allsvenskan.

Human resources are governed by three factors, especially in sports. They are all about *emotions, thinking* and *energy*. These were the elements I wanted to work with, and I tried to get those responsible to pay extra attention to them.

If you are constantly told how incompetent, clumsy and useless you are, how does it feel? When the newspapers were most critical, we reacted by retreating into our shell. I noticed that we lacked vision, and that our goals were set too low. Low goals yield low results — worse than you deserve or are capable of. With more losses, our self-confidence dropped. We had team spirit as we rose up the tables, but it dissipated once we got to the Allsvenskan.

The consulting company that sponsored these tests was willing to send their specialist to Ljungskile for two days, to meet each player. They would present the results and provide useful direction on how to change behaviours.

The test could predict how each player would act. You could see which were powered by high-octane petrol and which by diesel. The diesel-powered were energy-killers. They slowed the pace and pulled everyone down with them. This is why a coach has to act fast and replace a player who isn't in the best shape.

The results shocked many. They couldn't acknowledge what was really going on under the covers. Most were aware of their shortcomings, but some didn't even want to know their test results. They were the weakest individuals, who were performing unevenly.

Those under pressure either escape and show aggression (where the yellow and red cards come into the picture), or display offensive behaviour without outright aggression. The players with the most red cards did not want to take the test. They didn't acknowledge the problems, and if they did, they believed they definitely weren't theirs. Others with obvious problems would not take the test. What employer would accept such defiant behaviour from their employees?

After the review, some players, and especially the coaches, were very positive. They thought this was exciting and educational. But most did not realize the serious side of what we were going through. Many still believed the garbage the press had written about them. How can you win when you have that attitude? It permeated almost the entire team. No company could survive if they started every morning believing that nothing worked.

I tried to make everyone understand it was time to act. I'd concluded that the head coach must leave. To most associated with the club, this was unthinkable. It would be the scandal of the year. For them, it was easier to accept their incompetence than change. They closed their eyes and hoped that the other teams would not succeed.

Of course, it doesn't work that way. You waste your energy hoping that others fail. This kind of thinking is strongly rooted in the business world. Some of my competitors did nothing but watch me and hope that I would fail. My failure would give them a chance to survive. Imagine if they had instead invested all that energy in getting better at what they did. The winner wins by their own steam, and nothing else.

In hindsight, I should have been much tougher on the board. The club could have survived in the Allsvenskan professional league.

They had appointed a coach, Bo Wålemark, who had been the soul of the team and helped them on the fabulous journey to the Allsvenskan. He's the only Swedish footballer to have played in every division for the same team. I was against his appointment when I realized there were difficulties very early on. But how could I say no when literally everyone — the organization, the public — wanted it that way? "It is the will of the people!" I was told.

Unfortunately, a number of problems began to plague the club after they left the Allsvenskan. Financial issues from the arena's construction haunted management. Much of our energy went into finding temporary solutions. My great personal interest in football diminished as the soul-killing administrative work occupied my every waking hour and darkened my dreams.

I still hoped we would make a comeback. That gave me strength. I'd call from Paris to Ljungskile, checking on club business. I was up late at night following the matches from China. The bad results did not break my will, but the results were very bad indeed.

I began to realize that we had constructed the team the wrong way. Management's feelings and traditions took precedence over the team's best interests. I took advantage of my chairmanship and pushed the coaching issue again. Most gave a resounding "No" immediately. There were endless excuses. "He has meant so much to the team and the whole community." "Our other sponsors will drop out." "We just can't do such a thing." "It will be a scandal!"

This time, I was not in the mood for an argument. The goal was for my team to emerge a winner. There was only one solution: to win the series and return to the Allsvenskan. I couldn't cope with more sleepless nights. My family could no longer put up with my bad mood after each match. My children watched the matches and braced for my return home. We'd lose, and nobody said anything. They silently avoided me.

I decided to resign as chairman. I would still continue my commitment to the club, but I could no longer be that figurehead for them.

It reminded me again of *Zorba*, when the beautiful widow is slaughtered in front of her fellow villagers because no one dared stand up for what was right, fearing what others might think. I went home and watched the movie twice. I had now seen it 23 times. It gave me the resolve to leave the board. I like to build things with my own hands, but when someone ties my hands, rendering me powerless to make good things happen, I can no longer be with them.

The weeks rolled by, with one bad match after another. By now everyone realized that something had to be done. I called a meeting with the squad, and then the board.

The solution I proposed was to keep the current coach on the field while we worked on finding his replacement. "It's not possible," they said. "There's going to be a scandal."

I could not imagine what could be more scandalous than continuing on with this losing proposition, and disappointing our fans again and again, with no end.

"You asked me to solve this," I replied. "Why do you refuse to understand that you have to make a change to give new life to the team?"

I asked the board to let me take care of everything. There were not many matches left. We quickly found a new coach, and the old one accepted this without any pushback. He loved the team more than anything, and they needed him on the field. He was a leader. What team could survive without a leader?

As it turned out, everyone was happy with this change: sponsors, the audience, the team, and most of Sweden. What a comeback we mounted! The whole team shone. They were lively and full of energy through the remaining six matches; we didn't lose a single one! The results spoke more loudly than any fears of 'disruption' or 'scandal' the board may have had.

We all experience this phenomenon, avoiding change because we fear how others might react. Or, we're convinced that we ourselves might be the obstacle.

THE COACHING QUESTION came up again in the autumn of 2000. I realized in the first few matches that something was not right. I didn't sense the right attitude, even though we enjoyed a few initial successes on the field. The wins were down to coincidence, I thought. I pointed out what I thought was wrong, but again no one listened. I said they needed a new coach. The team now lost several consecutive matches. They struggled even against the worst squads in the series. I questioned the coach's tactics. Some players, who left a lot to be desired, remained, making the same mistakes game after game.

With two matches left, supporters called and wrote to express their disappointment. Why did I not do anything? It was painful to know that I had tried, but couldn't do what was necessary … yet the fans thought I had the power.

By the time the board asked me to talk to the coach and the team, I could see that the series was lost. I saw that the players had the wrong attitude, and there were no clear big-picture goals. They offered weak excuses. "We always have a hard time against Gunnilse," I was told, regarding a club from suburban Gothenburg. What do you mean you have a hard time, I wondered? Aren't they the same players and coaches you meet every time? Can't you figure out their weaknesses, play to your own strengths and send them packing?

We lacked a few good players in midfield, but we didn't acquire new talent. The club's proud visionary, Bosse Fagerberg, worked frantically and found several hot prospects. However, the board was close to a financial settlement with the municipality, and was hesitant to make changes. They were afraid that it would appear they'd bought new players with the municipality's support. I intervened and promised that I'd bear the full cost of the new players, because we absolutely needed them. Ideally, I would have liked to combine this with a change of coach, for maximum effect.

The answer was a resounding no. Settlement with the municipality took precedence.

They wouldn't believe me when I argued that we'd drop to the Super-ettan, a level down in the league system, if we did nothing. And then it happened: the team dropped to the second division. Management had taken the easiest path, for fear of having a difficult discussion and actually doing what needed to be done. And this was the unfortunate outcome.

THE EXPERIENCE highlighted what was wrong with so many organiza-tions and our news media. The disease was not confined to the old guard in Sweden's sports establishment. You see it play out around the world, in the tabloid press and privately-owned media. Clickbait for headlines. Speculation reported as fact. Opinion masquerading as authority. Pay-to-play coverage. All this, and worse, for the sake of a few more readers. To hell with truth, ethics or reputation.

The public, however, can often see the heart that goes into something, when it comes from a decent, hard-working individual. The attacks only served to enhance my reputation. My deeds touched the hearts of a lot of people and became deeply rooted in them. I had real feelings, and they sensed that.

I had invested my hard-earned money, made from honest work, to benefit one of Sweden's most loved sports. The team was worth it. They needed it, and while it didn't prove to be enough, my support extended their success for a little longer. If I were in the media's shoes, I would wel-come any positive, action-oriented example for our youth. **People should travel their own path and challenge the establishment.** Yet, I have the distinct impression that so many despise new thinking, and wish for nothing new to flourish. They are the face of cowardice and apathy in today's society. Some, like the young Swedish climate activist Greta Thun-berg, break free of this insistence that we all conform, and we're all clearly richer for it.

9
Marketing outside the square

In 1998, it was time for my own birthday celebration. I was about to turn 40, and had amassed a gigantic network that included big personalities, public figures and celebrities. I wanted to gather them together and show them a good time. A really good time!

I began planning a big party in Stockholm's trendiest place, La Villa, to be followed by another party in Gothenburg that would be more private. Rumours quickly spread that I was planning a party and several event organizers offered their services. I wanted to throw a five-star blowout that no one would forget. It was a unique opportunity to strengthen the brand and cement the success I'd enjoyed since the beginning of the '90s.

I gave the assignment to a popular Greek party fixer, Christos Neo. He listened carefully to my wishes and accepted that I would be the creative soul in that project. I was exacting about what the surroundings would look like, how the food would taste, what music would be played and how the guests would mix. Above all, we would set the bar high, to attract exclusive guests who didn't usually make an appearance. I wanted my party to be teeming with the hottest personalities of the moment.

Certain celebrities were commodities who would surface and disappear. They'd make a splash on various TV programmes, but it seemed that very few managed to remain in the limelight for more than a few months. Christos was a very creative personality, and absolutely fearless. He loved setting high goals and never asked 'why' or 'how' in reaching for the stars. He came up with a great idea, based on my life story and journey. The invitation would look like a plane ticket. Back then, these were long, wide strips, comprising many pages, all placed into a travel folder. He worked up a guest list with utmost care and we went through it together.

Now it was time to send the invitations. This would be a way for me to measure how strong my name was. Will the best come? How much of the press would show up? Would they want to 'advertise' me with all the free publicity? The gossip press would obviously come, but mainstream TV news programmes, daily papers, fashion magazines — would they find it captivating enough to cover the event?

The chefs had made sample spreads of the food, so we could taste-test it before giving a go-ahead for the menu. I decided that spirits and wine should be complementary all evening. Often, at these parties, you got a couple of glasses in the first hour and had to pay for the rest yourself. They were luxurious parties, but in my eyes poorly executed when it came to the quality of the food and drinks. You were perhaps treated to a beer or two, a couple of glasses of wine, and if you asked for mineral water you would have to pay for it. There would be no such annoyances at my party. It would be luxury and *filoxenia* straight through, down to the smallest detail.

Three days before the party, we discovered that we'd received too many acceptances. That was a big problem. Who could we now not permit to come, after having invited them? Some important people said on the phone that they'd met someone at another party who claimed they were coming, even though their names were missing from the list, and now they people wanted to be there as well

Christos said that it was a good problem to have, and not to worry about it, since on the day of the event a certain number would be no-shows. He added that some would inevitably have scheduling conflicts, as the party would start at 6 PM, and it was in the middle of the week.

By 1 PM on the big day, Christos appeared stressed for the first time. Even those who we never thought would accept our invitation were sending in last-minute confirmation that they would come. We would be hosting the mayor, politicians, ministers, actors, TV presenters, and celebrities. I even caught wind of some 'secret guests' that Christos didn't want to reveal to me, because he was unsure that they'd come. "What do we do now?" he asked, worried about what would be an over-flow crowd, which would challenge our plans and supplies and ability to manage things. Nonetheless, he appeared happy that it had grown into such a big thing.

"Make sure we have food for everyone, and order extra wine and spir-its," I told him. "Everyone can fit. It's summer, and we're lucky with the weather. It'll all be fine, but we have to have food. I don't want to run out of anything." There was panic in the kitchen because they had to find ingredients to make extra food for several hundred people, just hours before the start.

"Let us see this as a great, positive challenge," I urged everyone. "This is the best thing that could have happened, to have all these respondents." I thought back to the benefit concert I'd hosted, when only a few dozen people had showed up. I'd rather have this problem, any day.

La Villa's managers also saw this as a fantastic thing, even though they were used to welcoming celebrities. My party was different — this was going to be *big*! The beverage suppliers struggled to get more wine, and the venue was frantically looking for more staff.

I saw the list of journalists who would be there. There were many good names, but I lacked television and newspapers. It was known that they usually came at the last minute if they had time to send someone.

"Now," Christos said, "we bring out our strong cards. I'm going to call the press and tell them the names of some of the guests."

He waited until 4 PM, and started calling the editors and revealing which guests would be arriving through the evening.

By 5:30, we had a long queue outside. We had to have security guards, but chose to have them dressed in plain clothes. At the door were some Greek girls and boys in folk costumes. Deep down, I remember having felt depressed as an immigrant, and wanted to remind everyone about my origins. Christos ran around, tending to all the details that had to be just right before we would let the guests in. He came up to me and said that a number of guests had brought suitcases, and wondered why that would be. "Do you know how many press photographers are out there waiting?" he added. The TV crews tried to get in earlier than the other journalists, but we would not let anyone through before 6 PM.

I saw my party planner's big smile as additional cases of food and wine arrived in the kitchen, as the crowd grew outside. We opened the doors at the appointed hour, and I stood and greeted everyone, one by one.

We soon learned why some had brought suitcases. They thought I was going to launch a new airline when they saw the plane ticket-style invitation, and had packed for a trip! As they were standing in line they started whispering that we'd probably be flying to Greece. Those who hadn't packed a change of clothes debated rushing home to grab a fresh pair of underwear!

We planned for a maximum of 450 people and ended up letting in more than 700. The Greek orchestra played while everyone mingled, laughed, ate and drank. We had to inform them that there was no trip planned; the final destination was right there at La Villa. Everybody laughed at that and assured us that they were glad to be there.

Some had prepared speeches, but we wouldn't be doing anything like that. The only remarks would be my welcoming them in the receiving line, telling everyone how glad I was that they'd come, and encouraging one and all to have a wonderful time.

Some TV channels reported live from the party that night, and the next day the papers all featured considerable coverage. In fact, they continued to run stories and photos for weeks!

The publicity was overwhelming, and the quality of the guests exceeded all expectations, compared to other A-list parties that drew international celebrities. What really set us apart was that many of the most lavish parties had lacked passion, good vibes and love. We had it all, and no one wanted to go home. One article described my 40th birthday party as the best "of all time." It became a point of reference — the bash that all subsequent parties would be measured against. Imagine that!

IN THE LATE 1990S, I received a call from a TV production company that wanted me to participate in something fun. At that time, Kristian Luuk was a very popular Swedish television personality. His talk show on TV4 was watched by millions. They wanted to show me in my office, and Kristian would show up wearing a woman's swimsuit, posing as a model looking for a job!

Of all the experiences I'd had in marketing, I couldn't think of anything that had been nearly that outrageous, clever and funny. Sweden's most famous and beloved TV presenter would do a free promotion for my brand and me, and everybody would be talking about it!

They asked if I had an office in Stockholm, where they were filming. I said I didn't. They suggested that we rent some office space there, and said they would organize everything.

I sat at 'my' desk like a typical Greek boss, looking very puffed up and self-important. Kristian walked in, and I could not stop laughing. We had to do it over and over, until finally I got my serious look and the taping was finished. It was a success, and people would never forget my 'surprised' look (on the tenth take!) when their favourite TV personality walked through the door in that women's bathing suit.

THE SYDNEY OLYMPICS of 2000 were the big event on that year's sporting calendar, and Therese Alshammar was Sweden's greatest swimmer of all time.

By this point, the Panos Emporio brand had become remarkably strong. It was barely 14 years old, firing on all cylinders, and ready to conquer the world. My marketing always went in its own direction, and at that point I was really just competing with myself! I continually wanted to surprise myself and push the boundaries in every way.

In the '90s, the advertising agencies were kings. Digital media had not yet become mainstream, and all marketing and advertising campaigns tended to go through them. Companies large and small had few other options but to hire ad agencies for this work; it was unrealistic for them to think about doing it all themselves. It was hard to find the right skills to do any of that in-house, so everyone paid the agencies big bucks, even if the results left something to be desired. The agencies had huge budgets, bloated staffs, luxurious offices and enormous egos. This made me want to do something that would outflank them.

I believed that if you dared to create your own marketing philosophy, and act on it, you would be differentiated from everyone else.

By this point, I felt I had done almost all I could have dreamed of in marketing. I started to get tired of where we were, and wanted to challenge myself with bigger dreams. To me, it had become a game. That's probably why I didn't use all these ideas in the right way, to make more money or grow the brand. At the time, I didn't realize how much influence I actually had.

Some of our retailers had wanted us to make a collection for Sweden's Olympic swimming team. I refused. Back then, I used to say that I created fashion, not 'work clothes.'

As the games approached, I had my eye on the different swimmers who'd qualified to go to Sydney. One in particular caught my attention: Therese Alshammar.

Therese was an excellent swimmer, and a very cool person, with a nice media personality. She was one of Sweden's great hopes in the Sydney Olympics. I began wondering if I could change her last name from Alshammar to Panos Emporio. That may sound strange, but imagine how it would look on international scoreboards when Therese won!

I didn't have to think for long before deciding that I would find a way to make it so. The same day, I called my business lawyer and asked him to come up with a contract proposal. He went very quiet on the phone. After a long minute, he said, "Have you taken leave of your senses? This can create huge problems for you and your brand. The people of Sweden will not like it, and what happens when everyone gets annoyed at you for doing this?"

I interrupted him. "That's enough! Prepare a draft so I can present it to her, and leave the money amount blank. I'll decide on that during negotiations."

I found Therese's cell phone number and called her directly. She was in Germany, at a training camp for the Olympics, and she would be there for a long time. I checked on her interest in cooperating with me, but she said she had a long-term contract with a sports brand. I said she should be able to continue with that, because I'd thought of a completely new and different sort of campaign. She became very curious, but I told her, "No more in this first call. I'll follow up with you." I'd let her start wondering what I had in mind. Eventually, of course, her agent got involved.

I started dreaming about how this would be handled, and when I would release the news. Therese had a huge chance of winning a medal for Sweden, and perhaps its only medal. Imagine the moment when Therese stood on the podium with her medal in hand, and the whole world would hear her new surname.

Therese Panos Emporio … superstar!

Of course, some would mock this, but others would love it. I knew that loads of people would think this was fun — clever and funny and entertaining, in all the right ways. The whole world would know, and it would be a long time before they would forget it!

The few who became aware of my idea only thought of the downside consequences, not of the possibilities it would open up. Every time you have a new and innovative idea, the biggest obstacle is within us, or coming from those around us.

I realized the time was right and decided to try to negotiate, forgetting the idea of increasing international sales altogether. This was about the brand, and doing something innovative with it. It spoke to the daring and the adventurism that were part of Panos Emporio's brand values.

I talked at length with the agent and Therese, and we almost agreed on the sum, but there were still some uncertainties. For instance, there were various practical considerations: what about her passport, ID, driver's license and other documents? I realized that my adviser should have foreseen all that and proposed solutions to any uncertainties. He had not done so. And then, there was the question of when countries had to register their athletes' names with the International Olympic Committee.

We didn't have answers to a lot of these questions, and my lawyers didn't know how to deal with them. When I look back, that created uncertainty and slowed down my whole thought process. It cost us a lot of time. By the time we looked at the different dates and deadlines, it became apparent that we would never have time to complete the name change and properly register Therese.

Sweden won two silver medals in women's swimming, both thanks to Therese (almost known as) Panos Emporio.

I had a dream to compete against the giants of sportswear, those mega-large global companies who spend millions to be seen at the Olympics. I could have done it for considerably less. Nike founder Phil Knight once said that he could not afford to buy the back page of *Sports Illustrated*, but if he sponsored a top athlete, he could get on the cover. I wanted to do one better. Forget just one magazine ... this would have been on the Olympics' official rosters and scoreboards, and spotlighted by every medium covering the spectacle. Had I succeeded, I believe the public would have loved it. Billions would have smiled, because everyone loves an underdog story, especially when the little guy takes on big, global corporations and beats the officialdom of sports sponsorship at their own game. It would have cemented the idea that I was an unparalleled out-of-the-box thinker. That's the sort of positivity that can light up the whole world, and the sports media would have had to eat humble pie.

THE SAME YEAR, I launched a bag collection for men and women, including leather business briefcases. I chose to produce the men's collection in Småland, Sweden, where we could get very high-quality leather.

Bengt Westerberg modelled the men's line. He was a handsome, erudite Swedish politician, among the very few whom in my opinion held strong values. I appreciated that, and liked him as a person. He had been leader of the Folkpartiet (People's Party) from 1983 to 1995, a member of parliament from 1984 to 1994, and Minister of Social Affairs in Prime Minister Carl Bildt's government from 1991 to 1994. He had a lot of charisma: his party's share increased substantially in 1985, and that was credited to Bengt. Economically, he favoured a tight fiscal policy and tax reform, and helped steer his ministry through tough economic times. He also chaired the Swedish Red Cross.

Using a well-known party leader and former minister for the promotional campaign was a great success. When the photos were ready, they were released to the press in my trademark way: with the same carefully planned timing, using the same procedure, with strict conditions regarding positioning, visibility, captioning, credit to our brand, etc. Getting on the front pages of papers would not be a surprise, but we risked having other breaking news take precedence during the night, which would leave us with less space. That's why I always released the information late at night, and was careful to check what else might happen, choosing days when they weren't likely to write about any other major events. It tended to work.

Olympic swimmer Louise Karlsson modelled the women's collection — she had a number of European and World Championship gold medals at that point, and held various records, including one that stood from 1992 to 2014. She was particularly popular and a really nice girl.

We struck a deal to work together; Louise's pictures went out, and it all looked really good. She contacted me a week later, asking if I could call someone from ATG, the state betting agency for horse racing, who wanted to work with us. ATG had branched out into online betting, and was going to roll out a big outdoor ad campaign that featured Louise in a bathing suit. I learned that the pictures had already been taken, with Louise in a suit from a competitor's brand, which was sponsoring her. Now, with all the buzz around our new campaign with her, the betting agency wanted to swap out that photo for one of ours.

I asked how big their campaign would be, and when the ATG marketing guy told me what the budget was — in the tens of millions of kronor — I went silent for a while. He kept telling me that it would not cost me anything beyond them using a Panos Emporio swimsuit.

"I'm in a hurry," he said. "We're printing the posters tomorrow, so we have to decide today. We need to see some pictures of yours that we could use."

I sent over three or four photos from the shoot we'd just done with Louise, but he didn't like any of them. They were too complex and fashion-forward, he said. They wanted her wearing a swimsuit in a solid colour.

We had not photographed Louise in such a bathing suit, and it would be impossible to reshoot her the same day, as she was away. ATG's campaign could not be stopped or moved, even for a few days.

I was disappointed, because I didn't want to lose this gift that had come from the heavens. I wanted to hold on to the opportunity, and asked if they could come back to me for their next campaign, in a few months.

Now it was his turn to go quiet. I said nothing and waited.

"I've got an idea," he said. "Let me check on some things, and I'll call you back."

While I waited, I tried to think through possible solutions, but I wasn't going to be able to persuade them to use anything we already had. The designs were too daring and risque for their brand — the whole focus would shift to the bikini and their message would be buried.

It took him half an hour to get back to me. He reiterated that our photos were not suitable for their campaign, but they really wanted to collaborate with Panos Emporio and Louise, to bring the campaign more attention.

I asked if he could send over their original photo.

When it arrived, I saw that Louise was wearing a dark turquoise suit with the Arena brand printed across her chest. They sponsored Louise directly. I called the marketing guy back immediately. "We have a solution!" I said. "You work with an ad agency, right?"

"Yes, of course we do," he said. "They're the ones who produced this layout."

"Ask them to retouch the whole swimsuit in dark blue and erase 'Arena'. You aren't working with the Arena brand in any way on your campaign?"

"No, we're not," he replied. "Louise had just brought the swimsuit with her when they photographed her."

"Good," I told him. "Change the colour and replace the Arena branding with my signature, 'Panos'!"

He called the ad agency and was told that the rework could be turned around by that afternoon.

A few days later, on every billboard location imaginable, there were giant pictures of Louise in a Panos swimsuit! The campaign would have cost me millions, but we got it for nothing because the brand was so strong, and there had been no resistance to the idea. ATG knew we were riding high, and that the association with us could only be positive. It would boost people's awareness of their campaign, since we were already getting so much press. They saw the symbiosis, and weren't afraid to act.

Anything is possible when you have a brand that others want to be associated with. It's even better when you make yourself accessible, as the one person who can quickly say yes or no to a deal.

Great business isn't founded on densely layered bureaucracy. It's about making those quick decisions that are beneficial to the brand.

Better yet, in these cases, jump on opportunities that are beneficial to _both_ brands.

I DIDN'T NORMALLY choose professional models to be the face of Panos Emporio, and I often didn't want someone famous, who was already over-exposed. I loved the idea of selecting someone who could become famous. When you think about Jannike or Victoria, they hadn't become household names yet. I propelled them upward. You might think that there are a lot of beautiful women in Sweden — and there are, of course, as with most countries — not many can wear a bikini well in modelling shots.

There was one star who could have been a Panos Emporio face: Whitney Houston. I had a friend who made the connection with Whitney. She was performing in Gothenburg in 1999 as part of her *My Love Is Your Love* world tour. By this time, she had already been in *The Bodyguard, Waiting to Exhale* and *The Preacher's Wife*, and was a bona fide movie star. She was married to the singer and rapper Bobby Brown. *My Love Is Your Love* was her first studio album in eight years, and she was touring in the wake of its release. I met her, we hit it off, and we decided to do a shoot with her. She would wear a white swimsuit modelled after the one she'd worn on her first album cover, in 1985. I had designed a similar one, with a Panos print, for her to wear.

We never signed a formal contract, but both sides' lawyers were involved. Everything was ready. She had 2–3 hours set aside in her schedule for the shoot.

I was backstage at the Scandinavium, a large arena in Gothenburg, when she performed on the night of 1 October 1999. I witnessed the dynamic, and saw that she was under great stress. As it would later emerge, all sorts of bad things were happening in her life at the time. It was clear that she wasn't in a great place, personally, and I felt for her.

I immediately knew that it wouldn't be fair to Whitney, or for all my consumers who believed in Panos and everything I stood for, to go ahead with the photo session.

Whitney was scheduled to shoot the next day, but I made up an excuse and postponed the session. I didn't mention to anyone how down and dark and troubled I thought she looked. It was easier just to give her the space and let it pass. "Let's reschedule the shoot for another time," I told her. "We can take a trip somewhere."

It had been a simple decision for me to make, mentally, but it was tough nonetheless. Whitney could have opened the world for my brand and me. My whole life had been about living my values, and always trying to do the right thing, not about the money. The zeroes at the end of the balance sheet are just that: zeroes. It wasn't worth putting Whitney through more than she was already dealing with … and she was dealing with a lot. In a few years, she'd no longer be with us.

FRÖLUNDA HC (the Frölunda Indians) were Sweden's hottest ice hockey club, with the most medals. Their name was not the most politically correct through today's lens, referring as it did to the First Peoples of America.

Ulf Sterner, who was the first European-trained player in the US National Hockey League back in the '60s, was originally with the Indians before he played for the New York Rangers. He was inducted into the International Ice Hockey Federation's Hall of Fame in 2001.

Not many companies can afford to use a hockey star for advertising, but in the autumn of 2001, a bank director I knew called, wanting to talk about Frölunda HC. I declined, because I was not interested in hockey. I'd once attended a final, and was so bored I left halfway through. The next day, I heard how people had literally fought to get tickets to the game that I'd walked away from.

My acquaintance at the bank insisted that we meet, saying he had a mandate from his board to talk to me about a big idea. I relented, and he came to visit me in my showroom.

He looked around, evidently enjoying his surroundings, and asked, "Why is it so white in here?"

I like white. I always have. The room had large white pillars with some gold details, there was white marble from Greece, and the ceiling was in a Greek turquoise. The sofas were also white, and I had three small, white vases with red flowers in them.

"I'm not used to such a clinical office," he said.

"It is not an office; it's my showroom," I told him. "I usually receive important guests and journalists from around the world here. It is my special place — my home away from home."

He opened his bag and took out a pile of pictures and newspaper clippings. He pointed at some people and asked if I recognized them.

"No," I answered, to his disappointment.

I saw that they were hockey players, but told him, "*I don't follow the sport.* I can't know everything about everyone."

He described how important the players were, and pointed out two in particular: the Lundqvist brothers, twins Joel and Henrik. "Can you imagine those guys wearing your swimwear?"

"It sounds nice, but that just isn't something I would like to do right now."

He stared at me, and could no longer hide behind a façade of politeness. "Do you know what others pay just to meet them, or to be able to give them a product?"

I motioned for him to get up and walk with me, to break the tension and lighten the mood. I pretended to present what our new collection would look like the following year.

"Listen," he said, "I can arrange for the Lundqvist brothers and others — Sweden's best players — to come here, and for you to take photos of them in swimming trunks. We can then use the shots to produce a calendar."

I quickly figured out in my head what such a campaign would cost me under normal circumstances. He handed out pictures he had of most of the players. Everyone was physically fit, but they were lacking a certain something.

He saw me hesitate, and continued. "The campaign will be for our bank customers, and we'll see that the press gets pictures. You just organize the swimwear, styling and set-up here. We've already asked a photographer who has shot some of the players before, and it will not cost you anything."

A few days later, dozens of players arrived at my chalk-white showroom, directly from their training. The whole office suddenly had another scent, one that made my female staff stop whatever they were doing. After the photo shoot, the ladies went in to mingle with the athletes, and everybody was soon chatting and laughing. Only then, having witnessed that, did I understand how important they were.

BY THE EARLY 2000S, my creativity had been running on a high for 15 years. New models, new innovations, new fabrics and unusual colour combinations stimulated me, so that I could come up with new designs every year. The hardest part was stopping my creative burst and saving some ideas for the next collection.

Everything had been going so well, and the successes kept coming, but I began to feel an emptiness in my soul. I wanted something more. It dawned on me that I wanted to create a collection that would convey something bigger and deeper — a message of love.

It was a Saturday night, well past 3 AM. I loved the silence that was around me. Nothing moved, so my thoughts could be as they were, without distraction.

I did not know what bothered me, but I started writing a poem. I jotted down a few simple words, and soon entire sentences were coming from deep inside. I could not control it. The words just surfaced and I wrote them down. It seemed to happen mechanically. The pend guided itself across the page.

The poem came quickly. I read through it a couple of times and tried to interpret what it meant. Where did these thoughts and feelings come from? What did my subconscious mind want to say? I tried to change a few things, to make it flow better, but it didn't work. It felt impossible to change a single word.

I sat for a long time and read what I'd written. I just wanted to express a sense of unlimited love. But how do you express that in written words, in black and white, on a sheet of paper?

I put these sentences on my desk, and looked at them for a few months. I wanted to do something, but what? How could I send a philosophical message via a bikini? Was this possible? Would the shops want it? Was the whole notion absurd?

Two years later, I heard from some of my fans. I often received letters or calls, or people came up to me while I was out, letting me know how much my swimwear meant to them. Sometimes I asked what they were saying — how could a swimsuit can mean so much to a woman?

Over a short period of time in 2002, I heard the identical pronouncement more than once: "Once Panos always Panos." One woman told me, "I belong to you!" I remember women coming up to me while their boyfriends or husbands held their hand, and saying, "I will always have you on me!" Initially, it was a bit embarrassing, but over time I came to think it was fun. The men actually seemed to enjoy seeing their women light up like that. Some guys would use their mobile phones to take pictures of me, and then politely asked if they could get a shot with me as well. I started to think that "Belongs to Panos" felt really strong, and once that occurred to me, I actually started hearing it more often. I wrote it down on my idea board, and it ended up next to my poem about love.

In 2003, it was time to form a collection around this, and "Belongs to Panos" became a message on the tags in bikini bottoms and one-piece swimsuits. I made new labels with the poem. The message became clear: I wanted to tell the world that love is individually abstract and has no set form. Love can never hurt, it can only do good for humanity. No one has the right to tell anyone else what it means to them. Their love for someone is personal, deep, their own. It was part of who they were; their own, one-of-a-kind self-expression. Concerns such as gender norms didn't come into it — the binary system was a silly human construct. So were expectations of who we could fall in love with. **I wasn't talking about sex, I was talking about real, undiluted love. Love came from somewhere deep inside each one of us. It was the very essence of who we each are.**

It had been more than 35 years since the Beatles had sung these words, but I wanted to tell the world that all you need is love.

I SAT IN A TAXI with model, performer and creative consultant Rickard Engfors, who at the time was still doing a drag act. We were heading to a movie première and decided to grab a drink with a mutual friend beforehand. Rickard sat in the front seat and I was in the back, with a couple of ladies who were coming along. During the trip, Rickard turned and said to one of the women: "You have no idea! You're trying to impress Panos! You will not be his model, but I will be next year!" He looked at me and said, "I've always dreamed of becoming your bikini model!"

I gave a little smile and asked, "How are you going to wear a bikini? What are you going to do with your penis?"

He started laughing out loud. "I'm a drag performer. I can tuck it back and you won't see it! Of course I can do that!"

That evening, I observed Rickard walking around, engaging with everyone, spreading joy and good energy. People liked him — that was obvious. I waited for him to ask again, and he did, in the taxi as we left the after-party. I replied that I had an idea.

He shouted loudly that he just knew I'd have a brilliant idea. The idea took shape and grew during our ride, and within a few days everything was planned out, down to the smallest detail.

Rickard was to be photographed in secret, by a well-known photographer from one of the largest newspapers, and I would own the pictures as usual. The *Unlimited Love* collection was ready, and I had been waiting for the right idea for the launch photography. This was it!

The pictures were really nice, but I wanted them in a separate catalogue, as they were not the same as the rest of the collection. It had nothing to do with the choice of model, but because I began to see *Unlimited Love* as a sub-brand. It had to be distinguished from everything else. It would cost more, but the special catalogue was rendered in black, in an oblong format, and Rickard wore my colourful garments. There was a sort of perfection to it, a harmony in colour and shape, and there was a clear message physically in the garment itself. The whole concept breathed something big.

When it was all ready, I decided to double the retail prices for *Unlimited Love*. My salespeople did not like this, and some retailers were sceptical, but I had made my decision.

There was some thought behind it. We gave our retailers a gigantic, healthy profit margin. We had already sold the collection to them at the lower price, so they could keep the extra profit for themselves. Still, they had misgivings.

The catalogue went to print and I invested in a large media placement. It would be distributed via the hottest fashion magazines, like *Elle*, *Café*, etc. It was also packaged as an appendix in our regular catalogue, which would go to most Swedish homes.

In the meantime, I called around to some friends and acquaintances to get their reaction to what I was about to spring on an unsuspecting public. It was the first time a drag performer had been photographed in a bikini for a large, professional brand. I did not know what they'd think about it all.

The first call went to Thannasis, a friend in Stockholm. He was an older, traditional man who had worked for many years on the police force, and then at the Greek National Bank. He was also active in the Greek Orthodox Church. I knew Thannasis well, and could tell him exactly what I had done. I did not have time to finish when he shouted on the other end of the phone, "You did what?" I fell silent, wondering what would come next. He shouted even louder: "That was a brilliant idea! You have to show me the pictures when they're ready!"

I had planned to call about 40 different people, but after the conversation with Thannasis, I decided there was little point. He confirmed that my gut feeling was right — people were going to love it. I was 100% certain that women would have no objection, but I was worried about the older men who bought Panos exclusively, year after year — the same black or navy blue swim shorts that were popular at that time.

It was like an atomic bomb when the news came out, and we started selling the pictures to the press. Everyone who was sceptical of the high prices changed their minds quickly. The products sold out in the shops while the press published the photos with complimentary articles. No newspaper wrote about it negatively. Women of all ages loved the campaign. Every woman who provided feedback could see something good in the images and interpreted the campaign in their own way.

The news quickly reached other countries, such as neighbouring Finland. There, it began with a newspaper questioning the campaign and a major Swedish TV channel interviewing Finnish men in a sauna, asking what they thought about this. That prompted a back-and-forth 'media war' between Sweden and Finland.

The collection was a big seller in St Petersburg, and we and our retailers decided to use one of these images on outdoor advertising in the subway, among other things. There would be few words on the ads indicating that it was a man in the pictures, and everyone thought it was a woman.

The very image of a female-presenting man in a bathing suit on the balustrade of a Russian subway escalator was already provocative for that time, and we had to be very careful in choosing the photo.

The ad went up, but we had to quickly delete "Belongs to Panos." This was interpreted by some as a political, religious or cultist message, according to one retailer in St Petersburg. They told me that the ad agency's editorial board was concerned that the slogan was just too ambiguous. In order to avoid any misunderstanding, we slightly reworked the words.

The *Unlimited Love* collection was a resounding success. That's not to say there weren't concerns, though. One design, with a wildly eclectic pattern, reportedly sent one customer into a state of cognitive dissonance and she required medical treatment. The buttonhole seam on the front of the men's trunks was perceived as a defect; some believed that such a feature was permissible only on the inside.

The feedback included this note: "Dear Panos, your design ideas were innovative and original and we were delighted to introduce your beautiful collections to Petersburgers. Hopefully your work on the catalogue will bring you pleasant emotions and memories."

However, we seemed to have been a bit premature with our concept in some of the more culturally conservative countries. In several territories, our agents did not want to market the catalogue, or reveal that there was a man in the pictures. We were so successful elsewhere that I could deal with the more difficult markets going without.

As a person, I have always attracted vulnerable groups in society. I'm note sure why that is, but I like to think they felt my empathy and understanding. Or, maybe it's better to say that I bore no prejudices that would signal something untoward. But after this campaign broke, I became a topic of conversation in the gay community.

Each year, QX magazine hosts the QX *Gaygalan* gala for the LGBTQIA+ community, which is broadcast on network television. It's a big draw for many people, because everyone wants to be seen there. The Prime Minister of Sweden goes, and everyone who gets an invitation gladly accepts. I don't want to compare this to the Nobel Prize ceremony, but it arouses almost the same level of interest in terms of how exclusive the tickets are. No matter your title or role or industry, it's one of the places where you need to be seen.

QX published photos with Rickard, and asked if I wanted to attend. I was only offered one ticket, and was unsuccessful in trying to secure another, so I would have to go alone.

Rickard offered to sit with me, but he was part of the ceremony that evening so I was prepared to be alone for parts of the occasion. I'd never felt comfortable going to events alone, and called QX to decline, but they persuaded me by saying they had a good seat for me, and mentioning the names of other guests I would know. I decided it would be just fine, and confirmed that I'd be there.

I chose to wear a pink floral tie and a black jacket that night. I had seen the gala on TV, and how everyone tended to dress extravagantly, but saw no point in trying to do the same. It just wasn't me.

I made my entrance with Rickard and the press was quite interested when they saw me there. I could see it flashing in their eyes, and all the photographers tried to get lots of shots of me. I stood out by not wearing anything over the top: the only thing that really popped was my tie. I paled in comparison to the other guests, who were tricked out with extreme styling, from head to toe.

One photographer after another took shots of me, front, back and sideways, and then wanted even more. Each wanted me to stand in a different place than the previous photographer had used. Of all the events I'd attended through the years, it was the first time they showed such great interest.

The gala is a live broadcast and everything is programmed down to the second. I had the best seat in the house, in front of the stage, and next to me were a couple of people I knew, all scheduled to perform. The event lasted about two hours, with exciting appearances and presentations, and they gave prizes to people who had been brave in coming out. I saw many happy looks directed at me throughout the evening.

The broadcast started and Rickard disappeared for a while. It was hard to be still, and I could not get up to pretend to go to the toilet because I was so strategically placed. It was impossible during the broadcast to leave my seat. My mobile was on silent, but I saw several SMSs come in. I opened them discreetly, and saw friends and family urging me, "Don't look so angry!" When I'm not laughing, people interpret that as me being mad, when in fact I'm focused and thinking. That's just how I look!

The awards continued, and there were 30 minutes left. Now there were text messages from other friends. "You're kidding! You're not coming out on national television, are you?"

I smiled and continued watching the show. Rickard had come back and sat next to me. Then came even more text messages telling me that I should stop looking at my phone all the time, because the camera was constantly on me.

I learned that every time they announced someone new who had come out of the closet that year, the live broadcast would cut to me and stay on my face. My closest friends started wondering what was going on. What revelation was I going to make?

I put my mobile away and tried to think about not looking angry. I couldn't tell when the camera was trained on me, so I strained to smile constantly. When the programme was over, I took out my phone again. It was impossible to read all the messages; I'd received several hundred in the last few minutes. I saved these for the next day, but I never finished reading them.

I was simply an exciting, different and welcome person at the gay gala. That was all ... but all the coverage triggered a lot of speculation!

THE NEWSPAPERS knew they could get mileage out of showing the Panos Emporio brand. Carola Häggkvist, who had represented Sweden at the Eurovision Song Contest in 1983, 1991 and 2006, placing third, first and fifth respectively, had become a sought-after musical star. In 2006 she was pictured holidaying, recharging in the sea, by a paparazzo, and her photo wound up on the front pages of tabloids, including *Aftonbladet*. She wore her Paillot. Now, the papers could have easily cropped her photo so only her face and décolletage were visible, but they chose to include the Panos Emporio brand. Ten years after its launch, Paillot still looked contemporary.

I generated headlines, too, when I bought a 7% stake in Wedins, the re-tail shoe chain, later in 2006. The papers knew I'd sell copies, so I wound up prominently featured in the finance pages, even though I'm not a fi-nancial-industry figure.

Because I had bought more than 5% of the company, by law we had to issue a press release. It wasn't an easy purchase, since I'd negotiated to buy the stake from a state pension fund. I was a foreigner and an outsider, and they had to be sure that the sale wouldn't leave the company exposed to any risk.

The release came out late in the day, virtually at the end of trading. Within minutes, the share price went up by more than 30%. What it told me was that my name was so connected to good values and simple trust that if Panos was going there, he would work hard, make positive changes and, more than likely, succeed.

But when the board met on 18 January 2007, they didn't want me there. I wasn't given a seat at the table. At the time, I was quoted as saying, "It did not feel right to stay when I was not allowed to be involved and influence the company. This was not a financial investment, but a long-term investment where I hoped to be able to help turn the company around." I just couldn't believe in them if they weren't open to me. So, I sold the entire stake, at 11kr per share, netting myself a profit of 8,000,000kr. I was probably the only person who made any money out of Wedins for years. Their share price immediately fell by 4.2%, and continued to fall.

The next day, my photo made it onto the front page of *Dagens Industri*, the leading business paper in Sweden. I made for good copy and potentially added circulation.

HM King Carl XVI Gustaf, the king of Sweden, also did his bit to promote Panos Emporio. Entirely unprompted by me, he wore a Panos Emporio cap during a regatta. He gave an interview on live television that ran on multiple channels. My friends all called to make sure I was watching as I received 'royal promotion.'

A few months later, I got a call at 6 AM. A journalist had taken a photo of the front page of that morning's *Expressen* and sent it to me. I was at the airport and saw the image come in on my mobile, thinking, "So what? It's the king." Because the photo was so small, I really couldn't make out what it showed. I responded, "What is it?"

"Can't you see?" said the reporter. "We have the king wearing your cap on the front page."

"What happened?"

"He was riding a horse without a helmet, only your cap. It's not a good look."

It wasn't the first time members of royal families had been photographed in my designs.

LIKE THE ATG CAMPAIGN, for the state betting agency, BDO, the international accounting firm, used a Panos Emporio image for a huge 2009 marketing campaign. It included outdoor advertising, as well as major placements in the business press and general-circulation papers, and went on for half a year!

This type of marketing, with a large global firm, strengthened our brand enormously in all sectors of society. And it was BDO who had sought us out. We used the firm as our auditors, and they recognized how rare it was to go from zero in the 1980s to working with a big global name in roughly a decade's time. That was not something you could easily buy into.

I cannot remember anyone who worked in marketing, or among my competitors, who acknowledged such a unique collaboration. Yet, they themselves did nothing special in their promotions. I only heard, "Was it worth it?" "What does swimwear have to do with an auditing firm?" Once again, many seemed to waste their time gossiping about what I was doing, rather than focusing on their own businesses.

It pays to remember that doing your own thing — going on your own journey — is one of the most important ingredients in success. And that's true not just in business, but in everything.

During the Panos Ljungskile years, I tried to get our players to stop griping about the referees' decisions all the time and focus on their own role on the field. I showed them many examples of how you could see which team would lose a match because some players had the wrong attitude, and spun their wheels trying to get referees to change their decisions. At that point, you knew they were going to be the losing side, seemingly unable to roll with the punches and concentrate on how they could play better. Once they told themselves it wasn't their responsibility — that it somehow wasn't up to them to make things happen — you knew they wouldn't have the drive or motivation to better themselves.

WHEN MOST PEOPLE plan a marketing campaign, they have a demographic that they target. I never did so, and that's why the Panos Emporio brand became so big and touched consumers of every kind.

I broke all the rules in the marketing playbook. I was obsessed with my own, home-grown strategy, which everyone else questioned continually.

In the first year alone, I managed to attract different types of retailers, ranging from lingerie boutiques and department stores to sporting goods stores. The lingerie shops were the first to whine when they learned that you could buy Panos Emporio at Intersport, a popular Swedish sporting goods retailer. The more you grew, the more you got to hear from your buyers what was right or wrong. Many, in their criticism, contradicted their own sales force, who saw their customers' reactions and knew it was all about backing the consumer! I used to say that most of the battles you wrestle with in business are internal ones.

I was determined, I stuck with what I knew was right and I didn't tolerate any deviations. I used to say that I would wholesale to anyone who can sell my products at my recommended prices and can pay my invoices on time. Retailers who want to develop invariably have a clear vision and an aggressive survival philosophy.

When I look back, I have a fairly clear memory of my sales reps' facial expressions every time they heard this from me. I also remember the buyers' reactions. It could get very comical because I got angry every time I heard their doubts. I used to tell the important buyers, "We can discuss things if you cannot sell my products, but since you always run out, let's be prepared to talk about how much you can increase your orders instead!"

10
Beware of the job

As any businessperson will tell you, success and the high profile that comes with it often draw certain elements that you never expected. Some are friendly enough on the surface, while others can be rather sinister. Both give you pause for thought.

The 1996 Stockholm International Fashion Fair, and the launches of my Paillot and Symetric lines, generated unprecedented visibility for Panos Emporio. A few days after the fair, two muscular men in their 40s showed up at my offices. It was noon, and my employees were out to lunch. I was about to lock the door to head to lunch myself when these two big, smiling guys walked up to me.

"Hi Panos, nice to meet you," one of the pair said as he shook my hand, gripping it tightly. His palm was gigantic, and my hand disappeared in his long fingers. It hurt, and that seemed to be the idea. It was a show of their strength.

The taller of the two said, "Let's go into your office and talk a little. We need some swimming trunks for ourselves."

"I have no time now, but here, have two pairs," I said, grabbing a couple of samples that happened to be on a side table. "They're the latest. You'll be the most beautiful on the beach. But you get these under one condition: we share 50% of the brides who fall for you due to my creations." I laughed a little out of nervousness.

They looked at each other and asked, "Is that all we get?" They weren't laughing.

I felt I had already answered them. "If you want more, you can go to any store," I said. "We don't sell directly to consumers here." I locked the door and started walking slowly down the corridor, towards the exit. I had no idea who they were or why they had come, but I'd immediately understood that they were some strange characters and I reacted instinctively.

The tall one grabbed me by the shoulder and said, "You need our help, so we'll be back in a few days. We take care of our Greeks." He grinned at me, still squeezing my shoulder.

That evening, I went to a friend who might know what type of people they were and what they meant.

When I described their appearance, as well as their accent, he knew exactly who they were. "Balkan mafia," he replied. "Beware of them!"

They never returned, but a few years later I was having coffee and the man who had squeezed my palm so tightly appeared out of the crowd. "The Greek!" he said. "Tell me if anyone behaves like a dick towards you. We can take care of it! You're a nice guy, so don't think about reciprocating in any way! But what a damned insult that you just gave us two pairs of swimming trunks."

IT WASN'T my first contact with the mafia. In 1988, when I'd been in business for just a few years, a competitor called my office to say he had a Russian visitor who was interested in buying swimwear.

An hour later, he arrived with a man and a woman. Both were very tall, solidly built and strong looking. He introduced them, and then quickly left us, saying only that their English wasn't good but they understood a bit of it.

I started to talk about my design philosophy and wanted to know more about their way of working. They pretended to listen, but it was apparent that they weren't interested in such things.

I finally asked, "What is it that you want?"

The woman took charge and said in a thick Russian accent, "We want swimwear that we can take with us today. We do not work long-term. We live in the present in our country. We never know what could happen in the next hour."

I showed them the items we had in stock and they made a quick selection of designs that we had in larger sizes. They wanted a men's XXXL, but we did not have that.

We totalled up the purchase, and it came to around US$20,000 — quite a lot for that time. I said I could put it on account, and they could collect the swimwear later. The man opened his portfolio, and it was like something out of a mob movie: the satchel was packed with well-organized bundles of dollars. I said I couldn't receive such a large sum in cash, and had to check with the bank.

I called my competitor and asked in Swedish how he had dealt with them. "There won't be any problem," he replied. "Just give them the merchandise and take the money directly to the bank. The money is real." I followed his advice, and they left without incident.

A few months later, the woman called and said she wanted to come again to buy more. It had gone so well, she said, that they wanted to buy three to four times as much, and a truck would pick everything up the day after they had made their selections. It would be the same procedure: a cash payment, this time of around US$70,000.

Not long after, the Russian man came back to my office with two others, Kurdish guys in their 30s who said they had lived in Kiev for a few years. He told me that the two Kurds could buy directly from me now, as he no longer wished to be the intermediary and work with such products. His main line was in the arms industry, where he did big business, and the original contact had just been a case of happenstance for his wife. It was small pickings for him, he told me. He thought I was good to do business with, and said he would get his large customers to contact me directly.

The two Kurds seemed keen to work with the brand longer term. They didn't have the finances to pay in advance, but wanted to work as agents. They sat for many hours, going through everything to familiarize themselves with the collection, and pulled together samples to take back to Kiev and see what they could do. Despite the strange circumstances of our introduction, I felt that they were OK.

When they returned, they were exhilarated. "We received great interest from Ukraine's only private department store, Roksolana, in central Kiev. It is where the upper classes shop. There you can buy with dollars and credit cards." They told me that the store wished I could pay them a visit in Kiev, because they wanted to invest in Panos Emporio. They'd already bought some of my swimwear through the Kurds, and it quickly sold out.

I contacted the Swedish embassy there so they could help me with visas and the practical details. The embassy staff were happy that a Swedish brand would want to work with the department store, which was apparently quite prestigious.

I organized everything and packed some samples, along with all the necessary documents to be able to enter the country, and flew Lufthansa to Kiev. The embassy had connected with Roksolana's CEO and even arranged for a dinner. Our Kurdish friends were to meet me at the airport and drive me to the hotel that the embassy had booked. It was January 1989, with a lot of snow and a temperature of around –25°C (–13°F).

One of the Kurds sat in the car, with the engine running to stay warm, while the other came inside the terminal to meet me. As we left the airport, there were few cars on the highway, but it was late at night. Everything looked white but too dark and unlit to be a highway.

After a few kilometres I heard some noise and the car stopped. One of the Kurds got out and opened the bonnet, but they couldn't manage to start it again. It started to get really cold in the car and they tried to flag down another vehicle. It proved impossible in the dark and desolate conditions.

I did not have time to get worried, but I was properly freezing. Then I saw the driver stand in the middle of the road, wave his arms and stop an ambulance. He spoke Ukrainian with them for quite some time and then ran back to ask if I had US$30. I gave him the cash and he said, "Come out, you go with them." They packed my suitcase inside the ambulance and one of the Kurds went along with me.

I asked, "Wouldn't it be strange for us to pull up at the hotel and step out of an ambulance?"

"If you have money, nothing is strange here," he replied.

Sure enough, no one at the hotel raised an eyebrow when we rolled up in an ambulance in the middle of the night and stepped out with a suitcase. I was the only guest, it seemed. There was a person at the reception desk who barely spoke English. He took an extremely long time to register my passport's details, which he looked at over and over again before giving me the key. My contact had said that they would pick me up at 9 AM, and I was to have the bag ready with all the samples in preparation for meeting Roksolana's CEO.

My room was sparsely furnished. I never thought that a supposed five-star hotel would have worn towels with lots of holes, but it was the same with the bedding. It was suffocatingly hot, and I could not find a thermostat to lower the temperature.

The next morning, I was down in the breakfast room and three other hotel guests came in and sat down. They were part-Russian, from what I could tell. The waiter served the other three while completely ignoring me. I tried to wave to him but got no reaction.

I went up to him and said, "I want my breakfast."

"Yes, it will come," he said. Still, nothing happened.

I went up to him again and gave him US$2. Then things happened, very quickly.

I got a dry slice of bread, a little piece of butter, very sweet jam and strong tea. I tried to ask if there was anything else to choose from but he shook his head no.

The Kurds arrived, this time in a car that worked. We went to the department store's offices, located in the same building as the store itself. I thought it would be like the grand European department stores, but it was a modest, five-storey place. Outside were several security guards, who checked us in as we headed to the office. The CEO's secretary, a very businesslike woman in her 20s, received us. Inside, their office was really luxurious, a huge contrast to the shabby hotel I'd stayed at. Here they would serve coffee and snacks!

The CEO came after a short while, and had a nice, quiet manner. You could easily think that he'd grown up in some big city in southern Europe. He was polite and spoke good English. Everyone looked at the collection and asked many questions. The CEO said that they'd had my swimwear the previous year, and it appealed to their customers, who were rich people who could afford it. He said they were considering giving me 250 square metres of floor space to set up a Panos Emporio swimwear boutique. They wanted to know if I could deliver every month, and whether we had items that could sell during the winter.

I told him I'd brought some sweatshirt material and ladies' knitted sweaters that were unique, with their angora wool mix, plus they were machine-washable. I felt that this issue would come up, because few customers wanted a brand that was seasonal and so heavily dependent on good weather. They were clearly impressed by the products and their quality.

The embassy had planned a dinner at a Ukrainian fine-dining restaurant that night, for the Swedish trade attaché, the store's CEO and me. We were there for a long time, exchanging ideas on a major investment in Kiev for Panos Emporio. The whole thing was like a dream: I'd had hardly any time to become a big brand in Sweden, but it seemed that in Ukraine this could be realized overnight.

There was vodka and caviar that I did not really like, but I felt compelled to taste them. Later in the evening, the embassy car dropped me off at the hotel, and the next day my Kurdish friend would drive me to the airport.

At midnight I started feeling really bad, with a high fever, and I vomited. There was no minibar in the room. It was probably food poisoning, and you needed to drink a lot of water to cleanse the body. You could absolutely not drink water from the bathroom in Kiev. I was losing my strength and called down to reception. The phone rang but no one answered. I was dehydrated and continued to vomit.

I went down to the lobby to ask for help. The night concierge was lying behind the counter, watching a little black-and-white TV. I asked if they had a doctor, or some Coca-Cola, or any other kind of beverage. He just shook his head. "It's night now, there is nothing."

I went back to the room and tried to call my Kurdish friends, but no one answered. I tried to stay awake until they came to pick me up, and left the door half-open, so someone could see me in case I collapsed. At 5:30 AM, one of the guys knocked on my door, and then came in as it swung open.

He found me sprawled across the bed, hardly able to speak. "Water," was all I could whisper. "Water." He ran downstairs and came back with a drink. He went to the toilet and saw vomit everywhere. He ran away again and got his friend to help me.

I drank the first bottle of water and they brought me, and then more. One of the guys took my bag and the other tried to get me onto my feet. He felt my forehead and said I was boiling with fever. They asked what I had eaten, but I was in no mood for conversation. "Just drive me to the airport," I said. "I want to go home."

I downed more water on the way, but when we arrived, I could barely stand. I was racked with chills and my whole body shook. They checked my bag and literally propped me up all the way to the gate, walking one on each side.

We arrived at passport control and they presented my passport. I heard a few Ukrainian words, and the passport controller shouted something to the police, but we were waved through to the gate. The Kurds fetched more water as we waited for the flight to board.

The wait felt endless, but the time came to stand on my own two feet and make my way to my seat. I think I lost consciousness before we took off, but vaguely remember two flight attendants trying to talk to me. I managed to say that I had food poisoning and I just wanted to get home. "Don't leave me here," I gasped.

The pilot came out and tried speaking with me, and they gave me some tablets with a glass of water. The plane finally took off, and a flight attendant watched over me during the entire trip. When we arrived in Germany an ambulance was waiting for me. I have to hand it to Lufthansa for doing their job so well.

AFTER GETTING HOME, I started planning the deliveries to Roksolana, and we had received their floor plans so we would design the Panos Emporio boutique. I contacted a Danish interior design company that had experience decorating shops and hotels in Kiev. We created a unique design with a Greek theme, which of course included the beautiful, timeless pillars. I was in a hurry because I wanted to catch the summer season. It was a big investment for us, over US$150,000, but I was encouraged by the thought of conquering Ukraine in such a short time.

The store's CEO was involved in all the details, and said they wanted my face on a poster measuring four by six metres. I asked several times if I had heard the size right. I had! They wanted it on the front of the department store for a month, to promote the launch. That photo had been on the first page of my catalogue, and they thought it would appeal to the Ukrainian people. The interior designers did their work, and everything was to be delivered and assembled by their Danish staff on site. They were used to dealing with such things and going through customs.

The in-store boutique was completed on time and the deliveries began to arrive. We had close communication and as sales got under way I received information on what was selling well, so we could send new inventory. During the first month they made a couple of payments that we had agreed on, but then the problems started. No money came in, with several large deliveries having already gone to them, and more were on the way. I sought out the CEO but he was unavailable. His secretary would answer and say, "He's busy, but we will send the money soon."

I called the Swedish embassy and asked for help, and they tried, but they got the same sort of response. No clear answers, and the CEO was not available. I'd stopped all new deliveries by then, but they owed us US$250,000, including US$150,000 on the furnishings. It was too big an investment for me to swallow at that time.

The Swedish ambassador himself intervened and pressed the CEO for an answer, with phone calls and formal letters. Alas, the nice CEO we had the poison dinner with seemed to have slipped off the face of the earth.

After much pressure, we received word that they could not send foreign payments. I informed the embassy that we were willing to accept local currency, which the embassy could forward it to me. They told the department store, but it went cold again. The next answer to the embassy was that I could go there to personally collect the money. The embassy's advice at this point was dead serious: "*Do not come here*. We cannot guarantee your safety."

My frustration was immense, and I felt totally let down. But why was this happening? What would they gain by having a section of their store custom-decorated with Panos Emporio branding, with the entire inventory soon to run out? They knew my products sold well, and we could have made good things happen for years to come. Why would they ruin everything right out of the starting gate?

My Kurdish friends — who had acted in good faith all along, and stood by my side when I'd become ill — had some of what we delivered, in their role as the initial intermediary. But, they didn't have enough capital to really do anything with it. And so, they'd chosen to remain on the sidelines, letting Roksolana open the Ukranian market while they handled small customers in other cities.

The Kurds wanted to try to pressure the store themselves. They asked if they could act on my behalf, and if they could keep some of the money they might recover for their trouble. I felt used and abused, and was willing to do anything to get justice. I gave the go-ahead, and offered them 25% of whatever they could get back. A few days later, I heard from them that things were going badly. They said the department store was 'stronger' than they'd thought.

Weeks later, I received information that someone was on their way to Gothenburg to tell me in no uncertain terms that I should no longer try to contact Roksolana. If I did, I was told, things would get ugly, and the government could not protect me. Things seemed to have become increasingly complicated. I have no idea what the Kurds did, but I'd assumed they were going there to have words with the store's management. It appeared there may have been violence involved. It was now evident that the Ukrainian operation was run by their mafia, and they had their enforcers.

Coincidentally, the original Russian customer showed up at my office with another customer from Russia right then, saying the new guy wanted to shop. I told him what had happened in Kiev, and how bad the situation had become. He became really upset and said, "I will take care of this for you."

"No," I answered. "I've already been informed that they're sending someone to Gothenburg to deal with me. I'm afraid for my family. I'm afraid to even park my car in a public place. Have you seen all the terrorist car bomb blasts on the news?"

"I have to help you," he insisted. "I was the one who helped you enter the Ukrainian market. I know who they are, and I can get control over this. Do not worry. I'll stop this in a couple of days."

He asked, "What should I give to my guys who are going to do it? We can get the décor, the swimwear and as much money as we can."

I told him that I'd already lost, so they could keep everything they might be able to pick up.

A few days later, he came back to the office to tell me that everything had been resolved, and no one would disturb me again. He had secured the furnishings and wondered what they should do with it all.

"Keep it," I said. "Give it to different retailers who stock Panos Emporio, if you'd like." And today, you can still find some of the furnishings from the ill-fated Kiev boutique at retailers in Russia.

Months later, he was going to visit me again with a Russian customer. He reported what swimwear they had retrieved, and he was willing to pay for it. He wanted to put things right. It seemed that being a Russian arms dealer trumped being a member of the Ukrainian mafia.

The communist system soon fell, but it would be many years before I returned to beautiful Kiev, a place that had affected me so negatively early in my career. For me, it was for a long time a place haunted by bad memories.

WITH PANOS LJUNGSKILE, I had received far too much publicity. All kinds of media wrote about my football team, day after day, and certain journalists launched purely personal attacks on me, one after the other.

One summer's day, as I left the office and headed to the car park, I saw four men and a big Rottweiler hanging around my car. They looked rough, like the bad guys you see in American movies. It was late afternoon, and a few others were still in the building, but there was no one else in the parking lot. I quickly looked around and thought that there was no point in trying to run. I figured I might as well continue on to my car. As I got closer, they started walking slowly towards me.

The man with the dog said, "You've got a cool car. You must be the King of Swimwear." Before I had time to answer, they surrounded me. Oddly enough, I did not feel threatened. It was a strange situation.

I looked at the guy who'd asked me the question and said, "I like German cars. They're good quality. That's a new model, and it's really fun to drive."

He smiled and said, "We drove by and saw that your office was here, and then we saw the cool car and thought it must be yours. And suddenly you came out! We just want to say that we think you're a good guy, but we see that there are some people out there who aren't very nice to you. Take my phone number. We can take care of those bastards! Just call me if you need to." I thanked them, and they shouted "We like you!" as they walked away.

ONE NIGHT IN THE EARLY 2000S, there was a burglary. At 3 AM, Securitas, our security service, called to tell us that thieves had got in through the roof of our offices. The alarm went off when they exited through the front door, but as far as the guard could see, they hadn't taken anything. I headed to the office and found that they had stolen my computer hard drive. I didn't understand why, because there was no great value in it, and nothing else had been stolen.

The next day, the thieves called, asking if I wanted to buy back the computer drive. If not, they warned, they would expose the information it held. There were some photos and personal details about important personalities with whom we were negotiating, earlier agreements with models, etc.

I asked the thieves to call back in the afternoon, after I'd had a chance to think. They said I was not to contact the police, but that was the first thing I did. The officer in charge said I could pay the ransom and get the drive back, but if I was kidnapped during the exchange, or there was a further extortion attempt of some sort, they could not guarantee the safety of my family or me. In Sweden, it is impossible to keep your home address or your income secret. Anyone can learn almost everything about you in a few minutes. Readership skyrockets a couple of times a year when newspapers publish the names and addresses of those who made the most money in each municipality. This creates huge problems, and literally puts lives at risk, but if you're successful, their feeling is that you should be punished for it.

It seemed we would have to surrender to skilled blackmailers. I thought about my family, and the worries they would have to live with, so I chose not to negotiate with them or buy the drive back. Deep down, though, I did not feel good about my decision.

ON 20 SEPTEMBER 2007, I was having my morning coffee when I received some worried calls from friends. They had read in the papers that Panos Emporio had wound up on an al-Qaeda hit list. It seems that a Swedish daily, *Nerikes Allehanda*, had published a cartoon depicting the prophet Mohammed, and al-Qaeda announced that 100 Swedish companies were now their targets. Sure enough, there was Panos Emporio, alongside names like IKEA, ABB, Akzo Nobel, SKF and Volvo. This was a shock to me, all the more so since I had my Pakistani 'brother from another mother' back in Greece, who followed the Islamic faith.

The phone was hot for a few days, and it even made headlines in Greek newspapers. I had to cancel some trips and follow the Swedish Foreign

Ministry's advice on how to act and what to be alert about. It felt unreal that we were so interesting to al-Qaeda. The other companies had billions in turnover and thousands of employees, and operated globally, including in Muslim-majority countries.

Some of my friends were proud of this. "Can you understand how big this is?" one of them gushed. "There are hundreds of thousands of companies in Sweden, and they chose these 100, including you!"

Indeed, Panos Emporio had risen to the heights occupied by these other brands from Sweden. This black skull immigrant's company was now as much a part of the Swedish national fabric as IKEA. The nation had embraced me, and now I was so closely associated with it that we were being threatened by terrorists because of something a Swedish paper had published. It wasn't so much about any financial aspects of Panos Emporio, but the power of the brand, and how well I had cultivated it over the previous two decades. When the brand is right, the public isn't going to care about details like what's on your balance sheet or the colour of your hair. What they see is what you publicly present to them, and I had generated so many headlines in Sweden that touched consumers — far more than industrial groups like ABB, which might only be seen by a trade audience.

I was always consistent about how Panos Emporio was presented, and admittedly a lot of that was tied to my own personal image. That consistency forms ideas in people's minds; they begin to recognize that there is a person behind the label, and feel the passion that goes into it. This time, it put the business in danger, but it did illustrate how a company with millions in revenue could punch well above its weight, as a peer of those raking in billions.

Along with consistency, humanity — and the stories that go with it — will always be an ingredient that serves a brand well.

AS EARLY AS THE 1990s, I had some dealings with Lebanon. It was a difficult market to work in, because something unexpected was continually happening. There wasn't much business there, but I had met a Lebanese businessman, Michael, and his wife, Nada, in Greece. I really liked them as people. We had a friendly, humane relationship and business came second. They loved my collection, and that made me extra happy and patient.

After three years or so, they knew my thinking behind my design work and how I operated. We met every year in Athens for a few hours when I was visiting, and the rest we took care of via fax and, later, email. My brother's wife has Lebanese roots, so it was natural that I was interested in the country and followed what was happening there.

Every year Michael asked me, "When are you coming to Beirut? Some customers want to meet you. They've heard all of our stories about you, and now they want to see you in person."

"Next year," I would always tell them, "if there is time."

In August of 2012, I finally decided to go for a Friday-to-Sunday trip, and then proceed on to İstanbul, where a large customer had started working with us.

The Turkish distributor loved my designs but he was very worried about the name Panos. In both Greece and Turkey, stories are written daily about the problems our countries have had for so long, and the wars we have fought. "How could we sell your swimwear to the Turkish people?" he wondered. "Can you do another label for us? Maybe you could take away Panos and just leave the word Emporio."

"I don't think the people would have anything against us," I replied. "Let's test it." I told them that the name had met resistance in Russia, since *ponos* meant *diarrhoea* there. And in Finland, *panna* meant *fuck*. It wasn't the first time someone wanted to replace Panos with another name. I explained how it had gone in Russia and Finland, where in the long run everything worked out fine.

"But it is not the same," the Turkish distributor argued. "The problem here is that we hear on the news every day how close we are to war with each other."

I appreciated his concern but persuaded him to start selling the swimwear in his own 14 stores. If this did not go fantastically well, he would not have to pay me one cent. I was sure of success, and willing to take the risk to prove my point. I liked İstanbul and loved having a reason to go back. I always chose places to sell to that I enjoyed being in. That was my reward, I used to say, because I worked so much — I looked at places I wanted to travel to, and made plans to sell my collections there. It was a reward and a luxury for me to do so.

The first collection had been on the Turkish market for about four months and had already been a success. It was important to have a press event there. I would go to Beirut first, and meet with two important customers, before heading to Turkey to tend to the larger programme.

My friend Michael had planned every hour of my Beirut visit, so we could see the city together. I had great expectations, on both a personal and business level. We had a clear plan on how to conquer all of Lebanon, increasing our sales there by several hundred percent.

My flight landed on time at 1 PM and I stood in line at passport control while the policeman checked my Swedish passport several times. He asked me what my mother's name was, and I answered Maria. He continued with his questioning, and before I knew it, two officers came running towards us and handcuffed me.

They took me to an interrogation room and started asking rapid-fire questions. "Where are you from?" I was asked. "What are the names of your mother and father? When were you born? Where?"

I asked why they had arrested me, and they said Interpol had me listed as a wanted man, because I had done something criminal in Greece.

I tried to explain that I had just come from Athens — passing through the airport there, with all of its security controls — with no problem from the authorities. I said I'd conducted a big press conference there, and pulled out a couple of Greek newspapers with the coverage. I argued that I could not possibly be wanted if I was so accessible and everyone knew where I was.

The officer took the handcuffs off and we waited in the room with three plain clothes police officers, who in my eyes could easily have been criminals.

After a while, they took out a piece of paper and wrote something down in Arabic, which they wanted me to sign. I refused.

They kept asking what my mother's name was, and I said, "Maria," again and again. They asked if I could prove it. They were relentless.

"I am a personal friend of the Greek prime minister," I said, "and I can call his mobile right now, if you want to talk to him directly. He can confirm that I am not wanted in Greece, and I am not the person you think I am."

"Put the phone away. You're not calling anyone!" one of them exclaimed. Another one started in on my mother's name again. "Can she fax over her ID?"

"My mother is over 80," I told them. "She is illiterate and doesn't have a fax machine at home!"

"Then you can stay here!"

Eventually, they added something else to their repetitive question about my mother: "Help us so we can help you!"

"How should I help you?" I asked.

They shrugged their shoulders. "We need to know what your mother's name is. You need to help us with this."

This lasted for about three hours, until I was close to collapsing. I asked for some water. One of the policemen fetched half a glass of ice water and handed it to me. I was sitting on a broken plastic chair, behind a beige metallic desk, with the wood top peeling off and scratches everywhere. The room had grey linoleum floors and a jail-cell door in a colour that I could only describe as vomit. A worn mattress sat in the corner. It was one of the most miserable places I had been in, and perhaps that was precisely why they were interrogating me there.

They spoke in Arabic loudly, and laughed while staring at me. One typed something and wanted me to sign it. I and refused and said I wanted to call someone. They said it wasn't going to happen. They took my cell phone away and shouted back and forth at each other.

Then one opened a plastic bag and poured white powder over the desk, using a piece of paper to divide it between smaller bags. I didn't understand what this was, but I was really scared for the first time. How do I get out of here now?

We were locked behind a metal cell door, inside an airport. I could not escape. There was no point in screaming. I pretended to feel ill, sliding out of my chair and rolling onto the mattress on the floor. And then, writhing around down there, I discovered that they had not taken a small pouch where I had two more cell phones: one with my Greek number, the other with my private Swedish number.

They took me to a side room, a few metres from the desk, and kept the door open. However, they could not see me around the corner. I got out one of the cell phones and quickly typed an sms to former Greek prime minister George Papandreou, asking for help. Then I sent one to the Greek ambassador in Stockholm, whom I knew personally, and asked him to alert the Swedish authorities. I have dual Greek–Swedish nationality but I had entered Lebanon with a Swedish passport.

After half an hour, they came to me and opened my bag to see if there were other phones. They said nobody on the outside would be able to help, or have permission to get there.

The interrogation resumed, with the same questions and the same phrases. "Help us so we can help you!" they shouted at me.

It was past 11 PM, and I was exhausted and hungry. They had finished writing a report, consisting of several pages in Arabic. They pointed at it and said, "Sign here!"

"I don't understand what it says, so I can't sign my name to it," I replied.

What happens now, I wondered? What if they put the white powder in my bag? What did that corridor look like when they'd led me through? Would it be possible to escape? But I had no memory of anything. My body and brain were completely exhausted.

The phones were on and texts came in on the Greek one. The officer handed it to me, but ordered, *"Do not call anyone!"*

I read the SMS. It was from the Greek embassy in Beirut, advising me to stay calm and just wait. I texted back briefly, "They have drugs on the table — help now! Where is Sweden? Why are they not helping me now?"

The reply came: "Sweden has not had an embassy in Beirut for some years, but they have been informed. Stay calm and wait."

I slid back down to the mattress and cried. By now only one cop was still there with me, and I thought about jumping him, but where would I run to then?

At 2:30 AM, the others came back and gave me some papers in Arabic, and a little note in English that read: "You have four days before you go to court, and they will decide if you can leave the country."

They told me that if I signed the papers, even though I did not understand their contents, I would be released for now, under orders to remain in the city until my court date. I did so, and two policemen followed me towards the exit, past the customs desk. I walked out without my passport. I would have to collect it in court, they said.

"I can't show up at the hotel without a passport," I said. "They won't check me in."

They shrugged their shoulders and nudged me out of the door.

Outside, Michael was still waiting for me. He had been in contact with the Greek embassy and knew what had happened. He drove me to the hotel in the central Beirut, where we arrived at 4 AM. Surprisingly, they let me check in without the passport, and I collapsed into bed.

The next day was a Saturday, and we sought a court to get my passport back. The Greek embassy had sent a couple of people to help me, and serve as witnesses to my identity. We spent half the day looking for a judge, but nobody was working on the weekend. All of my press activity had been cancelled — how could I possibly look upbeat and positive, let alone concentrate on what I was saying, given what I was going through? I wanted my passport back and I wanted to leave.

The embassy folks warned that I could be arrested again at any time, for no reason. I was told that some countries did not observe international laws, and Lebanon was one of them.

We went around to different courts, trying to find a judge who was working that day. We got tips on where to go, where we might have better luck, and soon we were in a giant building. The structure had been scarred by grenades, bullets and fire, and certainly did not look like a courthouse. I was scared, and reluctant to enter, but Michael said, "Come," and we hurried in.

We ran around trying to find someone, but the place seemed empty. After a long search, we found a courtroom and a person who told us that a judge was on his way there to sign some other papers.

The embassy staff asked me if I had US dollars, to give to the judge. I had about US$1,000. They said that should be sufficient.

After a couple of hours, a burly man showed up. He reminded me of Savvas, the gruff manager of the factory in my home town where my mother and I had worked, in both his dress and his physique. Instead of shoes, he wore sandals. He shuffled his feet along. He had his daughter with him, a charming girl who appeared to be 10 or 12. Her eyes shone in the gloomy building, which looked like a war zone.

He asked what we wanted, and Michael, together with the embassy staff, explained who I was and what had happened. He turned to his daughter and asked her, "What do you think? Does he look nice, or is he the one they are looking for?"

She didn't answer, but he turned to me and said, "Yes, well, you seem to be a good person. Wait ... we will find your passport."

A court employee nodded at the judge and disappeared through a side door. The minutes ticked by, and I felt really uneasy.

He came back with my passport in his hand. It seemed impossible — how was my passport there, in this random, war-torn building somewhere in Beirut, which we'd come to after trying a half-dozen others?

The judge took my passport, checked it for a moment and gave it to me.

The embassy staff handed him the money. They asked him to write a certificate declaring that I was free to leave the country. They explained to him who I was, and that they had also talked to the Swedish Ministry of Foreign Affairs. If he wanted to talk to them, they had a foreign minister on standby, awaiting his call.

"There is no need," the judge replied. "Wait for me to write a verdict, and sign this, stamp it and give it to me."

It was just after 6 PM. We had been looking for this judge since 9 that morning. Time for dinner, which I wasn't particularly in the mood for, and at noon Sunday I would board my flight to İstanbul. The embassy staff advised me to go to the airport nice and early, and gave me several numbers to call, to confirm that I'd boarded the plane.

Michael drove me to the airport at 9:30 AM. We checked my suitcase and made our way to passport control.

This time, a female officer checked my passport. She stared at it for a minute, and I got ready to show her the written verdict from the judge.

Before I could, two officers ran over and arrested me again. One was from the first night. I tried to tell them that I had the judge's decision, but they would not listen. They were determined to take me to the same room as before. Once we were there, behind the locked cell door, they sat down and looked at the papers.

"Sit down and keep quiet," they said. "We'll check with the judge and see if you can go!"

I texted the embassy and told them I had been stopped again. They answered just as they had previously: "Do nothing. We're working on this."

I was out of patience and raised my voice. "I have the bloody judge's decision that I'm free to go!" They did not react at all, as though I didn't exist.

"What's the problem?!" I shouted.

"We looked for the judge, but he wants to rest now. When he wakes up, he'll call us."

"Wake him up!" I screamed.

"That paper is hand-written," said one of the officers. "It is not a valid document! He must confirm to us that it is OK to release you."

Another one of them said, "Why don't you help us so we can help you? What is your mother's name?"

Same fucking story ... over and over again.

It was now past 6 PM and I had lost all strength. One of the text messages from the embassy sounded even more hopeless. "We're trying."

There were several more flights that evening, with the last one — on Turkish Airlines — scheduled to leave at 9 PM. I asked the embassy to call and reserve a seat for me. They said they had already booked me on all possible flights that were available, to nearby countries or to Greece. On the outside, Michael was aware of what was going on. He would inform my Turkish distributor to cancel all activities.

The Greek Ministry of Foreign Affairs had been working hard, at a high level, to get me released. Meanwhile, the Lebanese police threatened that things would get worse because I had involved politicians, and it was still them who would decide. "You may not leave the country," one of them told me. "We will hand you over to Interpol next week, as soon as we can get in contact with them."

The Greek embassy had tried calling Interpol, to find out what had happened, but there was no answer. This was insane! Interpol, the international law enforcement agency whose stated mission included facilitating "worldwide police cooperation," were off work because it was a weekend? That seemed to be the situation. Until they could be spoken to, I would remain under arrest.

Just before 9 PM, I asked the embassy staff to check the possibility of a private chartered flight if I were to be released during the night. It was not easy to arrange, and it was dangerous flying out of Beirut under any circumstances.

It was utterly absurd to be arrested (twice!) and harassed for almost two days without reason. Every minute that passed felt like several years. My agitation grew and I began pacing back and forth, clenching my fists and muttering profanities.

One of them eventually turned to me and angrily said, "Sit down, you're annoying me!" Good, I had got on his nerves.

The clock ticked past 11 PM, meaning the last flight would have left two hours earlier. But then, miraculously, my phone pinged with a text message that I should get ready and run to the gate.

Shortly afterwards, they handed me my passport and the judge's written decision and pointed the way out!

I ran as fast as I could towards the gate. There was no one in the airport other than the cleaners. The gate was closed. There was no flight information on the TV monitors, either.

Then I heard, "Mr Panos, this way please!" I turned, and it was a flight attendant in a red uniform.

I ran toward her and she took my carry-on bag from me. "Come in," she said, pulling me onto a jetliner and quickly closing the door. The first row was empty, but the rest of the plane was packed. It was the 9 PM Turkish Airlines flight — it had been held for me. They'd received information about what had happened, and had kept several hundred passengers sitting there for more than two hours. I quickly sat down in the front row and put on my seatbelt. I saw a lot of activity as they closed the door, the flight attendants took their seats and the plane started taxiing.

A flight attendant took a seat next to me and looked at me. I could not get a single word out. I wanted to say thank you, but my mouth had stiffened.

I looked at a flight attendant who was sitting opposite me, reciting the routine take-off instructions into the microphone, looking back at me the whole time. Her eyes said something, but I didn't know what.

The plane was in the air and the flight attendants let their stressful, anxious expressions go. The one next to me asked if I wanted a brandy. I nodded yes. She brought it, followed by a water, and then another brandy. One of the pilots then came out and said to me, "You're safe now. You can relax," and I could hear some applause. I could not control my tears.

The plane landed in İstanbul. Turkish passport control quickly released me, before everyone else. It seemed that everyone knew what had happened to me ... but I still didn't comprehend it all.

A FEW YEARS LATER, I received a request to become the Consul-General of Greece in Gothenburg, which I declined. But after that, I came up with an idea that I absolutely wanted to implement. There was no Turkish consulate in Gothenburg. I wanted to be Consul-General for Greece and Turkey, and have both under one roof!

A wild thought? No, it was natural for me. I told my loved ones my idea and they thought it was fabulous. It was time to start exploring this politically — a little cautiously through my trusted contacts, so no one could ruin the idea.

However, the time wasn't right. The first calls I made, to my closest politician friends, weren't too positive. They thought it would be too difficult to implement. And, in retrospect, it wouldn't have been right for me. I had already begun thinking about selling my life's work and moving on to the next stage ... whatever that might end up being.

I would have loved it, and above all, I'm sure that both Greek and Turkish citizens both would have liked to experience something like this. What a symbol of love and togetherness that would have been, after all the conflict and strife between our two countries. It's a thought that remains close to my heart, and there's a chance that it could blossom again.

11
Angels, kings and queens

IN MY LONG FRIENDSHIP with Jean-Louis Dumas, the chairman of Hermès, I visited his home in Paris on many occasions. He was a very elegant man. You could tell he was an aristocrat, not so much from his clothes, or his face, but through his voice and his manner. He was so kind. I saw Jesus in his kindly personality.

I met Jean-Louis through a mutual friend. One wintery Sunday night in 1990, my friend Nikos, who lived in Stockholm, called me. I was already in bed — it gets so dark in Sweden in the winter that most people go to bed early. He wanted to tell me something important.

"Were you asleep?" he asked. "This might interest you." He went on to say that his father had met the Frenchman who owned a large fashion house in Paris. It turned out that Nikos's dad took care of the garden at the fashion executive's vacation home on the Greek island of Aegina.

"Dad just called to say he's invited you and me to his fashion show in Paris next month."

"But he doesn't even know me," I replied.

"No, but Dad gave him the bathrobe he got from you. He thought it was too nice for him, so he saved it in his closet. The Frenchman is very kind to Dad, so he gave it to him as a present. The Frenchman opened the bag and thought it was nice, and wondered where he'd bought it. Dad told him that we knew each other, and a little about you. He left his secretary's phone number, so we can contact her if we wanted to go," Nikos explained. "But of course it costs a lot to go to Paris. I have no money for that, but you might be able to go yourself."

"Who is the Frenchman?" I asked.

"He's the one who has the Greek trademark — the Greek god Hermès."

I went silent. I asked Nikos several times if he meant the 'real' Hermès.

"Yes," he answered. "Dad takes care of things at his summer house on Aegina."

I had been up and running for about four years, and 1990 had been a particularly tough one. I couldn't afford to go to Paris on a whim. But, to be invited to a fashion show in there — not just any show, but to one of the world's great brand's events — seemed too big to miss.

A few days later, I called the secretary of Hermès CEO Jean-Louis Dumas, who said she knew I would be getting in touch. I thought it was all a joke, but she pronounced my name perfectly, politely thanked me for calling, and asked if I needed help with hotels.

I decided to also get a ticket for Nikos, who had made the Hermès adventure possible, after all, and cover his expenses. The day of our departure approached, and my nervousness and anxiety grew. What should you wear? When you looked at magazine photos from fashion shows, all you could see was luxury and flair in those days. My best outfit cost a couple of hundred dollars, at most. What if the head of this legendary fashion house thought I was rich, and suddenly, in person, I looked like a fly in a glass of milk?

I called Nikos and expressed my doubts. "I might look completely ridiculous there, and the Frenchman will find it embarrassing that he even invited us."

"If you don't want to spend the money, that I can understand," he said. "But if you're concerned that he'd take the idea of two poor guys attending the show badly, don't be. I've met him. He's simply an amazing man. Take a chance."

"OK," I replied. "We'll go."

WE ARRIVED IN PARIS the evening before the show. Nikos managed to book a centrally located three-star hotel at a reasonable price.

We got up early the next morning to visit the flagship Hermès store, so we could see their current collections up close. There was no World Wide Web at that time, so you couldn't browse online. It feels like the Stone Age when you look back.

We were outside the store half an hour before they opened. I walked around and enjoyed their storefront. The feeling was indescribable.

Soon we were inside, and the staff's eyes turned politely towards us. It was quiet. I dared not touch any garments or their fantastic shoes. I was curious what they cost, but there were no prices that you could see.

We spent a long time there, and then hurried back to the hotel to get ready. I'd brought some souvenirs with me from Sweden, including a bathrobe for Jean-Louis. We produced these in Sweden and I was proud of the high quality. I had managed to mix Lycra in with the material we wove, and it had a luxurious feel. I asked Nikos if we should take it to the show, but he said he would leave it at the Hermès offices the next day.

The show would begin at 1 PM, and we were already in the queue by noon. After a while, they opened the gate, and everyone flooded in. What beautiful clothes and what handsome people! Everyone was happy and it seemed that they knew each other. Nikos and I felt a bit like outsiders, but at the entrance our names were on the guest list and the staff pronounced them correctly.

The show started, and it was like a beautiful fairy tale. It's difficult for me to describe the feeling. I was sitting among the fashion élite in Paris, at the world's hottest show, and on top of all that, we had been personally invited by 'Mr Hermès' himself!

After the show, Nikos spotted Jean-Louis, who was surrounded by photographers and lots of people. He acted very calmly and his eyes radiated great warmth and courtesy. You could see he was a fine soul.

I sat quietly, still trying to grasp where I was, what was happening and who all these beautiful people were. I don't mean that they were beautiful in the usual way, as simply something on the surface. It was a combination of being extraordinarily well dressed, acting kindly to each other, and creating good energy and positive vibes that radiated throughout the hall.

I figured it was time for us to go, but Nikos said, "No, wait! We'll go up to him. I've met him a couple of times when I helped my father in his garden."

I hesitated, but he pulled me toward Jean-Louis, who waved at us to come forward.

Jean-Louis slowly and surely started to walk toward us, and everyone else fell in behind him.

His face was from the kind planet that I would like to believe exists somewhere, with divine eyes and a soft smile. He extended his hand to Nikos and said, "It's great to see you!"

He turned toward me and extended his hand, and said, "You're Panos Papadopoulos! Thank you for coming!"

I don't remember how I answered, but I stood there in disbelief, wondering if this was all for real.

"Stay," Jean-Louis said to us. "We'll go and eat together in a while."

I was so nervous — in shock, really — but in a positive way. I couldn't manage to say much of anything, and just basked in the wonder of it all.

A short time later, a woman approached us. Nikos said it was Jean-Louis's wife, Rena. She greeted Nikos and introduced herself to me. She spoke Greek like she'd spent her entire life there, but didn't look like a typical Greek woman.

I learned that she was a famous architect and interior designer, and had her own career outside Hermès. She'd been born in Greece and had studied there, in France and in the US. When she opened her own practice in 1972, she already had some high-profile projects under her belt.

Jean-Louis returned, freed from the press and entourage, and said, "Now, let's go and eat. Can I decide on the restaurant? I can imagine that you don't want to have the typical French meal, so let me choose."

His driver was waiting outside the building in a Volvo. I was a little surprised that he didn't have a more luxurious car, but there was something special about this Volvo. The trip took only a few minutes, and we arrived at a simple but nice restaurant.

The waiter came with the menu, but I did not recognize any dishes. Jean-Louis noticed this and asked if he could help me choose, saying he knew what my Greek stomach would like.

"Of course," I answered. We sat for a couple of hours and talked about a lot of things. He was curious about my company, and saw that I was shy and did not say much. He told me that he thought the bathrobe — the one of mine that Nikos's father had originally given him — was quite beautiful. Rena interrupted him, saying, "I'm so mad at this bathrobe! He never takes it off at home, so I can't even wash it!"

Everything felt very comfortable, and it was eventually time to leave. Jean-Louis took out his card, and on the back he wrote his home phone number and address. "Call me next time you come to Paris," he said, "and let's have you over to our home."

I kept in touch with him, and a few months later I was on my way to Paris again, to see the next Hermès fashion show.

I was really curious what their home would look like. Would it be as luxurious as their store, or even more so? I wanted to see the colours, the furniture, the curtains. I wanted to see their balcony and how they were in their own environment, away from everyone else who demanded their attention.

The address was in central Paris. I walked around outside for a few hours, checking out the area. We were to meet at 7 PM, and I rang the bell promptly. The gate opened and a voice with an Indian accent informed me how to get to the right floor. I studied every centimetre as I made my way to their entrance. The door was half-open, and an Indian man was waiting there. He was very polite, and in a soft tone said, "Mr Jean-Louis and Mrs Rena are waiting for you." Jean-Louis came to greet me, stretching out his hand with a big smile, saying loudly in Greek, *"Kalos irthes!"* (Welcome!')

We sat down in their living room, which was lined with giant shelves with lots of books. We talked while the man who'd met me at the door prepared dinner. Jean-Louis had travelled extensively in India and was fascinated by everything about it. He loved to see the world and was sensitive to different cultures. There wasn't a single drop of malice in this man, and he never uttered a foul word. I could never have dreamed that there were such people. How divine. The gods might have been disappointed in us humans, and wanted to punish us for our sins, but Jean-Louis only had a friendly side ... nothing else. His heart was great enough for all humanity.

It was a long and pleasant evening. I brought along the new catalogue, featuring Jannike Björling, which I was quite proud of. I'd also brought along new bathrobes for both Jean-Louis and Rena. He was very curious about everything and managed to get me to tell him about my brand, my life and my dreams. He seemed fascinated by what I was saying and encouraged me to tell him even more. I opened up more than I ever had in my life. It was a great feeling to be asked to share these things by someone who knew so much and wanted to listen to you!

I began to really like Paris, and soon felt that it was becoming my second home. Jean-Louis, Rena and I were developing a true friendship, and talked comfortably about most things. Rena told me several times that her husband liked my energy and creativity. When I turned 40, I invited them to my big party in Stockholm, and the other big party I hosted in Gothenburg the following week. They absolutely had to come, I told them.

They told me that it had been a long time since they'd been in Sweden, and they looked forward to coming. However, a few days before the Stockholm event, Rena called and told me that Jean-Louis had to go to India, and then Hong Kong and Japan, so he couldn't make it. On the day I turned 40, there was a DHL delivery at home. It was a large package from Hermès, with a handwritten card offering good wishes from Jean-Louis and Rena. The box was filled with lots of Hermès ties and other beautiful items.

Our friendships developed, and I thought of Jean-Louis as my mentor from the moment we met. No matter how busy he was, he always called back. I have noticed since I was a little boy that the greater one's personality is, the more respect they tend to show for others, no matter who they are.

One time, Jean-Louis gathered together a couple of his design team and introduced us. He told me which of my creations he liked. He was particularly enthusiastic about Paillot, and liked the men's products, such as the Eros swimsuit. He wanted to get a couple for himself — one for Paris and the other for his summer place in Greece. He asked if I could tell his team my design philosophy, and how I think when I create new innovations. How incredible that the élite, world-famous Hermès design team was intently listening to my thoughts on design!

One night, Jean-Louis asked if I could consider moving to Paris. There was room for me on his team, if I was interested. The idea was for me to build my label under the Hermès umbrella, and it played heavily on my mind for several months. But did I really want to leave Sweden, just as I had started to establish myself? And my family was not interested in moving. I was blinded by the speed with which I had gained my standing. I was self-confident, but too immature to understand what this would mean for my career. Here I had a mentor, who would play ball with me and make me think before any big decision. Many of my decisions were purely emotional, which could be good for others, but not always for me personally.

I thanked Jean-Louis profusely, and politely declined the offer to become a part of the Hermès empire. I told him that I knew, deep down inside, that I had to make my way forward on my own, as I had done up to that point. He told me he understood, and that he was proud of me for holding on to my convictions. To my great relief, my decision didn't affect our personal relationship. Our friendship continued, and grew even greater over time.

Jean-Louis taught me to see all challenges as part of the journey. He showed me that everyone faces the same sorts of problems, headaches and frustrations, no matter who they are.

One day in 2003, one of my assistants resigned while I happened to be with Jean-Louis. I got a little upset. He asked what had happened. I explained, and he gave me a big, warm smile. "Let me tell you my situation," he began. "A few days ago, one of our designers resigned after working for me for many years. He wanted to start his own label, and it was not possible to persuade him to stay. I tried everything."

"What does it matter to you?" I asked. "If you advertise tomorrow, thousands will apply."

"It's a big problem," he said. "There are not many who can do that job, so it's not a simple matter of advertising for it. But I can tell you what I did three days ago."

Jean-Louis had concluded that the designer Jean Paul Gaultier was the best candidate for the position, and thought long and hard about how to recruit him. He decided that he'd ask Gaultier for his help in 'choosing the right person.' Gaultier agreed, and they made plans to meet for lunch the next day.

"After we'd settled in, Gaultier asked who was up for the job. 'He's sitting here,' I told him, looking him straight in the eyes. He was surprised, and flattered, and we aagreed that day how to proceed."

Jean-Louis said it wasn't only the small brands that had problems, but also the big ones. However, he assured me that with careful thought and calm deliberation — and a healthy dose of think-outside-the-box creativity — anything could be overcome. Gaultier was a case in point. An enfant terrible of the fashion world who'd dressed the likes of pop star Madonna in corsets, he was certainly an unconventional choice for a traditional luxury brand like Hermès. In fact, he went on to have a successful seven-year run there.

Some time passed and Jean-Louis called one day when I was in the car. He told me that Rena had cancer. I could hear from his voice that it was not the same Jean-Louis I had known for so many years. He had experienced other huge events in his life, but this had hit him hard. Naturally, you aren't going to be the same person, with the same joy and enthusiasm, when you face losing your life partner.

A few months later, I paid them a visit. Rena seemed all right, but there was no happiness in the home. Jean-Louis was more worried for Rena than she was.

A while later, I had plans to introduce Panos Emporio on the stock exchange, and wanted to see if Jean-Louis and I could work together in some way. I called his cell phone but there was no answer. I left a message, but he never called back. I waited a week or so, and then called his home. The Indian gentleman answered, and told me that Jean-Louis could not talk, and neither could Rena. I couldn't understand. How can such a dear friend just cut our ties?

Some time passed, but I couldn't let go of this. I called Jean-Louis's secretary, who knew we were friends. She said he wasn't available. He would get in touch with me, she said.

Why did they not want to talk to me? What had I done to lose him?

After a few weeks of waiting, I called their home and Rena answered. Her voice made me tremble. I knew immediately that something terrible had happened.

"He has had a cerebral haemorrhage and has lost his ability to speak," she said. "I'll call you when things are a little better around here."

I was devastated. Rena had cancer, and now Jean-Louis was incapacitated. Life was so unfair. I'd thought that the angels would never get such diseases. Both he and Rena were my real, flesh-and-blood angels.

A few months later, I went to their house and Jean-Louis was able to receive me. It was a profound experience. It was hard emotionally to know that my idol, my role model, my close friend, was so sick.

Rena had told me that I should arrive at 4 PM, but she was not certain that he'd be well enough to see me. I tried to prepare myself for whatever might happen. Unfortunately, he was having a bad day, so I had to go back to the hotel without seeing him. The next day, Rena called and asked if I could try again. After I'd arrived, he came slowly into the living room wearing a robe. I barely recognized him, and could not stop my tears. He said something, but I couldn't understand his words. Rena helped to translate: "Do you not see that he is wearing your bathrobe?"

He wanted us to sit in the living room. I followed and sat silently. I did not know how to act at that moment, and he had great difficulty talking. I asked Rena if it would be best for me to leave, but she wanted me to stay. "He wants you to be here for a while."

The Indian gentleman came in and said someone wanted to deliver flowers in person. Jean-Louis turned slowly toward the entrance, curious who was there. Rena went to the door. I heard a few hushed sentences in French, and she rejoined us.

Jean-Louis's eyes demanded to know who the visitors had been. Rena answered in French. I didn't even hear her words; my focus was on him. My thoughts scared me. Many people used to say to me, "*Stop running like this!* You're mortal like everyone else!" I'd been convinced that I was immortal. Now, this tremendously successful man, the absolutely nicest person I knew, sat across from me, completely helpless … waiting. I was staring mortality in the face. Life was unfair. Why was it like this?

It was after 7 PM and I felt I should leave. Jean-Louis signalled that he wanted to say a few words before I left.

Rena went close to him so she could help me understand what he was saying.

"Do you know who came and left these beautiful flowers?" he asked.

"No," I told him. "I caught a glimpse of their faces at the door but I don't know who they were."

"It was my competitors, who own the other big fashion houses. How funny that they would show their 'appreciation' to me now." I saw in his eyes that there was something else. He strained to continue. "They came to see how bad it is with me. They're like vultures — awful blackbirds that wait until you're done, and then circle in for a look. We have known each other for so many years. We're often on the same plane, at the same restaurants, in many of the same places, but they would never visit us."

I chose to walk the long way back to the hotel. It was all too much for me. In an instant, I had a completely different picture of the human race and, above all, people who didn't need more money. Surely they could be nicer to each other. I could not stop walking and walking, as my thoughts swirled. Death scared me again — that cruel fate you cannot buy your way out of. What was the meaning of life? Why do you get so exposed when you make the climb up? Why can't we humans take care of life the right way?

In April 2009, the cancer took Rena. A year later, I got a call from Jean-Louis' secretary telling me that he had passed away.

I never set foot in Paris again. 'The City of Light' was Jean-Louis and Rena for me. It was a destination with a warm home where I was always welcome. Now that this was gone, Paris does not exist for me either.

NOT LONG AFTER I'd first met Jean-Louis and Rena, I wound up meeting former King Constantine II and Queen Anne-Marie of Greece, though in this case it was less by chance.

I had been sitting in the lounge at Athens airport, on my way to Sweden. I always buy all the fashion and gossip magazines that I can carry, so I have something to browse on the plane. Flipping through gossip magazines would give me inspiration, seeing how celebrities act, what kind of clothes they wear, their hair, how their faces and bodies changed. These all inspired me to anticipate societal trends.

There were some pictures of the former Greek king and queen, from their holiday in the Greek islands. I saw that he wore a pair of my swimming trunks, and the queen was also wearing my swimwear. I looked again, wanting to be sure they were mine, and saw the PE logo very clearly.

I was excited, as it was the early 1990s and I had only been on the market for 5–6 years. I thought about how to take advantage of this, but the subject of royalty is a touchy one in Greece. Since the abolition of the monarchy in 1973, most Greeks, in both a 1974 referendum and subsequent polls, believed that the republic was better for them. The exiled former king had even been detained and questioned on his trips back to Greece, and had been denied Greek citizenship by the republic, since he'd refused to take a surname. For a long time he was not welcome in the country, and did not return to live there until 2013.

During exile, he and the former queen lived in London, and I decided to seek them out next time I visited there. I could see that their second son, Prince Nikolaos, was making a splash in the gossip rags, and everyone wondered when the partying young bachelor would get engaged. The prince, meanwhile, seemed to live his life without much thought on the subject. There were not many marital contenders in royal circles, and newspapers speculated that Sweden's HRH Crown Princess Victoria might be a suitable match. Many years later, the prince married Venezuelan writer and publicist Tatiana Blatnik, who is descended from the 19th century German royal Wilhelm II of Hesse.

I wrote to the former king's secretary, told her I was on my way to London, and requested an audience with him. I told her I had seen him photographed in my swimwear.

I was very nervous about this. I did not know how to address a king or how to dress for a one-on-one meeting with one.

His office was in central London. The guards received me and I waited in a room of typical English design, with nothing that reminded me of Greece. Even in exile, I suppose I had expected him to be immersed in a world of classical Greek design.

My décor aesthetic, most proudly displayed in my Gothenburg showroom, was a mixture of ancient and modern Greece: white marble, proud pillars with gold details, and Greek blue on the ceiling. People who were allowed to enter that room often stood silently for a long time, looking around with their mouths open. It was a great contrast to the environment in the rest of Sweden, and it was my inspirational place. Some questioned why I had such a lavish retreat, and seldom let people in, though every now and then a journalist from a major newspaper or TV channel, or an important customer or supplier, might have the doors opened for them. Most had to rely on reports of what it looked like.

The former king's secretary greeted me and asked me to follow her to his quarters. She opened the next door and there he sat, behind a large desk. He got up, took a few steps towards me and stretched out his hand. I took his hand and stared intently into his face. It felt great to shake hands with the King of Greece. He led me to the sofa and seated himself in a giant, royal armchair. Between us was a side table, and the secretary asked if I would like to have coffee. I declined, as I always had since childhood, and she asked if I wanted Greek coffee instead. I said no, but asked for water.

On the table was a large bowl of pistachios from Aegina. I recognized these because the best ones came from there. The king began opening one as we 'mortals' usually do: you hold the pistachio to your mouth, lick the salt on the shell, and then split the shell with your teeth to get the nut out. The king handed me the bowl so I could take some. I didn't have time to recall my parents' words — "You don't have to accept anything when you are with someone" — and grabbed a few.

I wondered if I should eat them like the king, which was exactly as the rest of us did in Greece. Could I really do that, in front of royalty? I commented that they were from Aegina and he nodded his head. "They are the best," he said. "I love *fystikia* ('Greece's peanuts') and eat them regularly. You cannot stop once you start!"

You'd hear these words from ordinary people, but now I was hearing them from a king! I stayed for about 30 minutes and answered his questions about my business and me. He already knew something of me, as both his secretary and the queen had told him a bit of my story when they knew I would be visiting. I told him about my recent success in Thailand, and he seemed impressed that I was so Greek in how I thought and carried myself, and how, through my design, I wanted to promote Greece.

I left feeling a great deal of energy and pride. A few months later, a Christmas card from the king arrived at my office. The staff opened the envelope and could not believe their eyes. There was a picture of the Greek royal family and a handwritten message from the king, wishing me a merry Christmas and happy New Year!

I felt badly that I'd forgotten to send him holiday greetings. I used to do so, and more than just a card. I'd send nice gifts to all customers, suppliers, journalists — everyone. For a couple months in advance, some of my employees would sit and prepare Christmas cards and presents for a wide range of recipients. I wanted them to breathe the same ideals I had throughout my journey: *passion, respect,* and *love.*

I struggled every year to find some gift to surprise people with their Christmas card. The cards themselves were memorable, and the recipients reacted happily to them. We used to drown in Christmas cards in those days, when everyone sent them out to show how many people they knew and thought about. It's sort of the same as today's Instagram 'likes.'

Giving gifts to buyers, customers and journalists is strictly regulated under the law. The maximum allowable amount was US$20–US$25, and some large companies had a policy that prohibited the staff from receiving any gifts at all.

I decided to go to London and personally give the king and his family a Christmas card and some presents. I called his secretary, to ensure that

I'd be able to greet them and hand over the gift. She confirmed they were in London, but warned that his agenda was full, so it might not work out.

Two days later, I managed to hand over Christmas presents to the entire Greek royal family in their London residence. I took the opportunity to mention to the king that I had thoughts of asking his son, Prince Nikolaos, to go with me to Thailand to attend my 'Greek' fashion show there. I knew they had a very good relationship with the Thai king, and thought it might be a draw for the prince to accompany me.

A few months later, it was time to start planning for the formalities associated with Prince Nikolaos's trip to Bangkok. I went to London a couple of times, the last time being a couple of months before the fashion show. Prince Nikolaos was to come to the king's office and meet me, but he never showed. The king's secretary called him several times but didn't get an answer. I was sitting in the king's quarters when she mentioned this to us. "He will be late," the king replied. "He has fallen asleep or forgotten your meeting!"

Later that afternoon, I went back to Sweden without meeting the prince. I let go of the idea that he would come, and focused instead on planning my trip. I would not be able to cope with the uncertainty of 'Will he or won't he?' He never bothered to mention it or follow up with me in any way, and I put a big red 'X' through his name.

In 2002, I was invited by the Swedish Ministry of Foreign Affairs to join a business delegation to Mexico. The group would accompany the Swedish royal family on an official state visit, at the invitation of President Vicente Fox.

My first thought was to say no. I called my travel agent to check what the trip would cost. This was just 20 years ago, but you couldn't book a ticket online, and had to go through an agency for everything. In the meantime, I mentioned to some friends that I had doubts, and told them how expensive it would be. They got angry with me. "You'll get the money from us for the trip if necessary. Go! Don't you understand how big this is?!"

After a few days of back and forth, I decided to go, and booked a business class ticket after I learned what other companies would be represented. There were Volvo, ABB, Electrolux, and a name that really caught my attention: Marcus Wallenberg. Wallenberg was from one of the most prominent families in Sweden, with interests in banking and industry, but on a massive scale. They held controlling interests in the likes of Ericsson, the banking group SEB, Electrolux and ABB. On top of that, SAS, SKF, AstraZeneca, Husqvarna and the aerospace arm of Saab were also under the Wallenberg sphere of influence, and at one point they employed 40% of Sweden's industrial workforce. Being invited along on the same trip as Marcus Wallenberg was a big deal indeed.

I contacted the Export Council in Mexico City to prepare for meetings there. I wanted to see if there were any opportunities to establish Panos Emporio there. I read everything I could find about the country, because the only link I had had with the place was through tequila. I have said repeatedly here that I am not a drinker, but I've always had a taste for tequila. To this day, it is my absolute favourite drink.

As our date of departure approached, I started feeling really anxious. It was the first time I would travel with the Swedish royal family, and I would be sitting with the President of Mexico and other government officials for dinner.

My English was not that good. How do you greet a president? Who will sit next to me? I did not know any of the Swedish business delegation personally, and when I checked the names, I became even more worried that I was lacking in credentials and clout. Had they invited me by mistake? Would they come to regret it?

I signalled that I wanted to pull out, and a senior government official responsible for the Swedish delegation called, wondering why I'd had a change of heart. He said they wanted me to be there, that I was a good addition to the line-up, and that the other businessmen would appreciate my participation. I took a deep breath, pulled myself together, and it was all on again.

I asked the travel agency to book me as far back in business class as possible, and wound up in the sixth row. As I sat wondering how the king would travel to Mexico, he and the queen walked onto the plane, surrounded by their entourage. They sat in the front row, and behind them sat two members of their court. They had blocked the left side of the first row so that it would remain unoccupied. There was no pomp or ceremony: the staff just welcomed them, as they'd welcomed us all. I sat and pondered the differences between countries, and how they handled famous people.

Here, HM King Carl XVI Gustaf of Sweden stepped aboard like everyone else, without fanfare.

I remember being in Athens, and had media attention because of my interest in buying the big Greek football club PAOK. It was impossible to find a moment of peace. On the days of heavy media frenzy, I didn't dare go out without a bodyguard, and the hotel had extra security positioned to stop reporters who wanted to come up to my room. It wasn't enough: TV reporters materialized outside my door, waiting to catch me. Restaurants invited me to dine free of charge, and treated me like a king … or better. In Greece, big names received special treatment everywhere they went.

But in my new homeland, Sweden, no matter who you are, you are treated the same way. I have been torn over what is right. In the beginning, I liked the sense of equality, but over time I realized that it lowers even the most basic courtesies to a common denominator. It's too exaggerated in this direction, in contrast with my homeland, which swings too far in the other direction.

The flight to Mexico was a long one. I could have fallen asleep, but I was excited and didn't want to miss anything. I wanted to experience every moment. After a few hours, the lights were turned off and everyone in business class got ready to sleep. Even the king and queen. I was curious what their assistants would do. In my little world, they would sit and watch their backs, but that wasn't the case. It was time for them to unwind, too.

Upon arriving at the hotel, I noticed that the royal couple stayed where the rest of us did. There were many heavily armed police officers outside, and you could see some inside the lobby. We'd read how dangerous it was in Mexico, and had been advised to follow only the planned activities and nothing else. We were warned not to go out by ourselves.

We had arrived in the middle of the day and there were only a few hours until the first official engagement, where the king would receive about 500 guests. We barely had time to go up to the room, unpack and take a quick shower before going down and getting into a line of minibuses. During the journey, we were surrounded by police cars and motorcycles. There were even helicopters overhead. It was like the president's motorcade in an American movie.

I wondered if the king would be on time, after such a long journey. I hadn't seen him when I boarded the minibus. We arrived at our destination and the venue, which was also heavily secured by police officers.

Everything was well organized and our bus stopped right at the entrance. After I disembarked and walked up the stairs, the king and queen were already there, greeting the guests one by one! When it was my turn to be greeted by him, I was surprised that he welcomed me by name. The king knew my name! I was dumbfounded. I do not remember if I whispered something back or just shook hands with Their

Majesties. That day was certainly a major highlight of my life. Incomprehensibly so!

I, a poor immigrant who had managed to make a career, shook hands with the King and Queen of Sweden, and he addressed me by my first and last name. "Welcome, Panos Papadopoulos," he said. "Nice to have you in our business delegation!"

At that moment, I felt so proud, and wished my parents could see me with the royal couple. I felt like a man, like my Dad. I felt I had reached a level of achievement, and maybe a level of personal maturity, that my parents would have wanted for me.

There were many Swedes who lived and worked in Mexico who had been invited, and some Mexican citizens who did business with Sweden. It was a good atmosphere. I was focused for the rest of the evening on what the king would do and how he acted. Seeing him in top form at the entrance, especially after a long journey, was impressive. It would have been enough to give a generic welcome speech, but he greeted us each by name. I admired his energy and strength, and wondered if the Swedish people were aware of how hard he worked. He remained active all evening, through to the end of the event.

On the way back to the hotel, I tried to analyse the king's actions and what they meant in practice. Suddenly, I started smiling and said a word out loud: "Touch!"

Next to me on the minibus sat the CEO of a large multinational, and he turned to me with a look of surprise. "Did you say something?"

"No, I'm OK," I replied. "I was just wondering why they'd wear out the king by placing him at the entrance to greet several hundred guests. I wouldn't be able to shake hands with 500 guests, and say, 'Welcome,' along with their names!"

He looked at me without answering.

"I know why I said that! **He and I have the same marketing method! It's something we have in common: *touch*!** Everyone who took the king by the hand, they will never forget it. Even if they aren't royalists, they'll still have a positive impression of him."

"What do you mean, you do that, too? Do you greet all those who buy your swimwear?" asked the CEO.

"No, but it's like I've touched them," I said. "I don't know how, but that's what they all tell me. That I've touched them deeply and they will never leave me! They'll always follow me, but it has nothing to do with my swimwear — it's about me as a person. That's what they like. It's just me.

My swimwear is the way through which they show their appreciation to me as a person. It is my feelings, my values, my way of acting, how I appeal to them, my way of being. It's just like the king. We touch them unconsciously."

The executive gave me kind of a funny look, and a little nod, and went back to reading whatever it was that he'd been reading. As for me, I was convinced of every word of it, and meant it sincerely. It filled me with pride and happiness. I felt pumped up and on top of the world, all the way back to Sweden.

When you're in business, your backstory sums up everything about you. Mine had become well known: the immigrant who had come to Sweden, stared prejudice in the face, and succeeded through hard work and values. It was easy to tell the truth. People, consciously or unconsciously, recognize it when they hear it. It was never marketing hype. The truth has a way of being consistent and unwavering, and that's what I've always told about my journey.

Everything else then becomes connected to that story. When I talk about my inspiration for a collection, people recognize that it comes from the heart, and it's consistent with everything I've said before. They know my feelings are genuine when I put this into one of my catalogues or a media statement. And, when they put on one of my designs, they can physically feel that it's comfortable, more so than the competition's, and that also reminds them of how much soul I've put into it. It reinforces what I've promised them about a great fit and making them feel good. And that then reinforces the understanding that I've always told them the truth ... and on it builds, over years, over decades.

The Panos Emporio brand is closely tied to me and my personal identity and journey. We are inseparable. *That's* what people purchase, more than the designs themselves.

Panos Emporio wasn't big, but the knowledge of the brand was huge. It was so strong, in fact, that I've even found myself on the lists compiled by financial journalists of the richest people in Sweden. I can tell you for a fact that I'm not up there. For example, one magazine put me on the top of a list of rich foreigners in Sweden and mentioned a half-billion dollar fortune. You can see that that's an invention because, as I've noted, you can't hide the figures in Sweden. It's easy enough for anyone to do a quick web search and find the turnover and profit figures each year.

Why would that happen? It wasn't the only time, and if you were to ask how big Panos Emporio was, there are people who'll say it's a multi-national company with a huge turnover! That's a myth, but one that's not made up by my company or me. It is a reflection of the image and strength of the brand, pure and simple. It's why some companies have the brand value as a single entry on their balance sheets — as intangible, intellectual property. If you factored that in, maybe I was richer than I thought! Still, any way you look at it, I was never in the same league as these massive companies.

The other wealthy people who were on the trip to Mexico never asked me about my revenue or profitability. They only said, "Pleased to meet you!" "You are amazing!" That was at a time when I wasn't as big as I am now. Nevertheless, Mexican ministers, Swedish government representatives, Marcus Wallenberg and other extremely wealthy, successful, connected people seemed fascinated by me. It was all sort of confusing — it was like a dream.

The power of the brand was unbelievable. It inspired thousands of people. It moved and empowered people who had hard lives. It made them want to try to have a better life. I'd touched students, foreigners, criminals, politicians, royalty — people from all walks of life, not only here in Sweden but in other far-flung countries. Even if they knew just a small part of my story, there was enough in there to make them connect with my life.

When I look back, it's a pity I didn't fully understand that at the time. Why? Was it from my childhood? I was conditioned to work hard and keep running. I never stopped because I wanted to do so many things. That makes me sad sometimes, when I look back. In hindsight, I wish I had done some things differently ... not to build a bigger company and put more money in the bank, but to enrich my private life.

I've never really been a child, in that I never found time for myself. My Mum always used to say that about me. "Stop thinking about us," she'd say. "Think about you! Don't always try to make other people happy. You are forgetting yourself."

Maybe this is something entrepreneurs have in common. But am I an entrepreneur? I don't see myself as one. Why not? Maybe it's because I'm not attracted to money. Maybe it's because I put so much passion into whatever I do, and I think too much about how to be a good person. I follow my heart over my head, and that has caused me to lose a lot of money, because I based decisions on feelings rather than cold, hard facts.

Back to the myth. I exist, but people seem to believe I sit on some lofty perch, far away from where they are. They're shocked when they meet me. Not just everyday consumers, but, as I said, people much richer and better educated than me. Lawyers and managing directors have said they were nervous about meeting me! Sometimes, people who come to business negotiations or meetings — whom I might label 'powerful older people' — have actually said that. They're conscious of how big the brand is, and they associate that with someone who must wield tremendous power.

It's not an advantage for me, to scare people and keep them at a distance. It's been happening since the early days. I've seen competitors at airports, and could overhear them discussing whether to approach me and ask about cooperating in some way, perhaps on a licensing deal, to produce items using my name. But they didn't dare approach me or call!

I always reply to all my emails. It doesn't matter who sends them. I return all my calls, even if it's just with a few words. I'm always polite. Why I scare so many people — business leaders, journalists, even police officers who've pulled me over for speeding, one of them visibly shaking when she saw who she'd stopped — I cannot fully grasp.

My staff frequently got strange questions about me after they told others where they worked. People couldn't believe they'd even met me. If only they knew that I was always the first into the office and the last to leave, and was open, friendly and conversational with everyone there.

All kingdoms operate behind a myth. I don't think all myths are necessarily concocted. They often swirl round people who authentically turn them into reality. It doesn't matter if we like it, or if they're true. **Myths aren't fully representative of reality, but there is often some truth at their core. That's the only way they endure. Any insincere attempts at fame, or infamy, quickly fall apart, never rising to the level of myth.**

When I think about my brand awareness, and the myth, there are some parallels with Tesla. Tesla is an unbelievably huge brand, but a very small company compared with the power of its name and image. Why? It's surrounded by a myth that's constructed by people who like the product and the vision. *We've* created it!

The downside is that myths are hard to change. Some people will believe them forever. Take HM the King. Good myths have put him in a very difficult position all his life. He must live up to them, and that's something monarchs and successful people of various stripes have in common. People have concocted their own idea about who you are, and how you act, and they will not change their mind about it, even if they see proof to the contrary. The myth doesn't die.

But the stronger the myth that surrounds you, the more alone you will feel. I've met many successful people in my life, and loneliness is one thing we all have in common. That's because the myth serves to keep your friends, and potential friends, away. Giorgio Armani has spoken about it many times in interviews. He would book models to spend time around his pool so he wouldn't feel alone.

I noticed it very early in my career. One Sunday, I called the leader of a political party, whom I knew quite well, while he was in Gothenburg. I asked him out for a coffee and he immediately said, "Yes! When? Now? I'll be there!" As we walked to the café, he said, "I'm glad you called me. It's a nice day and I wanted to take a walk, but I didn't know whom I could call. I thought about calling you, but thought you'd probably be busy." And here I was, thinking the same thing!

He's there, nearby, and we know one another ... but he's such an important politician that he must be booked solid with meetings and VIP engagements. Maybe I shouldn't bother him now, as 8:30 in the morning would be too early for someone like him. I couldn't possibly ring him up and suggest a casual chat at a café. All those thoughts circled before I made the call.

The more different you are, the more differently you act. You don't walk on the same wide roads as all the other people. And so, you try alternative routes, the more interesting ones, and come upon surprises you could never have anticipated. The winding paths end up making your life more interesting, and you feel richer for the journey in many ways. That's what my journey has looked like, and how it's felt.

BUT, BACK TO MEXICO. The second day, following our arrival, was the most important of the trip. We were scheduled for a state dinner at the Presidential Palace.

We met at 3:30 PM in the hotel lobby. Everyone was on time. The entire crowd seemed to be well-dressed men in dark suits and blue ties. I was immediately aware that I had too colourful a tie. Everyone seemed to be looking at me ... at my tie. Jacob Wallenberg was the only one to comment: "Nice tie!"

"Is it too colourful?" I asked.

"No, you can dress as you like. You're a designer," he said, in a very friendly and determined voice.

I felt safer after that. I did not have many, but I loved a Hermès tie that I'd received from Jean-Louis Dumas on my birthday. The floral pattern was small and stylish, I thought.

A convoy of minibuses surrounded by police cars made its way through the teeming streets of Mexico City, toward the Presidential Palace. Streets were cordoned off so that the motorcade could pass easily through the chaotic city. Several helicopters circled, guarding the airspace.

The large gates opened and all the cars pulled through, stopping one by one in front of the main entrance. My eyes went around to see the different people waiting for us, and to admire the beautiful building we would enter. It was a magical moment, and my body and brain were in full swing, registering everything that was happening. The king was already there, and together with the President of Mexico, he received us.

Eventually, after a short mingling session, we were seated at a long table. On my right side sat a woman from their Ministry of Export, and on my left a man from the Ministry of Finance. Both knew my name and were well informed about my business and me. Not having to answer boring, formal questions put me at ease. The woman was quite pleasant, and told me she was an admirer of my designs. "I know that you're very popular in Europe," she said. "We look forward to you establishing yourself in our beautiful country as well." The whole evening was made so much more pleasant by their interest and friendly conversation. My self-confidence grew and I was able to relax a bit.

I find it embarrassing when I'm at events and am suddenly bombarded with lots of questions: "Are you the one who makes the nice swimwear?" "What goes into making a great swimsuit?" "What colours are in this summer?" I usually want to shut myself off and not deal with any of that. As I've said, I'm basically a shy sort of guy. Not this time, though. Now, I wanted to socialize! What a difference!

Dinner lasted two hours and they held to the schedule, down to the second. We then started our journey back to the hotel, where a new adventure would await me.

I was curious to see how the Mexican people dressed, acted and partied, and had decided to go to some nightclubs with another attendee. I knew I'd feel at home in the clubs and would find inspiration, because I've learned to interpret people's behaviour when they're out having fun. Visiting a number of nightspots would give me a clear picture of their fashion prowess, their bodies, the way they moved and interacted, and the possibilities for my designs to conquer Mexico.

We changed into lighter clothing and went to reception to ask them to write up a list of the best clubs. It was a Tuesday night, and I thought it would be pretty quiet doing a round of the hotspots.

The receptionist asked me to wait, and within a minute, one of our security team came and asked what I was doing. I replied that I wanted to visit three or four nightclubs, but did not intend to stay out for long. I planned to pop in for a drink, have a look, and move on.

"That's not possible," he said sternly. "You're not allowed to leave the hotel." After much negotiation, and talk about their responsibility for our safety, they decided we could go, but security personnel would have to accompany us. We went in their car, and soon arrived at the first club. One guard went in front of us and the other walked behind. There was a bit of a queue, but they swept past everyone and discreetly showed their credentials at the door.

We ended up in the cloakroom, where I thought a sign that said "Hidden Camera" was a joke until I read the next line: "Leave your weapons here!" It was a little worrisome how uptight the security guards seemed as we moved into the crowd. They stuck tightly with us and constantly scanned the surroundings. They steered us through the place, and after ten minutes said it was time for us to leave. There was a fair-sized crowd, but mostly guys, and I was ready to move on.

The next place was the same. On the way there, I pressed the guards for more information on the security situation. "It's dangerous, and this is really too big a risk for you," one of them said. "I strongly recommend that we go back soon."

"Can't we go to ordinary clubs where regular people go?" I asked.

"These are regular clubs," he said, "but they're a big security risk for you."

We visited two more clubs, but I came away without any inspiration, or a clear impression of how Mexican people look and dress. The only thing I remembered was, "Leave your weapons here!"

I did conclude, from seeing a few girls that night, that it would be difficult to sell my swimwear to them. Their physique was distinctly different, and we'd have to adapt the designs accordingly. I had that experience in Thailand as well. I learned to study the target audience carefully before deciding how good our product would really be for them.

After an hour and a half we were back at the hotel, and I could see the relief on the guards' faces.

The next day, I had a meeting with a couple of big retailers, but I had already decided that I would not return to Mexico, at least not to do business. I always chose customers in countries that I would enjoy visiting. I was in a position of being able to steer clear of some markets, for all the right reasons. This was the luxury of freedom of choice.

The following day, at lunchtime, I met the king in the lobby and we exchanged a few words. I could read in his face what a tiring schedule he'd had. His Majesty's soft, polite voice was clearly fatigued. I thought about how hard he had it, not only during that trip, but every day, year after year. My thoughts went to all the great personalities whose lives are one long, tough schedule, as others control their every waking hour. They are prisoners of their greatness and success. It's impossible for them to maintain any sense of balance. It often reminded me of my great mentor Jean-Louis, and the constant demands on his time. Being famous all over the world does not necessarily mean more happiness, but more responsibility and less time for yourself.

After that trip, I had a much greater understanding of what our king does and how much he takes on for his country.

IT WAS DURING the writing of this book that I put on my Instagram Stories a news report that said I was selling the Miss Sweden contest — which we'd bought the rights to in 2004 — and discussed my pageant-related dispute with Donald Trump. As usual, I looked for a Greek song to post online with the image, and the right one popped up. I had never heard it before, even though the artist, Vertis, is a favourite.

It featured a sentiment I had expressed in hundreds of interviews, and have mentioned in these pages: I act with my heart rather than my brain! I have chosen to create my own journey, and pursue it in my own way. I wanted a rich and exciting life. My first goal, although money was never the driving motivation, was to get to the first million, to ensure an OK standard of living. That money in the bank would provide for security if something happened.

But then, I forgot everything to do with money. Running profitably was something I did not have to concern myself with; my values and habits just naturally steered the business in that direction. I never worked up a budget and never liked balance sheets. I knew without checking the books that I was in the black. Every year, when the auditor reviewed the financial statements with me, he could not understand why I didn't want to listen to the details. "You have earned many millions," he would say, and wait for me to react. I never did. He used to say he'd never had a customer who did not jump for joy when they were profitable. "You don't seem to care!" I heard, again and again.

At the end of 2020, I sat for a long coffee with a friend. It was sunny that day and the coffee was good. It was late afternoon in Sweden, and soon the US stock market would open. I then decided to buy into Tesla. My friend talked a lot about the revolutionary electric car and rocket maker, and I had a gut feeling about it, so I bought a US$1.5 million stake as we sat there chatting. I bought the shares, via my mobile phone, without thinking that I should check with my advisers. I pressed the 'Buy' button. A couple of hours later, Tesla had gone up many percentage points, and I sold.

"How much did you earned just now?" my friend asked.

"Wait, let me see," I told him, clicking into the Tesla chart. "It looks like I made about 3.5 million kronor (US$350,000)."

He stared at me, and then exclaimed, "You made that much money by pressing a button, and you don't seem to care! Most people don't make that much in their entire lifetime."

The same friend was with me on another day, as a stock I'd invested in went the other way, and I lost a significant amount. Again, he seemed shocked that I didn't seem to blink an eye, and wanted to know why I behaved so nonchalantly.

I told my friend not to think that I'd lost all respect, or appreciation, for money. I explained that it wasn't the money that provided the pleasure, but the feeling of pressing the right button at the right time. That gave me deep satisfaction, like an orgasm. I was never a gaming man — I don't play cards, or the lottery, or gamble on anything else. But I explained that I got a gut feeling, correctly interpreted the little information we had before the stock market would open, and dared invest in my interpretation. And that gave me a thrill. It's that simple. I compete with myself in these situations, and put myself to the test. I have an explosive personality. All my life I have acted before the information in front of me was fully processed in my head. My heart moved faster than my brain, and controlled my decisions.

When I bought the Fröken Sverige (Miss Sweden) beauty pageant, it was a similar story. I was sitting one day at my favourite spot, Café Centro, in central Gothenburg. Hans, who owned the café, made an extra effort that day to prepare the perfect Panos Cappuccino. His employees had undoubtedly thought, "Here he is again." They would make my coffee if Hans wasn't there, and when they were done with the last drop of milk, they would bring it to me and watch my face, to see if I approved or if they had to make it again.

The place was quite crowded that morning. It was a hot summer day, and I sat outside with my business lawyer, Bob. As Hans placed that expertly prepared cup in front of me, he lingered for a moment. "You look bored," he asked.

I didn't answer, but Bob said, "I agree with Hans. You need an exciting new project. You've talked about Miss Sweden; you said you might want to acquire it. What about that?"

"Yes, well, I don't have the time," I told him.

"This would suit you," he said. "You need new challenges and stimulation. You're stuck in a daily grind, and the routine is killing your creativity. You need to do something else to get your energy back."

He observed that the business was booming, and said I deserved all the credit for that, but observed that I lacked community involvement.

"You said you wanted to change the concept of Miss Sweden. To shake things up. Do you want us to check if they want to sell?"

After he left, I sat there quietly thinking. Hans fetched me another cappuccino. He knows I drink it with much less milk than normal, and made with double espresso ristretto — a short, concentrated shot. I savoured it, and I began feeling joyful. I pondered what my lawyer had said: "Buy Miss Sweden."

After a few minutes, I decided to call the MTG-TV3 channel, which owned the rights to Fröken Sverige. Despite being owned by a television channel, the contest no longer aired. By then, the once-popular event was said by some to have become 'unofficial.' As I waited on hold to be connected to the general manager, I made the decision: *I would buy it that very day!*

His secretary asked me to call back the following week, because he was on his way to their head office in London. I insisted on speaking with him.

She patched the call through, and he answered, but asked that I call back when he had time to chat. "No, I can't wait," I told him. "I want to buy Miss Sweden … and I want to do it right now!"

He laughed, and said in a friendly way, "Come on, now … can't you wait until next week?"

"No. I asked you two years ago, and offered you x million. Now, I'm offering half that amount. If you take it, here and now, I'll send the contract by the end of the day. Next week the offer will go down considerably."

He went quiet. I knew they were having difficulty keeping the pageant afloat, and once the brand sank much further they'd be forced to shut it down entirely. He began to explain that this had to be taken up at a higher level, at the head office. When I make a decision, though, I'm ready to rock, and I have little patience. I pressed on.

"Call your boss, and don't come back with a counter-offer. The deal is on the table. Either you take it or you don't. You'll get the money today, when we sign. I'm serious."

And with that, he was off and running.

To think, a huge, listed company was now working frantically — under pressure from me, on a weekend — to make such a momentous a decision and get everything ready in a few hours! And, I'd offered them half as much as I had two years earlier.

Everything came together, and Miss Sweden belonged to me that same day! Me, an immigrant who came from nowhere and was boldly challenging large establishments. A black skull who had gained people's sympathy for what he did. People loved my way of taking decisive action and making remarkable things happen. It gave me extra power, because people asked me all the time what I was going to do next. There was always a spotlight on me. And now, this small designer dictated the conditions to a multinational, which agreed in an hour to sell him the Miss Sweden brand.

It wasn't just a case of 'Where there's a will, there's a way.' It was the right evolutionary step, the logical next move, because it brought me community involvement.

I realized that that's important to any business, having a greater connection to people. And it was *people* who ultimately drove my business, not their wallets. I had come to realize that it wasn't just about my heart … it was about the public's, too.

It cost what it cost, but I wanted to realize a dream I'd long been formulating: to elevate better female role models!

I had used a negotiation technique I'd developed naturally since child-hood. Push hard and make it happen. No hesitation or dithering. Early on, it had literally been a matter of survival for me. Buying Miss Sweden was connected to my curiosity about society and interest in the psychology behind it all. But to spontaneously decide on a price while I waited for him to pick up the phone, without a business plan, without any of the usual, sensible steps, and spend millions that I'd earned with hard work? I did have respect for this hard-earned money. However, this was the excitement I wanted: something completely different to challenge myself with, and to succeed at. Something new and interesting to put all that money to work on! I knew it was not possible to revive a dead brand — dead is dead — but Miss Sweden was on life support, and here I was, ready to prove that miracles really do happen.

My self-confidence was at its peak, and I was certain all my decisions could be implemented. It cost what it cost, and that was just fine, because I could afford it! I felt independent of money: whenever I didn't have much, I knew that I could create it. I'm sure that my childhood helped me a lot in that regard. I'd already made money when I was ten years old. It is so difficult to explain that feeling and not be misunderstood. I supposed I could compare it to a young circus acrobat who tests the limits. He risks his life when he hangs in the air from a rope, but he is so confident that it feels like a steel cable

I knew I had to retool the pageant. Tv3 had run the event for three years, taking over from *Vecko-Revyn*, a respected women's magazine, and couldn't make a go of it. The 2004 event, run by the publishers of *Slitz*, was controversial, to say the least. Times were changing, and with them, the concept of the beauty pageant.

When feminist groups heard of the purchase, they got in touch with me. I suspect there was a fear that I would take my lead from the 2004 event, and head in an even more extreme direction. That never crossed my mind. The pageant had to be revamped in full, and we would delay the relaunch until 2006, to give it a fresh start.

To begin with, I had to get rid of the idea of objectifying women, with everything revolving around their looks. The swimwear segment was the first casualty. I understand the irony here, but swimwear designs have their purpose, and I didn't see them playing a part in what was now being called Nya Fröken Sverige (New Miss Sweden). The parade of women in swimwear felt woefully out of place in the 21st century, especially in a country that prides itself on social progress and liberalism.

A freethinking woman does not need to twirl around in a swimsuit to prove herself.

When we advertised for contestants in the want ads, becoming the only pageant in the world to ever do so, we used gender-neutral language, as is the law in Sweden. Anyone could apply, even men, but they wouldn't get particularly far in the process because the winner would head to Miss Universe, which barred transsexual contestants.

The purpose was to break away from the 'pageant circuit.' In most countries, there are minor pageants, and you get the same type of young woman entering them, competing in one after the other, eventually getting to the national event. I wanted to capture as broad a section of the population as possible, though there were limits.

If you ever had a chance to read the Miss Universe rules, you'd see that the eligibility requirements are quite stringent. The winner must never have been married or given birth to a child. At the time, the age range was 18 to 27, although you could be a year younger as long as you reached 18 by the time the final took place. And, you had to be a national of the country you represented, and live there (with exceptions made for women who studied abroad). While I couldn't do anything about Miss Universe's rules, I could at least try to address things on my own turf.

Therefore, my second change dealt with what the contestants had to do. The traditional pageant construct had them dress up, and judges scored them in swimwear and evening wear. They then had an interview session where they were scored again. Instead, I put them through a series of leadership contests and seminars, and they were scored on those, as though they were completing exams for a scholarship. I arranged for them to do the interviews in English and Swedish. Remember when Candice Bergen's character insists in *Miss Congeniality* that her competition is "a scholarship programme"? I really brought that to life. A Star TV series, *Vägen till Fröken Sverige 2006* (*The Road to Miss Sweden 2006*), followed their progress, in a reality format.

I got rid of the tiara and sash, too. When Josephine Alhanko was declared the winner, she came up to accept her prize in a smart-looking business blazer.

She was a fitting winner, having two master's degrees, and was at that time pursuing her Ph.D. She was exactly the sort of role model I had been looking for.

Miss Universe was a limited liability partnership in which Donald Trump had a share, although both the NBC TV network, who broadcast it, and Trump himself liked to overstate just how much of it he owned. They tended not to meddle too much in each country's competitions, provided they got their licence fee each year. They also offered next to no support through the licence: if you were to study the logos of the Miss Universe-affiliated competition in each country, you'd find there's no consistency. Part of why Nya Fröken Sverige always looked different was that there was never a template provided by New York.

Once we changed the concept, the Trump Organization was informed of every detail. Initially, they were positive: since their motive was getting the licence fee out of me each year, they were happy that I was making Fröken Sverige bigger in Sweden. They knew just as well as I did that the old concept was all but dead, not only here, but in many European countries.

I did get some benefits and discounts, and they even accepted that the Swedish contest's swimwear segment was gone.

Josephine headed to Miss Universe's 2006 final in Los Angeles and placed in the semi-finals. She was the first Miss Sweden to place in nine years. While in LA, she did have to get into swimwear and wear a sash, but there was nothing I could do about it. It was necessary if Josephine was to have a shot at the international title, which she very much wanted. During this time I met Trump, and everything was cordial between us. In my opinion, it was no coincidence that Josephine placed. I was good for the money, and I was netting them a lot of publicity in Sweden.

However, the revolution I pushed for in pageants didn't go unnoticed by the American media. ABC News, one of the top-three commercial evening news programmes in the US, came and did a story on us. When we started making waves in their own country, this positive promotion began to work against us in New York.

Miss Universe wasn't prepared for a shift. They had a business model and appeared fearful of change, especially if my concept were to spread to other parts of Europe. They would eventually have a problem with elimination of the swimwear section, because the international rules prescribe that the national winner must have gone through it.

Once the reality of the situation hit home, they couldn't fathom that we didn't have a swimwear segment. And come 2007, I felt it was inappropriate to send the winner to Miss Universe if they couldn't accept that we had to do things differently in Sweden. After Josephine, three more women held the Nya Fröken Sverige title.

In the meantime, I saw how the Miss Universe Organization ran Miss USA, and it was a low-grade production. That was the final straw. I couldn't spend so much money, keeping things at a high level, when the organization itself — including the Trump Organization — resided at such a low level. I sent Azra Duliman, the 2009 winner, to the COP 15 climate conference in Copenhagen instead of to Miss Universe.

The knives were out at Miss Universe, and they unilaterally sought to end the connection between Nya Fröken Sverige and themselves. A rival Swedish organization had approached them for the licence, and they were more than happy to award it to someone who was prepared to toe the line. This came despite letters of support to Miss Universe from around the world for our pageant. The new group, calling themselves Miss Universe Sweden, became the official licensee. Miss Universe continued on its old-school, pre-feminist way, with Trump remaining in place until he began his run for the US presidency. How passé it had all become.

My stint with Nya Fröken Sverige had implications elsewhere. In 2013, Miss Universe New Zealand was taken over by a new company, and they, too, discontinued the swimwear segment, directly inspired by what I did. They got around Miss Universe's requirement by shooting a swimwear calendar on a closed set, with female chaperones, and the judges would examine the finished photos. Any contestant could opt out, but between 2013 and 2019 only one ever did. Prior to the takeover, the contestants paraded around in bikinis in a suburban Auckland bar, which the new organizers found disturbing. By the end of the 2010s, Miss World, the older international pageant, also banned the swimwear competition. Sometimes it takes fresh thinking from an outsider to see what is wrong, and to remedy it.

Even though Miss Universe ultimately proved immovable, there's pride in being the first, and paving the way for others to follow suit. All it took was courage, and knowing where you wanted society to head. It was part of the same journey that led me to work in prisons, schools and the healthcare sector, although it was frustrating to see such inaction at other levels of the system.

IN 2012, I was in Los Angeles to participate in *Top Model Sverige*, one of the many licensed versions of *America's Next Top Model*, created by Tyra Banks. I was one of the judges, and the models would compete to become Panos Emporio's next model.

Every time I travelled to the US, I had problems with jet lag. It was hard to sleep and the time difference wrecked me. It always took a week before I was feeling reasonably normal again.

On the first day after the long journey, I sat at a bar next to the hotel with a friend, Musa, who had accompanied me to California. It was only 8 PM, but I was completely exhausted. My mobile rang, and I saw that it was Malik, a friend from New York.

I answered, and he asked if it was true that I was in LA.

"I arrived today," I replied.

"Fantastic! You're invited to a big celebrity party tonight. I'll text you the address. Be there at 11 PM."

"Malik, I can't even stand."

"You have to go. There's a guy there named Chris who will take care of you. Everyone will be there!"

Musa agreed that we should go to the party. "You can't sleep anyway," he laughed, "so why not?"

Malik sent an SMS with the address and some additional details. I didn't even read it. I handed my mobile to Musa and asked him to check with the receptionist how far away it was. I could see her looking at my phone, and looking surprised. Musa pointed at me. "Yes, my friend has been invited there. Where is it?"

"If you have a car, it'll take about an hour," she replied.

I told Musa that was crazy, but he refused to take no for an answer. "I'm going to drive. It won't take an hour. We'll be there in no time. Come on!"

We got ready and Malik called from New York again, to see if we were on our way. He gave me a mobile number for Chris, who would be our contact there. "Call him when you're close," Malik said.

En route, Musa talked non-stop to keep me alert. We arrived in a residential area, and the sat-nav showed that we were there. We looked around, but all we could see were darkened houses. We couldn't hear any music, and didn't see any cars or people moving about.

"It can't be here," I said.

"Yes, it's here," replied Musa. "We just have to find it."

We drove around the neighbourhood, looking for any sign of life. Suddenly, we were surrounded by three police cars, with their lights flashing. An officer called through a loudspeaker, "Get out of the car with your hands on your heads!"

What was this? We hadn't done anything. I hoped they wouldn't get rough, as we'd seen in so many American movies.

We got out of the car and I told Musa, who is good at talking and joking, that he should keep quiet so nothing would happen. The police had drawn their weapons and a couple of officers approached us cautiously, asking what we were doing there.

I tried to answer that we were on our way to a party, and tried to show them the address on my phone.

"What's the name of the person you are going to meet there?" he asked.

"Chris," I answered.

"Chris what?"

"We don't know his last name."

We had had a light shining into our faces, and they searched us. Satisfied that we weren't armed, or carrying drugs, they told us to take down our hands.

We began to see people looking out of their house windows. One of them had probably alerted the police to a suspicious car prowling the area.

I handed them my phone, with the original text from Malik. When they saw the address they said it wasn't here, but up in the mountains. "And you say you were invited?" asked one of the cops.

"Yes. We were told to be there at 11, and that a guy named Chris would be expecting us," I said.

"Follow us," one of them said, signalling to the others that they could leave.

We followed our police escort to the address, and when we got to the gates, the security guards took over. My mobile rang and it was Chris, wondering why we were taking so long. "We're here, out front," I said.

"Hand your phone to security," said Chris.

He spoke to a guard for a moment, and the gates opened. Inside we saw a person shouting at us from his quad bike. "Follow me, Mr Panos!"

We arrived at a giant mansion. Next to the magnificent entrance were a Bentley, a Rolls-Royce, a Ferrari and other beautiful cars. They reserved a spot for me between the Bentley and the Rolls. Musa started laughing, but I was so tired that nothing really registered.

Chris — it had been him on the four-wheeler — welcomed us as if we'd known one another for years. I got a good feeling and my energy came surging back in a flash. We followed him inside, where there were plenty of beautiful people everywhere. They had makeshift bars set up with champagne and other drinks, and Chris introduced us to some people near us. The bartender wondered what we would like to drink. I mumbled that I didn't drink champagne but I liked tequila, if they had it. They didn't, but Chris said, "Wait here, I'll get some."

A few minutes later he came back with a bottle in his hand, told me whose tequila it was, and said I could have it for myself. I couldn't catch the name. Chris told the bartender that it had to be served "only to Mr Panos." The man served me a glass and hid the bottle under the bar. He would refilled my glass when I wandered by again, and then return the bottle to its hiding place under the bar.

We walked around and looked at the beautiful mansion. It seemed like an A-list party, but I did not know whose, or if it was a special occasion of some sort. Chris said nothing because he thought I knew where I was.

In some rooms there were lots of different trophies on the shelves — an Oscar, a BAFTA, a Screen Actors' Guild award. Musa started joking that someone liked to buy souvenirs, but I was too tired to think about any of it. Many people came up to us and Chris introduced us to several of them.

I needed the toilet, but there were long queues outside every one I found. I went to Chris and asked if there was another one I could use. He paused thoughtfully and said, "Come with me."

We walked through different rooms and he knocked on a door. Two big guys opened the door. He said something to them, and one of them gestured that I should come in. It was a large square bathroom, maybe 60 square metres, with a guy sitting outside on a chair, guarding it. "Go ahead," I was told.

I tried to go, but it wasn't easy, with three men there in the room, suspiciously watching me. "What were they guarding?" I wondered.

I returned to the party and Chris shouted to me to come greet the host. He said his name, but my fatigue made it difficult for me to hear.

Suddenly a man in his 40s entered the room and everyone made way for him. Chris introduced us, and we shook hands. He thanked me for coming, and said he had heard a lot about me. He wondered if I wanted to come back the next day, at noon, so he could show me around the house. I replied without thinking, saying I was going to have a big day and wouldn't be able to. Sure, it was a spectacular mansion, but so what? The *Top Model* taping would follow in two days and I'd have to be well rested and in good shape. There were long days ahead and I had to do well. I saw on Chris's face that my answer wasn't the best, but no one said anything further.

At 1 AM, I wanted to leave, but Musa did not. They were so many nice people, he said, and we left the mansion at 2 AM. We thanked Chris and he followed us to the car. When we came out, there were people taking photos of the Bentley and Rolls-Royce, with our rental Chrysler parked between them. We stayed for a little while longer and Chris joked, "Your car has been the theme of the evening! Do you want me to take a picture of you, too, as you walk towards it?"

Looking around at dozens of the finest, most expensive cars, I saw how out of place ours was. No wonder security didn't want to let us in, even after we'd showed them the invitation on the mobile.

When we were halfway back to the hotel, Malik called and asked how we were. "We're fine," I replied. "We'll be back at the hotel soon."

Malik asked, "Why did you say no when Jamie invited you back for lunch, and to show you around?"

"I was tired, Malik. And, by the way, who is he?"

"Jamie, you mean? You don't know who that was?"

"No," I said. "I shook hands with him, but I was jet-lagged and dead on my feet. I didn't recognize him."

"But I wrote in the sms that you were invited to the movie star Jamie Foxx's mansion. It was the big wrap party for Quentin Tarantino's *Django Unchained.*"

Now I understood why the receptionist wondered if we were really going there, and why the police escorted us to the gate. It was Foxx's mega-mansion, in an exclusive area north of Malibu that's home to many actors and celebrities. That was his own, special bottle of tequila that I got to drink. It was his private toilet that they guarded. And those were his fabulous cars mine was parked between.

It was time for dinner with a friend at the luxurious Hollywood Roosevelt Hotel, located on the Hollywood Walk of Fame. On the way in, I saw someone looking at me. I could see that she was not sure if she recognized me, but she continued to look. And soon, she beamed a smile. We walked toward each other and she asked, "Is it Panos?"

"Yes," I replied, "but I'm afraid I don't remember you."

"I'm Alice Cooper's assistant," she told me. "We've been to your shop in Gothenburg. He loves it, and always wants to go there when we're in Sweden. It's the only place he absolutely has to visit there."

She asked how long I'd be in LA, and said she wanted to let Alice know.

I told her we were on our way in to dinner at the hotel, but she was welcome to join us. "No, wait here for a minute," she said. I watched her walk across the lobby, typing a message into her mobile.

She returned and said, "Alice wants to invite you and your friend to dinner in his suite, right now. It's only 15 minutes away."

"Of course we accept!" I said.

I had seen Alice in Gothenburg a couple of times, and had known that he loved my business called Shock. People can be shocked when they see the two different worlds I've built. There is of course Panos Emporio, which is glamorous and sensual. Shock, on the other hand, is an alternative fashion and lifestyle store. It features hard rock, punk, metal and goth themes, selling clothing, shoes, hair colours and accessories. As you've probably gathered, I like bold people, who dare to be independent and different, and Shock gives them a chance to express themselves the way they want to.

We joined Alice for dinner, and had a fun, easy-going time. I was impressed by his openness, down-to-earth personality and kindness. And, I loved that an international rock star would visit the store in Gothenburg, again and again, to buy gifts for others and things for himself. One that I'd been aware of was a T-shirt with a big Shock logo across the chest. He told me he'd chosen it to wear on German TV. He asked his assistant to send me the footage! It was an amazing evening, and confirmed what I've learned through the years: good people, no matter how successful they become, remain fundamentally who they are, and their goodness only grows over time.

Epilogue

WHEN YOU GROW UP POOR, and you go on to bigger and better things, that journey is more meaningful, and infinitely more enriching. I've even had rich people tell me this, including billionaires who'd had a privileged start in life. They may have been rolling in cash, but seeing their millions grow into billions didn't enrich them spiritually. It didn't touch their soul.

Life is made up of countless small moments that define who you are and set you on the right path. I was blessed to have the parents I did, because their principles and values always kept me on the straight and narrow. They worked hard, but we never felt deprived or unloved. They shared their love and affection with my siblings and me. So many kids who are born into poorer families don't have that chance, and the temptation to stray becomes too strong.

I'm reminded of my fellow Greek émigré, the famous American basketball star Giannis Antetokounmpo. He grew up in Sepolia, a tough Athens neighbourhood, where plenty of youngsters took the darker path and were lost to drugs and suicide.

When you watch interviews with Giannis, he emphatically says, "What I am today is because of my family. For me, family is everything." He stayed true to his values.

He and his brothers hawked watches and sunglasses in the streets of Athens. A café owner who felt sorry for the brothers would give them water, or something to eat after school. These small moments must have made a difference, and he has never forgotten them. He often returns to Sepolia, where he hands out food parcels to those in need, and he does it at night, in a very low-key way, to avoid media coverage or any suggestion that it's a publicity stunt.

Actions like this have meant a lot to me in my life, too. When you're fighting to survive, they give you hope. They become some of the most important events in your life. There were countless moments where I was presented with two very stark alternatives. I like to think that I always chose the ones that aligned the most with my values. The athlete Giannis has done the same.

All the marketing and business statements that have run in bold type in this book can be connected back to my childhood. So many are about creativity and respect. If my parents had never given me the freedom to think, and if they'd pushed me in the other direction, I don't think I would have excelled. That day when I painted the wall in the house, it was downright ugly, but my father never doubted me. That remains so strong in my mind and that I consider it the day I became an artist.

Those lessons still apply today, with my newest ventures. Conquer each struggle, one by one, and never give up. Don't borrow, if you can manage, and prioritize what you need. Don't wait for someone else to solve your problems: your life is in your hands. If you can find someone with whom you have symbiosis, that's a win–win. Listen to your inner-self and let the best values guide you. Keep your word and respect others. Those qualities, values and priorities were all imparted to me by my parents, before I had even left home.

The other boldface lessons are ones people might pick up at business school, but I adopted them early in my working life. Research your competitors and study the environment. That includes putting yourself in the customer's shoes and figuring out what they want. If others have a lead on you, then make up for it through hard work and training. Redouble your effort! Make your products so good that your customers become your viral marketers. Tell a story about your business: this combines the narratives of who you are and what your brand stands for. Outflank the competition by doing things your own way. Stay close to those who support you, and give extra attention and care to those who pay on time. Invest your profits back into your business. Always tell the truth, as people will recognize it when they hear it.

Then there are those personal goals and guidelines that I find inside myself, that drive me ever forward. And maybe these are the marks of the successful entrepreneur. The big one, which will make all the difference, is 'No risks, no history.' Make your own journey; it's the key to success in everything. A more rewarding life is one where you take the winding road, not the straight. If you know that you want to survive, then you'll fight for it. Leave no room for error, because that will give you focus. Do what you love, not what you 'should.' Respect is important in business, but so are honesty and simplicity. Be someone who customers want to connect to and let your good deeds speak for themselves. That is authenticity.

Your journey will touch them. Learn from children, who know how to have fun, and who don't know how to hate and be suspicious. And, don't be afraid to challenge the establishment. Look for opportunities to do so!

And these, my friends, are just the beginning.

As YOU'VE SEEN, when I was having fun, I had the most success. If I had to do it all again, I'd probably would walk away from Panos Emporio at the 25-year mark. After that, it wasn't as much fun, and I could see that I knew it in how I approached each day. Nevertheless, in the later years, I still innovated, with things like the men's Meander swimming trunks, for which I won a silver prize in the Swedish Design Awards in 2016. I noticed that men were rolling up the legs of their trunks, for movement, practicality, fashion or more complete tanning, so I came up with a design that allowed them to roll up the legs and fasten them. Why hadn't anybody thought of that before?!

Now that I have moved beyond my swimwear adventure, I've set out to do other things. I can't sit still — I have to make the most of my day and my life. House of Panos is my vehicle for inspiring and mentoring others. Over the years I've given many speeches on what my secrets to success were, and I want to keep sharing them. It's important to impart them to the next generation, too, so I've made it all accessible to young people.

The Panos Panos Tavern is my new restaurant in Gothenburg, a place where you can dine on quality Greek and international food, and, above all, be joyful. Human relationships are at the heart of everything we do, so why not have a place where we can form them, and revel in them, and have good, hearty food, too? At the Tavern you can taste two unique craft beers, one lager and one IPA, which I've created with a Swedish brewer. Craft beers are fashionable these days, and I can still spot the trends — you can't take away that innate ability.

I also can't erase the memories of how insulted and mistreated I'd been in the underbelly of this same city's restaurant scene, as a young immigrant potato-peeler and dishwasher. But I endured and pushed on through, climbing step by step to greater things. Who could have imagined that one day I'd stand in my own fine-dining establishment, right there in Gothenburg, welcoming guests from around the world?

When the time came to inject some fun back into life again, I took my own advice: do something you love, not something dictated by convention. Once again, I found the inspiration inside me, and it has driven me to do things differently. My way.

I still worked 18-hour days to get Panos Panos Tavern opened before my own self-imposed deadline in September 2021. While walking away from swimwear was meant to give me more leisure time, you can't stop me from creating. This is who I am, and to deny it would be to deny my very soul.

This latest venture was designed to give me a social life. It was the only way I knew how to achieve a degree of real work–life balance. For me, the solution was to work hard at creating something that would allow me to get out there and meet people.

And even now, there's no stopping me. There's still so much more creating to do. Even back in fashion.

So, HOW DO YOU KNOW what will bring you love, and give you joy, in this life? And what will bring you success? Is there a Venn diagram where you can figure out where these two intersect? Were these last six decades pure happenstance, or did I somehow create my own destiny? Is there a mindset you adopt in order to be successful?

We've only touched the surface of these questions. They are concepts and principles that would take another volume to write about. Those ideas are worth exploring, but there's only so much I can tell in this one volume. But, I want to keep the dialogue going.

IF THERE ARE too many concepts here to distil, you can at least focus on these three: *passion, respect,* and *love.* These are the core words that guide me, in everything I have done in life, and I believe in everyone living their fullest lives.

Passion is a strong emotion that prevails over logic. It emerges when you have great love and enthusiasm for something, and you're willing to devote all of your energies to achieving your goal. I felt this when leaving Greece, and I felt it countless times as I was starting up Panos Emporio. It was always there as I grew the business. It has always been hard to dissuade me once my passions spoke to me and I'd made up my mind about something. And, I believe I always chose the right path when I'd reached a crossroads.

You need to respectfully remember that we are only a temporary guest on this earth. We're custodians of our little patch for mere moments in time. We don't own anything forever.

In Ancient Greece, the concept of *aidos* might equate to what someone feels when they go against the prevailing social code. It is not about guilt, but more about respect and modesty. It is an integral part of one's soul, causing feelings of fear and shame when faced with the prospect that one's actions could be detrimental to others.

In modern business, respect meant seeing my customers and suppliers as partners. I was always ready to listen to them, and did my best to understand them.

Remember that when you are out to do right, you can see past any objections that are founded in fear rather than reality.

I tended to base my decisions on whether they would affect my environment, the place where I am a temporary guest. What about those who come after me? Whatever I did, I had to ensure that others would not be deprived of what I'd had the privilege to enjoy.

I still remember my father objecting to that neighbour using a chemical on their trees. He used the word *respect* all the time. It's a powerful word that I always keep in mind.

Our children will follow our example, not our words. Respect is the opposite of ego.

Take love, for instance. It doesn't matter if we are humans, animals or insects, or where on this earth we were born or where we live. Love between each of us starts at a very young age in certain ways, and ends when we are old in other ways. It constantly evolves. It is different for a teenager, for newly-weds, for a middle-aged couple, for an older couple, for a single person. The amount of love within and around us affects our health, our business and our overall success in life, on so many levels.

I cannot imagine any one of us saying that love isn't important. Without love we can't find harmony, mental equilibrium or physical balance. Love has to be the main focus of our lives; everything revolves around it.

I think back to old Giannis at the factory. He was poor, but he stood proud. I could see love in his eyes, even when I was a young boy. When we are in love, our eyes light up and people around us feel the power of this light. Others are attracted to us. When love is in the air, material things around us grow and business improves.

I asked Giannis many times about love. I wanted to know because I thought something was missing. But every time he spoke of it, he was short with his replies. He never explained why. Maybe he wanted me to figure it out for myself. There is nothing like a lived experience.

Let the word *love* emanate from your lips. You feel something nice just saying it, and hearing it. Millions of poems and songs and novels and paintings, in every culture around the world, have been about love.

It's been that way throughout human history. Remove it, that most crucial of ingredients, and suddenly everything collapses!

In this book you've read so many details about me, and secrets that only I knew about. They had been buried in my heart for a long time. I had not understood how heavy a burden it was to carry them alone for so many years. As I wrote, one memory after another flooded into my consciousness, as though they'd happened only yesterday. As they came to me, I had the strong sense that *love* formed the biggest part of my life's journey. I've made thousands of notes about it — I often wrote them down when I travelled for endless hours on planes.

When we next meet, maybe this is the subject we must discuss and explore and try to figure out. How the word *love* has been misused, and how it isn't always the core value with which we live our everyday lives. How it can be applied in all our life's endeavours ... in relationships, in business, in society. And, how we can use it to solve society's most pressing issues.

Love is invaluable, available, and free of charge.

It is always there, for us all.

Acknowledgements

To MY BELOVED CHILDREN Anna, Maria, Andreas, and Melina, I was at work or on the road a lot when you were growing up, but you were never far from my thoughts every day. I never wanted any of you to go through the hardships that I did, and working hard was the one thing I knew how to do to ensure you each had a brighter future. Thank you for your love and support.

Index